The Palgrave Lacan Series

Jacques Lacan is one of the most important and influential thinkers of the 20th century. The reach of this influence continues to grow as we settle into the 21st century, the resonance of Lacan's thought arguably only beginning now to be properly felt, both in terms of its application to clinical matters and in its application to a range of human activities and interests. The Palgrave Lacan Series is a book series for the best new writing in the Lacanian field, giving voice to the leading writers of a new generation of Lacanian thought. The series will comprise original monographs and thematic, multi-authored collections. The books in the series will explore aspects of Lacan's theory from new perspectives and with original insights. There will be books focused on particular areas of or issues in clinical work. There will be books focused on applying Lacanian theory to areas and issues beyond the clinic, to matters of society, politics, the arts and culture. Each book, whatever its particular concern, will work to expand our understanding of Lacan's theory and its value in the 21st century.

More information about this series at
http://www.palgrave.com/gp/series/15116

Gautam Basu Thakur · Jonathan Dickstein
Editors

Reading Lacan's Seminar VIII

Transference

palgrave
macmillan

Editors
Gautam Basu Thakur
Boise State University
Boise, ID, USA

Jonathan Dickstein
Westfield, NJ, USA

The Palgrave Lacan Series
ISBN 978-3-030-32741-5 ISBN 978-3-030-32742-2 (eBook)
https://doi.org/10.1007/978-3-030-32742-2

Cover illustration: DEA/ARCHIVIO J. LANGE/Contributor/gettyimages

This Palgrave Macmillan imprint is published by the registered company Springer Nature Switzerland AG
The registered company address is: Gewerbestrasse 11, 6330 Cham, Switzerland

Preface

Reading Lacan's Seminar VIII: Transference is a collection of short commentaries on Lacan's Seminar *Le transfert*. The seminar was delivered to training analysts at Sainte-Anne Hospital between 1960 and 1961 in twenty-seven weekly sessions.

English readers of Lacan's work remained teased about "transference" since the publication of Seminar XI where this was featured as one of the "four fundamental concepts of psychoanalysis," and the other three being "unconscious," "repetition," and "drive."[1]

But the significance of this particular concept, i.e., transference, extends beyond psychoanalysis and the clinic. Loosely understood as love for the subject supposed to know, transference is integral to psychoanalysis as theory and praxis: The "concept directs the way in which patients are treated." And it is conversely the way in which analysands are treated that ultimately governs the concept.[2] The curiosity about a full seminar devoted to the topic was therefore high among readers both affiliated to and beyond the clinic, including those in the disciplines of literature, film, cultural studies, and philosophy. This is because "love" is at the core of our most common cultural experiences and representations.

Most English readers picked up bits and pieces of this fundamental concept from the *Ècrits*, other translated pieces, and secondary scholarship, but nothing quite matched the anticipation for an actual English translation of the seminar. Consequently, the publication of Bruce Fink's English translation of the seminar *Transference: The Seminar of Jacques Lacan Book VIII* (2015) was greeted with enthusiastic responses, including the formation of an online reading group by Derek Hook and Calum Neill. The initial push for this book comes from this group and its members who all wanted to see their thoughts and ideas about the seminar represented in a peer-reviewed format. That said while many of the commentaries in this book indeed derive from the notes produced by the members of the group, this book also contains an equal number of "new" contributions from a larger Lacanian community spread across the world.

Written by clinicians as well as scholars working in fields as seemingly disparate as philosophy, literature, culture studies, and computer science, the commentaries in this book represent a wide range of disciplinary perspectives on and approaches to the concept of transference. Generally, these commentaries range from 2000 words to 6000 words. Some focus exclusively on one session and others on thematic concerns across multiple sessions. For this reason, the book cannot be identified as a collection of essays in the strict sense of the term.

Neither though is it a compendium to Lacan's seminar. Though many of the commentaries focus on explicating the main points of one or more sessions, the main aim of this book is to capture through shorter contributions, a spectrum of diverse voices debating, deliberating, and learning with Lacan the concept of transference and expanding the theoretical and philosophical consequences of this concept in the contexts of clinic, the classroom, and contemporary global society. These voices do not seek to establish any authoritative reading of the seminar nor are they homogenous in their understanding and interpretation of Lacan.

The incentive for the editors in curating these commentaries—working-thoughts, responses, and spandrels—has been actually threefold. Firstly, to collect different disciplinary perspectives on Lacan's transference insofar as this concept interests not only Lacanian analysts but also members of the larger academic community. Secondly, it has been our hope that this book will capture diverse, even contradictory readings of Lacan's seminar and thus offer in process different ways of thinking about love. Relatedly, and third, this project attempts to inaugurate a new paradigm in academic publishing by bringing out a collection of shorter writings that capture the developing thoughts of writers committed to reading Lacan with minimal reference to secondary criticism.

We are thankful to everyone who responded positively to this project, who encouraged us, and especially those who persevered in spite of this book's innovative structure and our editorial quirks. We have been especially fortunate to have received the support of Joanna O'Neill, editor at Palgrave, as well as Derek Hook and Calum Neill, the series editors of the Palgrave Lacan Series.

We have had nothing but love for this work. This is to say that we have had faith that when we release it in the world it might stand to abolish chance. In another sense, however, this means that we know better than to question the limits of probability.

Boise, USA Gautam Basu Thakur
Westfield, USA Jonathan Dickstein

Acknowledgements We thank our family and friends for their support through the crafting of this book. A big thank you to the wonderful editorial team at Palgrave, especially Joanna O'Neill and Beth Farrow, and the series editors, Derek Hook and Calum Neill, for showing faith in us yet again.

Notes

1. Jacques Lacan, *The Four Fundamental Concepts of Psychoanalysis. Seminar Book XI* (1973), trans. A. Sheridan. Routledge, 1981: 19.
2. Ibid., 124.

References

Lacan, Jacques. 1981. *The Four Fundamental Concepts of Psychoanalysis. The Seminar of Jacques Lacan, Book XI* (1973). Translated by A. Sheridan. London, UK and New York, NY: Routledge.

Lacan, Jacques. 2015. *Transference: The Seminar of Jacques Lacan, Book VIII.* Edited by Jacques-Alain Miller and Translated by Bruce Fink. Cambridge: Polity.

Praise for *Reading Lacan's Seminar VIII*

"This detailed and wide-ranging commentary on one of Lacan's most fascinating seminars—Seminar VIII: Transference—provides a useful outline to the often meandering series of lectures Lacan gave as he broached the topics of love and transference. The variety of contributors from different backgrounds—aesthetics, ethics, clinical psychology, psychoanalysis, etc.—helpfully contextualize what Lacan is up to here in relation to the broader trajectory of his work. The reader will not find in these pages a synthesis of Lacan's views, but rather discussions of the myriad main streets and byroads he explores in the Seminar, and keys to more profitable reading."

—Bruce Fink, *Lacanian psychoanalyst, translator of Lacan's* Transference: The Seminar of Jacques Lacan, Book VIII *and author of* Lacan on Love, *amongst other works, USA*

"This indispensable collection is requisite for making one's way through Lacan's Seminar VIII. This pivotal seminar's role in the turn of Lacan's thought after the Ethics seminar has long been unexplored territory. But the essays included here make it clear that this seminar on the transference displays Lacan at the height of his powers. If one wants to understand what he's thinking at the key turning point of his thought, this volume is an absolute necessity."

—Todd McGowan, *Professor of English and Film, University of Vermont, USA, and author of* Emancipation After Hegel (2019) *and* Only a Joke Can Save Us (2017)

Contents

Contributors

Frederic C. Baitinger Department of Romance Languages at Hunter College, The City University of New York, New York, NY, USA

Anthony Ballas University of Colorado Denver, Denver, CO, USA

Gautam Basu Thakur Boise State University, Boise, ID, USA

Jonathan Dickstein Fort Lauderdale, FL, USA

Ivan Ramos Estevão School of Arts, Sciences and Humanities and Institute of Psychology, University of São Paulo, São Paulo, Brazil

Rodrigo Gonsalves European Graduate School, Saas Fee, Switzerland; Universidade de São Paulo, São Paulo, Brazil

Owen Hewitson London, UK

Derek Hook Duquesne University, Pittsburgh, PA, USA

Dan Mills Woodstock, GA, USA

Calum Neill Edinburgh Napier University, Edinburgh, Scotland, UK

Ed Pluth California State University, Chico, Chico, CA, USA

Miguel Rivera Tufts University, Medford, MA, USA

Joseph R. Shafer School of English, University College Cork, Cork, Ireland

Jelica Šumič Riha Research Center of the Slovenian Academy of Sciences and Arts, Ljubljana, Slovenia

Stephanie Swales University of Dallas, Irving, TX, USA

Zachary Tavlin Department of Liberal Arts, School of the Art Institute of Chicago, Chicago, IL, USA

Hue Woodson Tarrant County College, Fort Worth, TX, USA

Cindy Zeiher School of Language, Social and Political Sciences; Sociology and Anthropology, University of Canterbury, Christchurch, New Zealand

List of Figures

1

Toward an Erotics of Truth: Commentary on Session I

Derek Hook

Introduction

Three themes predominate in the first session of Lacan's eighth seminar. Firstly, Lacan squarely foregrounds the topic of transference, summarily dismissing then dominant approaches—including Melanie Klein's (1952) notion of the "situation of the transference"—to this crucial clinical phenomenon. A series of links with the previous year's seminar (*The Ethics of Psychoanalysis*) are, secondly, set in place (particularly the themes of beauty, ethics, and the rejection of Plato's idea of the Sovereign Good). Lacan then, thirdly, moves on to foreground the importance of conceptualizing transference as *experience* and the experience of love and, furthermore, erotic love by highlighting a series of parallels between Freud and Socrates—who, of course, questioned those he came into contact with, claiming to know nothing other than how to recognize love—so as to assert that both men chose to operationalize love in the search for truth.

D. Hook (✉)
Duquesne University, Pittsburgh, PA, USA
e-mail: hookd@duq.edu

G. Basu Thakur and J. Dickstein (eds.), *Reading Lacan's Seminar VIII*,
The Palgrave Lacan Series, https://doi.org/10.1007/978-3-030-32742-2_1

In the Beginning...

Lacan opens the seminar with three rapid-fire qualifications, immediately distancing himself—in characteristic fashion—from prevailing clinical conceptualizations of transference. Transference, he insists, is to be discussed in its "subjective *disparity*"—a term that Lacan uses to stress that he is dissatisfied with both intersubjective frameworks and the ideas of transference as a *dissymmetry* between subjects. He likewise highlights the idea of "supposed situation" of transference, striking distance thus from Melanie Klein's ideas as expressed in her influential 1952 paper "The origins of the transference" (included in *Envy and Gratitude*, a subsequent collection of her writings). It is useful here, in grounding Lacan's opening comments, to offer a brief description, drawn from Klein (1976/1997) herself, of this idea of the transference situation:

> We are accustomed to speak of the transference *situation*...in unravelling the details of the transference it is essential to think in terms of *total situations* transferred from the past into the present, as well as of emotions, defense and object-relations.[1]

So, whereas transference has typically been understood in terms of direct references to the analyst, Klein insists on a broader purview whereby clinicians become aware of how a transference is not limited merely to the parameters of a projected relationship, but includes affects, defensive arrangements, and broader patterns of object-relating. Klein's views involve a series of developmental assumptions. And while she suggests that transference is more than an ego phenomenon—a view Lacan would likely agree with—her comments imply a far broader interpretive latitude than Lacan would be likely to prescribe:

> My conception of transference as rooted in the earliest stages of development and in deep layers of the unconscious is much wider and entails a technique by which from the whole material presented the unconscious elements of the transference are deduced.[2]

Lacan's prioritization of signifying material cannot be squared with such a free-ranging attention to "the whole material presented [by] unconscious elements," inclusive, one must presume, of affects and fantasy approached without attention to the structuring influence of the symbolic domain.[3]

Existing ideas of transference "technique" are likewise problematized by Lacan. Technique must be viewed in relation to principles that must in turn be derived from a correct topology, that is, with reference to the foregoing theoretical constructs (most notably the registers of symbolic, imaginary and real) established by Lacan himself in his previous seminars. The goal in rectifying the notion of transference—something that is extremely familiar to clinicians albeit inadequately theorized—"is to relate this notion to an experience."[4]

Plato's *Schwärmerei*

Lacan toys with his audience, evoking variations on the Biblical pronouncement from John 1:1: "In the beginning was the word." This enunciation has value in its demonstration not only of the *ex nihilo* character of creation, but of the evocative power of speech so intimately connected to it. Frustrating the expectations of his audience however, Lacan uses the statement to point not—as one might have expected—to the primacy of the signifier (that is, of the *word*), but to direct us to what the term "in the beginning" might more specifically invoke in the sphere of analysis, namely: "there was praxis." More directly: "In the beginning of analysis practice was… love"—as was made so painfully apparent in the inaugural case of Breuer and Anna O—and this love was not simply of a performative variety, that is, it "was not akin to the self-transparency of enunciation."[5]

This interest in *ex nihilo* creation clearly links to Lacan's (1992) previous seminar (*The Ethics of Psychoanalysis*), and Lacan glosses the objective of that seminar as explaining "the creationist structure of the human *ethos* as such, that is, the *ex nihilo* that subsists at its core, constituting the 'core of our being'."[6] *Ethos* (i.e., the subject's ethical substrate, their way of being) "wraps around the *ex nihilo*" and subsists as such in an "impenetrable void."[7] This is a reference to the notion of *das Ding*, which played such a central part in the first half of Seminar VII. *Das Ding* can be described as a voracious absence, which can, following Freud's (1950) comments in *The Project for a Scientific Psychology*, be identified with that thing-like element of the other that cannot possibly be retrieved into symbolic or imaginary registers.

The reason that this notion plays such an important role in Lacan's seminar on ethics is that with *das Ding* we are dealing with the radical alterity of the *Nebenmensch* (neighbor), with a blind spot in psychical and moral apprehension that cannot be overcome by attempts at empathy or intersubjectivity. Ethical commonplaces such as "loving the neighbour as one's self," the ideals of utilitarian ethics, the notion of the "right action," and Plato's notion of the Sovereign Good will not suffice here. Why so? Well, *das Ding* cannot be reduced merely to "otherness"; it is tantamount instead to a cavity of desire, a "swallowing abyss" that induces a response—a vacillating economy of attraction and avoidance—within the subject. With this concept, Lacan effectively supplements Freud's idea of the lost primordial object of *jouissance* with *a place*, with a power of emptiness which, like the astronomical configuration of a black hole, both mesmerizes and yet potentially spells the doom of the subject. It is this "non-object," this elevated position—incidentally, also that of the sublime (hence Lacan's refrain, according to which an object, once raised to this position, assumes the dignity of *das Ding*)—that takes center stage in Lacan's rethinking of ethics.

We can appreciate thus how Seminar VII pivoted around Lacan's rejection of Plato's *Schwärmerei*, that is, Plato's imagined notion of the Sovereign Good which he, Plato, is thought to have projected onto the impenetrable void. This rejecting of "the [Platonic] notion of a Sovereign Good to be found at the very center of our being" forms the backdrop to a psychoanalytic ethics centered on the notion of *das Ding*.[8] Lacan can be said to reverse Plato's priorities, focalizing "the impenetrable void" and relegating the idea of the Sovereign Good to a something akin to a defense against *das Ding*.

Lacan then turns his attention to Aristotle, noting that the latter's shift away from Plato lay in relocating the Sovereign Good, finding it instead in the contemplation of the stars, "the world's outermost sphere"—or indeed, to the realm of the Gods, the domain of the divine—which has been expanded in our own time into a "shimmering expanse of galaxies."[9]

While Lacan of course also distances himself from Aristotelian ethics, it is worth noting that with this juxtaposition of cosmological and scientific frames of reference Lacan is perhaps indicating that we remain within the territory of the Freudian notion of sublimation (sublimation pertaining to both the production of works of great artistic and scientific achievement).

The history of ethical reflection—at least, it seems, for Lacan—remains largely wedded to the notion of an ideal Good to which various secondary forms of good and pleasures remain associated. A similar reoccurring motif in philosophical discussion of ethics is the principle of right action (*Wohltat*). Lacan makes short work of such notions of the Good and the right action; Freud's observations on the aggressiveness underlying moral satisfaction are called upon as a means of problematizing such notions (Freud's [1930] proposed maxim from *Civilization and its Discontents*, "Man is wolf to man," springs to mind). The psychoanalytic question that emerges from discussion of ethical action is, then, as follows: How are we to handle desire, or more directly yet, how are we to *keep desire in our deeds, to preserve the relationship between desire and action* particularly so when action so often means the collapse or demise of desire?

This relationship between desire and action is all too often burdened, "infected" even by the "seething ground" of every social institution. From this follows a series of disparaging comments about the vacuity of certain sociological models, "exercises in futility," which quite clearly cannot attain the degree of ethical specification that Lacan has in mind.[10] One might guess that Lacan keeps prioritized here the absolute particularity of the desire of the subject, and that this underlies his rejection of sociological conceptualizations. An echo of this idea appears later when Lacan invokes the death of Socrates, who does not compromise on his particularity, a particularity that threatens the social harmony of the city, even though it costs him his life.

It is via Sade's reflections that we might have access to the frontier of something akin to a Freudian ethical terrain. Lacan recalls here the idea of a "zone between two deaths" discussed at length in Seminar VII. This position is exemplified by Antigone, who—in defiance of the laws of the city—refuses to give way on her desire to bury her brother; persisting beyond her symbolic death but prior to her actual physical death, she exists precisely "between the two deaths." With this concept, Lacan claims to have "introduced a guidepost in the ethical tradition," a "reflection on the motives and motivations for doing the Good" which entails an ethical type of fidelity to *das Ding*.[11] Beauty here is viewed as a final barrier to, indeed, a type of defense against "the final or mortal thing" [that is, *das Ding*], and Freud's death drive is accordingly cited as the point at which "Freud's thought made its ultimate admission."[12] The topic of beauty thus provides a link between the meditations of Seminars VII and VIII.

The hypothesis of the seminar that Lacan will go on to deliver is that Plato's *Schwärmerei*—his belief in a Sovereign Good—constitutes the effect of a type of immortal mourning, an immortal mourning which remains forever tied to the death of Socrates. This event is said—a large claim on Lacan's part—to lie at the source of all that has since been articulated in Western history in respect of the idea of immortality. More to the point yet, this mourning is tied to Socrates' wager of sustaining his (as yet unnamed) question—which is also seemingly *the* question of all who speak. Lacan makes reference here to his own earlier description, in Seminar I of "the essential form of the human message"[13] by noting that this question can be "received [from another]….in an inverted form."[14] Socrates can thus be placed at the origin of the longest transference that history has known. We are left with the tantalizing suggestion: "Socrates' secret will be behind everything I will have to say about transference this year."[15]

Socrates and Freud

In view of Socrates' secret, Lacan reminds us that the famous philosopher claimed to know nothing, except how to recognize what love is, and how to know who assumes the positions of beloved and lover in any given couple. Breuer's first sensational experiment with the talking cure would have been an interesting case for Socrates to speculate upon, for Breuer's experiment amounted to a love story, and the love it engendered was not, as Lacan stresses, unrequited. Lacan's gossipy and almost lascivious tone here is a clue perhaps to the dimension—indeed, the *form*—of love and the erotic that is so essential to the psychoanalytic relation.

Breuer's romantic misadventure foreshadowed, for Lacan, the break between Freud and Breuer a decade later. Eros struck the frightened Breuer first, and subsequently found its master in Freud. After a series of anecdotal and somewhat catty observations about the love lives of Freud and Socrates (Freud's wife described, for example, as "an element of the permanent picture of Freud's thirst," Socrates is said to have had "dealings at home with an unmanageable shrew"), Lacan highlights a common denominator between both men.[16] "Like Socrates, Freud chose to serve the god [Eros] in order to make use of him." Freud's approach was to make "himself master of this fearsome little god Eros."[17] But, to what end?

The link to the previous year's seminar is again crucial here inasmuch as the realm of Eros goes far beyond the field that the notion of Sovereign Good can cover. A more primary analytical imperative comes to the fore here: One should not posit as the primary aim of the analyst's actions the goal of their patient's good, but rather the goal of their patient's eros. The Socratic and Freudian endeavors have this in common: Socrates, like Freud, *chose to serve Eros in order to make use of him.*

Lacan cites the "seething ground of the social infection" stressing that Socrates was fully aware that what he was doing was going against the tide of the social order within which his daily practice was situated.[18] The historical echo with Freud's situation is clearly intended: "Wasn't his behavior truly insane and scandalous, despite the praiseworthy light his disciples devotedly cast…?"[19] In the social bond, opinions that run against the city's equilibrium have no place, and as such Socrates had no place, indeed, effectively *was no place.* (Hence, the historical reference to Socrates' *atopia* is the placelessness or unclassifiable nature of that which is so highly original as to be threatening.) It is not surprising in retrospect says Lacan that Socrates was sentenced to death; where though—an odd question, it seems—does Socrates' fate "take him now?"[20] Freud's own experience of scandal toward the end of his life came with his insistence on the controversial construct of the death drive. In this insistence on not avoiding death (ethically or within the practice and conceptualization of psychoanalysis as praxis), the two masters are again shown to have something in common.

Reminding us again of the previous year's seminar, Lacan returns to the difference between the idea of an eternal death as opposed to the death of the body, noting that "the body uncompromisingly obeys Eros. Eros is that by which bodies come back together, according to Plato into a single soul, according to Freud with no soul at all."[21] Moving between registers (of Platonic philosophy and psychoanalysis), Lacan insists "Eros is what unites intuitively."[22]

If Lacan by now seems to have confused the issue, that is perhaps the point. His "methodology" seems clear enough: to explore psychoanalytic issues not through the terms of the prevailing literature, but via the more de-familiarizing terrain of Plato's *Symposium*, where we find pre-psychoanalytic concepts apparent in what is at once both a foreign and an oddly familiar configuration of features. Eros can be seen as the same in both (Freudian and Socratic) cases. Moreover, if the question is raised regards the prominence of either the death drive or the dialectic, Lacan's answer is: "Yes," implying thus that the one necessarily brings the other in its wake.

Lacan makes a few further disparaging marks on the ineptness of the concept of intersubjectivity for psychoanalysis ("I intersubjectivize you, you intersubjectivize me"), as a way of fending off the claim that his recourse to Socrates should enshrine this notion.[23] That Socrates went against the tide of the masses is stressed by Lacan; this is something (going against the masses) that "should always be our guide."[24]

A Critique of Intersubjectivity

Lacan posits that intersubjectivity is foreign to the analytic encounter: "Freudian practice congeals as soon as intersubjectivity appears…The former flourishes only in the latter's absence."[25] This may appear to contradict certain of Lacan's earlier characterizations of psychoanalytic practice. In his *Seminar on "The Purloined Letter"* as contained the *Écrits*, he even refers to his L-Schema (which represents in diagrammatic form the co-ordinates of the clinical encounter inclusive of the crucial element of the symbolic Other) as a "This dialectic of intersubjectivity."[26] Intersubjectivity is also, as Fink (2015) notes, the topic of considerable discussion in Lacan's "The Function and Field of Speech and Language in Psychoanalysis" (2006). A crucial qualification should be made here so as to clear up any confusion.

Intersubjectivity, certainly inasmuch as it implies a "two-body psychology" or a type of ego-to-ego dialogue cannot work as an adequate basis of analytic practice. This is what Lacan often refers to as dyadic—or, we can add: *imaginary*—intersubjectivity. By contrast, the dialectic of intersubjectivity invokes a more complex relationship (as depicted in the L-Schema) in which the symbolic dimension of the big Other plays a crucial role. This latter form of subjectivity, which prioritizes the symbolic register and the role of the big Other above and beyond any ego-to-ego bonding between patient and analyst, is infinitely superior to situations where "I intersubjectivize you, you intersubjectivize me."[27] This form of relationality, which never exceeds the joint ego parameters of analyst and analysand, is anathema to Lacan. It is only via highlighting the functions of the signifier, stressing what is unintentionally said within the enunciative properties of speech itself, highlighting thus how the unconscious is the discourse of the Other, that we may reach beyond the deadlock of dyadic intersubjectivity. More simply put: If analysis is the domain where two individuals are preoccupied with wondering what one another is thinking in relation to themselves, with second-guessing one another, then there is no possibility of attaining the level of the *trans-subjective*, that is, of hearing the Other. It is for this reason that Lacan argues that the second-guessing of poker, like "diplomatic negotiations and ambushes," will prove a disastrous basis for a clinical treatment.[28]

An adequate *symbolic* transference is in fact conditional precisely on the avoidance of imaginary ego-to-ego modes of intersubjectivity between patient and analyst. As Lacan put it:

> [dyadic instances of] intersubjectivity....[must be] withheld or, better still, put off indefinitely to allow another handhold appear, whose essential characteristic is that of transference itself.[29]

Hence the difference between an imaginary mode of transference, where the analysand remains preoccupied with the enigmatic imaginary figure of the analyst, on the one hand, and a symbolic mode of transference, where—via prolonged attention to the discourse of the Other—the analysand becomes preoccupied with the enigma of their own formations of the unconscious (parapraxes, bungled actions, unintended enunciations, etc.). Hence Lacan's preference for the game of bridge over that of poker as an illustrative example. Bridge, unlike poker, cannot be reduced to dyadic intersubjectivity (consider here the role of the dummy); as such, it "formalize[s] the subjective alterities involved in the analytic setting" and opposes notions of interpsychology (interventions based on the ideals of a two-person psychology [see Rickman 1957]).[30]

There is, however, one unintended benefit of the notion of a "two-body psychology." It alerts us to the attraction of bodies, which again reminds Lacan of Socrates, and the constant reference he makes to the beauty of bodies which "animates the moment of questioning" (13). What is implicitly in question here is the intersection of the erotic and knowledge, the intersection between the beauty of bodies and the search for a type of truth.

We find something unexpected here, however, because while an "impassioned questioning…characterizes the beginning of the dialectical process," we also find that "this relationship is highlighted by traits whose value derives from their negative value,"[31] such as Socrates' ugliness. Analysis is thus "the only praxis in which charm is a disadvantage."[32] The negative features of the analyst—physical or otherwise—seem to function as a type of hook, as a kind of bait for a transference relation which itself entails what we might call an "erotics of truth."

Lacan muses about the neutralization of the body, both as it occurs in medical situations and, more broadly, as a goal of civilization. Such precautions seem to assume that the body can be abandoned, and Lacan, by contrast, considers the value of a given form of erotic charge—even if sublimated—for a viable analysis. Psychoanalysis requires from the outset "a high degree of libidinal sublimation at the level of collective relations."[33] Lacan is leading us to consider the role of such a libidinal charge in establishing transference. This is something that goes unexplored in Kleinian conceptualizations of the transference situation, a characterization Lacan again refutes in the closing pages of this first session of the seminar, insisting rather that the "analytical cell…is nothing but a bed for lovemaking."[34]

Lacan thus rejects the conceptual parameters implied by thinking analysis as a "situation," preferring instead that we conceptualize it along the lines of love. Love, however, has, according to Freud (says Lacan), a precarious and clandestine status. We can thus appreciate that "in the most protected context of all…the analyst's office, the status of love…[is] even more paradoxical."[35]

Toward the end of the session, Lacan poses a question which takes up the issue of transference in a novel way: "what is presupposed by the fact of isolating oneself with another in order to teach him what he is lacking?" The factor of transference presumably exacerbates this experience, because, as Lacan stresses, it is "by the nature of transference" that the analysand "will find out that he is lacking insofar as he loves."[36] This emphasis on love replaces the simplistic notion that the analyst is there for analysand's own good: The analyst is there in order that the analysand *love*. This poses the question of the difference between what it means to love, and what love is. Surprisingly, this is not something analysts seem to know much about—love (like hate) is all too often used as a self-evident term. It is for this reason that Lacan directs his audience to read Plato's *Symposium*, a text in which we will find evidence of "the first psychoanalytic transference" and "all the possible keys" to this analytical phenomenon.

Notes

1. Melanie Klein, *Envy and Gratitude and Other Works, 1946–1963*. Vintage, 1975/1997: 55.
2. Ibid.
3. Ibid.
4. Jacques Lacan, *Transference: The Seminar of Jacques Lacan, Book VIII*, trans. Bruce Fink, Polity, 2017: 4.
5. Ibid.
6. Ibid., 5.
7. Ibid.
8. Ibid.
9. Ibid.
10. Ibid., 6.
11. Ibid., 7.
12. Ibid.

13. Jacques Lacan, *Freud's Papers on Technique 1953–1954. Seminar Book I* (1975), trans. John Forrester, Norton, 1988: 51.
14. Lacan, *Transference*, 8.
15. Ibid., 7.
16. Ibid., 9.
17. Ibid.
18. Ibid., 9–10.
19. Ibid., 10.
20. Ibid.
21. Ibid.
22. Ibid.
23. Ibid., 11.
24. Ibid.
25. Ibid.
26. Jacques Lacan, *Ècrits: The First Complete Edition*, trans. B. Fink, Routledge: 40.
27. Lacan, *Transference*, 11.
28. Ibid., 12.
29. Ibid.
30. Ibid., 13.
31. Ibid.
32. Ibid., 14.
33. Ibid., 14–15.
34. Ibid., 15.
35. Ibid.
36. Ibid.

References

Fink, B. 2015. Translator's Endnotes. In *Transference: The Seminar of Jacques Lacan, Book VIII*, ed. J.-A. Miller Cambridge: Polity Press.

Freud, S. 1930. Civilization and Its Discontents. In S. Freud (1966–1974) *The Standard Edition of the Complete Psychological Works of Sigmund Freud*, vol. XXI, trans. J. Strachey. London: Hogarth.

———. 1950. Project for a Scientific Psychology. In S. Freud (1966–1974) *The Standard Edition of the Complete Psychological Works of Sigmund Freud*, vol. I, trans. J. Strachey. London: Hogarth.
Klein, M. 1952. The Origins of Transference. *International Journal of Psycho-Analysis* 33: 433–438.
———. 1976/1997. *Envy and Gratitude and Other Works, 1946–1963.* London: Vintage.
Lacan, J. 1992. *The Seminar of Jacques Lacan, Book VII: The Ethics of Psychoanalysis, 1959–1960.* London: W. W. Norton.
———. 2006. *Écrits: The First Complete Edition in English*, translated with notes by Bruce Fink, in collaboration with H. Fink and R. Grigg. New York and London: W. W. Norton.
———. 2015. *Transference: The Seminar of Jacques Lacan, Book VIII.* Edited by Jacques-Alain Miller and Translated by Bruce Fink. Cambridge: Polity.
Rickman, J. 1957. *Selected Contributions to Psycho-Analysis.* New York: Basic Books.

2

"Set and Characters" and "The Metaphor of Love: Phaedrus"—Commentary on Sessions II and III

Dan Mills

Session II

Set and Characters

As Lacan establishes the setting and characters of Plato's *Symposium*, he states that his focus on the body, particularly "when beauty may be one of its attributes," is an important part of his understanding of transference.[1] He further explains that movies frequently depict attractive psychoanalysts when analysis is meant to be comedic. Throughout this section, Lacan mentions historical French and Greek writers and philosophers to establish his knowledge of the relevant historical and philological issues at stake in his upcoming discussion of Plato's *Symposium*. This chapter will focus on the ancient, early modern, and modern authors, figures, and texts to provide context to the ancient material Lacan only mentions in passing.

Lacan, however, admits his training is in psychoanalysis, which limits his ability to engage with Plato's text without a "long detour" to provide

D. Mills (✉)
Woodstock, GA, USA

G. Basu Thakur and J. Dickstein (eds.), *Reading Lacan's Seminar VIII*,
The Palgrave Lacan Series, https://doi.org/10.1007/978-3-030-32742-2_2

an adequate introduction to the work, with which he concedes his audience might not have familiarity.[2] Lacan says that first time readers of the *Symposium* might feel "flabbergasted" [*etre soufflé*].[3] The text, according to Lacan, brings with it an "historical imagination" preserved by "generations of monks and ignoramuses [*de moines at de grimauds*], all of them vocationally unsuited to transmit" a work that he characterizes as a kind of "specialized literary genre" that resembles a "police investigation."[4] Lacan believes that the interaction between Alcibiades and Socrates "goes beyond the limits of the symposium itself."[5]

Lacan Introduces the Symposium

Lacan begins his analysis with a definition of the Greek symposium, which he labels as a "ceremony of rules" [*cérémonie avec des règles*] and "a sort of ritual, intimate contest among the elite, or parlor game."[6] Lacan notes that this ceremony/ritual is governed by "regulation" whereby everybody present "must do his share by giving a short speech on a specific topic."[7] Those present are not to drink excessively, which Lacan supposes is because they are already hung over from the previous day's drinking, although this also makes the reader aware of the "importance and gravity" of the "elite group" that has assembled. In spite of this gravity, Lacan notes, something unexpected happens that causes "pandemonium" [*un désordre*].[8]

Lacan here is referring to the new group of people that arrive as Aristophanes is about to make his speech. Among this group is Alcibiades, and he and the group are, according to Lacan, "completely smashed" [*complètement ivres*].[9] Plato writes (212d) that Alcibiades arrives "very drunken and bawling loud" [σφόδρα μεθύοντος καὶ μέγα βοῶντος].[10] Lacan then refers to Plutarch's "commonly accepted" description of Alcibiades "general character."[11] But Lacan cautions against relying upon Plutarch's account, which Lacan says is "Alexandrian," meaning a "funny time in history where everything seems to transform characters into mere shadows of themselves," by which he means the "moralistic tone" of surviving texts from that period. These texts involve a "coming out of the shadows," *νεκυία* as it is known in the *Odyssey*. Alcibiades, according to Plutarch, was the πρῶτος ἐραστής, the "first lover."

Plutarch was a first-century Greek Platonist biographer whose *Parallel Lives* provided idealized biographies of eminent Greeks and Romans. The real Alcibiades was an Athenian politician who lived c. 450–404 B.C.E. Lacan likens Plutarch's description of Alcibiades to Alexander, as Alcibiades was a man who could win victories for others but who would also end up being "chased away or exiled" [*pourchassé, exilé*] for various misdeeds.[12] Alexander the Great lived 356–323 B.C.E., so Lacan is pointing out an important complication in reading Plutarch's characterization of Alcibiades, as Plutarch based his biography of Alcibiades on whatever existing texts available to him and ultimately compares him to Alexander, who by Plutarch's time had become more of a mythologized figure than a real historical person. Plutarch writes (1.2) that "the favour and affection which Socrates showed him contributed not a little to his reputation" [Σωκράτουςπρὸς αὐτὸν εὐνοίας καὶ φιλανθρωπίας οὐ μικρὰ πρὸς δόξαν ἀπέλαυσεν].[13] Plutarch offers (2.2) a story about how Alcibiades as a boy bit a wrestling opponent, prompting the opponent to say, "You bite, Alcibiades, as women do!" [ὦ Ἀλκιβιάδη, καθάπερ αἱ γυναῖκες]. Plutarch characterizes (6.1) Alcibiades' relationship with Socrates as very dysfunctional:

> But the love of Socrates, though it had many powerful rivals, somehow mastered Alcibiades. For he was of good natural parts, and the words of his teacher took hold of him and wrung his heart and brought tears to his eyes. But sometimes he would surrender himself to the flatterers who tempted him with many pleasures, and slip away from Socrates, and suffer himself to be actually hunted down by him like a runaway slave. And yet he feared and reverenced Socrates alone, and despised the rest of his lovers.

> ὁ δὲ Σωκράτους ἔρως πολλοὺς ἔχων καὶ μεγάλους ἀνταγωνιστὰς πῄ μὲν ἐκράτει τοῦ Ἀλκιβιάδου, δι' εὐφυΐαν ἁπτομένων τῶν λόγων αὐτοῦ καὶ τὴν καρδίαν στρεφόντων καὶ δάκρυα ἐκχεόντων, ἔστι δ' ὅτε καὶ τοῖς κόλαξι πολλὰς ἡδονὰς ὑποβάλλουσιν ἐνδιδοὺς ἑαυτόν, ἀπωλίσθαινε τοῦ Σωκράτους καὶ δραπετεύων ἀτεχνῶς ἐκυνηγεῖτο, πρὸς μόνον ἐκεῖνον ἔχων τὸ αἰδεῖσθαι καὶ τὸ φοβεῖσθαι, τῶν δ' ἄλλων ὑπερορῶν.

Plutarch refers several times to Alcibiades' great ability in the art of speaking, but he also refers (16.1) to Alcibiades' effeminate behavior: "But all this statecraft and eloquence and lofty purpose and cleverness was attended with great luxuriousness of life, with wanton drunkenness and lewdness, with effeminacy [θηλύτητας] in dress,—he would trail long purple robes through the market place,—and with prodigal expenditures" [ἐν δὲ τοιούτοις πολιτεύμασι καὶ λόγοις καὶ φρονήματι καὶ δεινότητι πολλὴν αὖ πάλιν τὴν τρυφὴν τῆς διαίτης καὶ περὶ πότους καὶ ἔρωτας ὑβρίσματα, καὶ θηλύτητας ἐσθήτων ἁλουργῶν ἑλκομένων δι᾽ ἀγορᾶς, καὶ πολυτέλειαν ὑπερήφανον]. Lacan notes that Athens lost the Peloponnesian War specifically because they recalled Alcibiades from the middle of the fighting to punish him for the "so-called mutilation of the ερμαι" [*de la mutilation des Hermès*], which amounted to an insult to the gods. Like Plutarch, Lacan points out that Alcibiades was quite attractive both as a child and into his later years and that he was able to seduce people with his looks as much as his "exceptional intelligence."[14]

Lacan says that Alcibiades "provides a backdrop of constant eroticism to the speeches on love" in the *Symposium* and that Alcibiades tells those present at the gathering about the "vain efforts made when he was young, when Socrates loved him, to get Socrates to fuck [*baiser*] him."[15] Lacan notes that Alcibiades uses crass language to describe how he wanted to "make Socrates lose control [*à perdre son contrôle*], show some emotional turmoil [*trouble*], and yield to direct corporal come-ons [*à céder à des invites corporelles*]—physical contact [*approche physique*]," all of which he says drunk in public. Presumably, Lacan is referring to Alcibiades' request (213e) for a "big goblet" [ἔκπωμα μέγα] and his comment (214c) that Socrates has "drained" [ἐκπέπωκας] this cup. According to A. D. C. Cake, Alcibiades' "transgressive presence" shows how eros can overpower the "most thorough sublimations of its power" as symbolized in Socrates, who acknowledges only "sublimating activities."[16] Socrates, in other words, sublimates Alcibiades' lack of composure and control.

Lacan then offers an analogy concerning a hypothetical book about a celebrity like John F. Kennedy, "who is simultaneously a James Dean," that describes how everyone who knew Kennedy in college wanted to have sex with him. Lacan suggests comparing Socrates to someone like the nineteenth-century French Catholic Islamic scholar Louis Massignon and the twentieth-century American erotic-surrealist novelist Henry Miller, whose *Tropic of Cancer* was banned in the United States as pornography. Twentieth-century French publisher Jean-Jacques Pauvert (1926/1927–2014) would publish the book, Lacan says, likely in some kind of pun on *pauvreté*, French for poverty, and *perverti*, French for *pervert*. Pauvert was famous for publishing the controversial writings of the Marquis de Sade in the 1950s, about whom Lacan would write a few years later in his essay, "Kant avec Sade."

Lacan then ruminates on the "admirable edition" created by sixteenth-century French printer, publisher, and classicist Henri Estienne, whose contemporaries also had an interest in love. Referring to his previous year's seminar, *The Ethics of Psychoanalysis*, and its engagement with sublimation as it relates to "love for women," he reminds us that he had alluded to the sixteenth-century princess of France and Queen of Navarre, Marguerite de Navarre. In the *Heptaméron* (1558), Navarre depicts a symposium similar to the one Plato describes.

Lacan tells an anecdote about how seventeenth-century French dramatist Jean Racine received a translation of Plato's *Symposium* and believed the text "untranslatable."[17] Lacan then relates how he received "handwritten notes" from a course on Plato given by French philosopher Victor Brochard (1848–1907)—notes Lacan says were "well taken, the writing exquisite and, concerning the theory of love." Brochard had dealt with all of the relevant texts, which Lacan lists as *Lysis*, the *Phaedrus*, and the *Symposium*. *Lysis* was an early dialogue, but Plato wrote the *Phaedrus* in about 370 B.C.E., around the same time as the *Symposium*. In the *Phaedrus*, Plato in part engages with rhetoric and its relationship to the soul. Leo Strauss argues that "if the art of how we speak were the other side of psychology," it would lead to "knowledge of the soul," which would mean that the "science of how to speak would be full of content," that it is to say, Platonic rhetoric and its focus on how to "influence or persuade other people" by connecting to their soul.[18] Lacan apparently was a reader of Strauss, as he mentions reading Strauss' book *Persecution and the Art of Writing* in "The Instance of the Letter in the Unconscious."[19] But Brochard, according to Lacan, does not deal with Alcibiades.

Lacan says that French classicist Léon Robin (1866–1947) "rallies" to the fact that in the scene with Alcibiades Plato wanted "to make people give his master his due" [*c'est que Platon a voulu là faire rendre justice à son maître*].[20] Lacan notes that after Socrates' death, the Sophist Polycrates produced a "pamphlet in which one sees Socrates collapse under the weight of various accusations that are conveyed by three people," one of whom was Polycrates himself.

Lacan Analyzes the Symposium

Lacan refers to Alcibiades as "bursting in" in several places [*l'irruption*]. Lacan says that he considers the *Symposium* as "a sort of account of psychoanalytical session [*compte-rendu de séances psychanalytiques*]" in which the progression of the speeches means that "each flash is illuminated by the one that follows [*chacun de ces flashes par celui qui suit*]," and when Alcibiades "bursts onto the scene [*l'irruption de la vie là-dedans*]," Plato reports it as a "raw and even disturbing fact" [*de fait brut voire gênant*].[21]

Lacan points out that Plato's account of this symposium occurs 16 years after it happened through the perspective of a character who "extracts from his memory the verbatim text" [*extrait de sa mémoire le texte littéral*] of what everybody present said.[22] This means, according to Lacan, that Plato wishes the reader to "believe in this brain recording" that many people practiced. Aristodemus says (178a) he could not remember what those present said any more than Apollodorus could [*ἃ δὲ μάλιστα καὶ ὧν ἔδοξέ μοι ἀξιομνημόνευτον, τούτων ὑμῖν ἐρῶ ἑκάστου τὸν λόγον*], as "parts of the tape were damaged and there might be gaps."[23] Therefore, Lacan says, "If it is a lie, it is a pretty one" [*Si c'est un mensonge, c'est un mensonge beau*], because "only liars can fittingly respond to love" [*seuls les menteurs peuvent répondre dignement à l'amour*].[24] This slippery intersection of memory and lying is what Lacan says is most relevant to psychoanalysis in the *Symposium*.

Lacan understood memory through the 1950s as existing in the symbolic order and connected to the signifying chain and he contrasts it with recollection and remembering, which he situates in the context of "imaginary reminiscence."[25] In *Seminar III: The Psychoses*, Lacan had said that the kind of memory relevant to psychoanalysis is different from what psychologists mean when they reveal "its mechanism to us in an animate being in an experiment."[26] In *Seminar VII: The Ethics of Psychoanalysis*, Lacan had said, "the structure engendered by memory must not in our experience mask the structure of memory itself insofar as it is made of a signifying articulation."[27] This is because "history presents itself as something memorable and memorized in the Freudian sense, namely, something that is registered in the signifying chain and dependent on its existence."[28] Lacan says that neurosis leads to the formulation of "the realm of the Freudian unconscious *qua* register of memory."[29] The signifying chain refers to the fact that a signifier cannot exist outside of the context of its relationship with other signifiers, a relationship Dylan Evans claims, "expresses the eternal nature of desire," and is therefore metonymic.[30] Lacan uses metonymy, the substitution of an attribute or quality of the thing referred to, as a way to express the signifying chain of signifiers.

Lacan says that Socrates claims to know nothing except the *σμικροῦ τινος*, the "little thing" about science, [*μαθήματος*], the "course" concerning "matters of love" [*τῶν ἐροτικῶν*]. Phaedrus announces (177a–c) the topic of the *Symposium*, but this actually comes from Eryximachus:

> The beginning of what I have to say is in the words of Euripides' *Melanippe*, for "not mine the tale" that I intend to tell; it comes from Phaedrus here. He is constantly complaining to me and saying,—Is it not a curious thing, Eryximachus, that while other gods have hymns and psalms indited in their honor by the poets, the god of Love, so ancient and so great, has had no song of praise composed for him by a single one of all the many poets that ever have been? And again, pray consider our worthy professors, and the eulogies they frame of Hercules and others in prose,—for example, the excellent Prodicus. This indeed is not so surprising but I recollect coming across a book by somebody, in which I found Salt superbly lauded for its usefulness, and many more such matters I could show you celebrated there. To think of all this bustle about such trifles, and not a single man ever essaying till this day to make a fitting hymn to Love! So great a god, and so neglected! Now I think Phaedrus's protest a very proper one. Accordingly I am not only desirous of obliging him with a contribution of my own, but I also pronounce the present to be a fitting occasion for us here assembled to honor the god.

εἰπεῖν οὖν τὸν Ἐρυξίμαχον ὅτι ἡ μέν μοι ἀρχὴ τοῦ λόγου ἐστὶ κατὰ τὴν Εὐριπίδου Μελανίππην: οὐ γὰρ ἐμὸς ὁ μῦθος, ἀλλὰ Φαίδρου τοῦδε, ὃν μέλλω λέγειν. Φαῖδρος γὰρ ἑκάστοτε πρός με ἀγανακτῶν λέγει οὐ δεινόν, φησίν, ὦ Ἐρυξίμαχε, ἄλλοις μέν τισι θεῶν ὕμνους καὶ παίωνας εἶναι ὑπὸ τῶν ποιητῶν πεποιημένους, τῷ δὲ Ἔρωτι, τηλικούτῳ ὄντι καὶ τοσούτῳ θεῷ, μηδὲ ἕνα πώποτε τοσούτων γεγονότων ποιητῶν πεποιηκέναι μηδὲν ἐγκώμιον; εἰ δὲ βούλει αὖ σκέψασθαι τοὺς χρηστοὺς σοφιστάς, Ἡρακλέους μὲν καὶ ἄλλων ἐπαίνους καταλογάδην συγγράφειν, ὥσπερ ὁ βέλτιστος Πρόδικος—καὶ τοῦτο μὲν ἧττον καὶ θαυμαστόν, ἀλλ᾽ ἔγωγε ἤδη τινὶ ἐνέτυχον βιβλίῳ ἀνδρὸς σοφοῦ, ἐν ᾧ ἐνῆσαν ἅλες ἔπαινον θαυμάσιον ἔχοντες πρὸς ὠφελίαν, καὶ ἄλλα τοιαῦτα συχνὰ ἴδοις ἂν ἐγκεκωμιασμένα—τὸ οὖν τοιούτων μὲν πέρι πολλὴν σπουδὴν ποιήσασθαι, ἔρωτα δὲ μηδένα πω ἀνθρώπων τετολμηκέναι εἰς ταυτηνὶ τὴν ἡμέραν ἀξίως ὑμνῆσαι: ἀλλ᾽ οὕτως ἠμέληται τοσοῦτος θεός. ταῦτα δή μοι δοκεῖ εὖ λέγειν Φαῖδρος. ἐγὼ οὖν ἐπιθυμῶ ἅμα μὲν τούτῳ ἔρανον εἰσενεγκεῖν καὶ χαρίσασθαι, ἅμα δ᾽ ἐν τῷ παρόντι πρέπον μοι δοκεῖ εἶναι ἡμῖν τοῖς παροῦσι κοσμῆσαι τὸν θεόν.

Melanippe refers to the daughter of Aeolus who appears in Euripides' tragedies, *Melanippe The Prisoner* and *Melanippe The Philosopher*, which only survive in fragments. Plato labels Phaedrus in the *Symposium* as the πατὴρ τοῦ λόγου, literally "father of the word."

Lacan makes a side comment about his wish to lecture on the *Phaedrus* and its "absolutely essential trait without which there is no way of understanding how what I call the lit circle [*le cercle éclairé*] is situated in everything Antiquity has bequeathed us."[31] Lacan briefly talks about the nature of night and how in the *Phaedrus* someone wakes Socrates before dawn and Socrates fumbles around in the dark. Lacan says the same thing happens in an Aristophanes play, most likely *Clouds*, the play in which Socrates himself appears as a character. Ellie Ragland-Sullivan argues that "Lacan teaches us that Plato put profound words in Aristophanes' mouth," which he reiterates in *Seminar XI: The Four Fundamentals of Psychoanalysis*: "the unconscious (sexuality) finds itself on the opposite side to love," which is ironic because people "are characterized by lack and loss" and "In nothing are we total, neither in our speech, our bodies, our fictions, or our gender 'identity.'"[32] This is certainly true of Socrates, the master analyst of every dialogue in which he appears who nevertheless does not pursue his own love interests and in effect sublimates himself in spite of what readers of Plato are to assume is his psychological health.

Lacan says that Marguerite de Navarre's *Heptaméron* depicts bed trick stories, a plot trope in which a man could slip into a woman's bed at night and pass as her husband or lover, which Lacan claims happened frequently. Lacan then refers to what he calls "the spreading of light" [*la diffusion des lumières*] that "changes many things in the realm of human relations" [*à la diffusion dimension des rapports êtres les etres humains*] because "To us, night is not a consistent reality—it cannot be poured from a ladle [*louche*] or form a blanket of darkness [*épaisseur de noir*]."[33]

Lacan Analyzes Greek Love

At the beginning of this section, Lacan bluntly says, "You'll have to get used to the idea that Greek love was love for pretty boys [*beaux garçons*]. And ... that's it."[34] Lacan says that the Greeks accepted love for boys universally and that some of his own contemporaries have claimed so, "regretting that they weren't born a bit earlier." But, as Lacan notes, different regions of Greece had different attitudes toward this practice. Lacan says that in the "totalitarian" regions of Greece, which included the Spartans and Boeotians, "where everything that was not prohibited was compulsory," it was a "mandatory from of service" that was accepted as well as expected.[35] The Spartans of course were always preparing for war, and the Boeotians were self-contained like the Spartans and fought against Greece during the Peloponnesian War. The Boeotians were wealthy and the Athenians often mocked them.

Lacan says that courtly love served an "analogous function of society" as a type of sublimation, and he refers to his previous year's attempt to provide a "slight rectification in your minds regarding the real function of sublimation."[36] Sublimation involves the redirection of socially unacceptable sexual impulses or neuroses into socially acceptable behavior. In *Seminar VII*, Lacan attempts to connect sublimation to ethics by departing from Freud's belief in the possibility of "perverse sexuality as a direct form of satisfaction of the drive," which means sublimation is necessary only because of societal prohibitions. Lacan, however, "rejects the concept of a zero degree of satisfaction" by arguing that perversion is not merely a "brute natural means of discharging the libido, but a highly structured relation to the drives which are already, in themselves, linguistic rather than biological forces."[37] Lacan also believes that because of our instincts' malleability the subject can never completely achieve sublimation.[38] Lacan disagrees with Freud's mandate that sublimation redirects impulses to a non-sexual object, as he believes that the object itself does not change but rather "its position in the structure of fantasy."[39] This means that the nature of the desired object must change, not the object itself because if "the drive allows the change of object, it is because it is already deeply marked by the articulation of the signifier."[40] The object's "sublime quality" does not rely upon an "intrinsic property of the object," but rather the "effect of the object's position in the symbolic structure of fantasy," meaning that sublimation repositions the object into the position of a thing and, in Lacan's formula, it elevates the object to the "dignity of the Thing."[41] This elevation "exerts a power of fascination which leads ultimately to death and destruction."[42] According to Lorenzo Chiesa, Lacan in *Seminar VIII* shows how "real love somehow *sublimates* real desire for death without erasing it: real love has to come to terms with real lack. In this sense, love is a messenger of the Real, a *metaxu* between the order of the Real (qua lack) and reality (in which the structural lack is necessarily veiled)."[43] Plato depicts Socrates as having the ultimate *sprezzatura* in all his interactions with other people but one gets the sense that Socrates is lonely and that there is a lonely dysfunction lying underneath his public persona.

Lacan states that the Greek love for boys does not reside in the "register of repression on a societal scale," although psychoanalysis relies upon a "fraternity among men as the basis of the social bond," with homosexuality connecting man to the "neutralization" of this bond and a return to an "innate form." Lacan notes that the "masters of Greece" [*des maîtres de la Grèce*] practiced this kind of love, men of a "certain social class and milieu, people at a level at which culture reigned supreme and was developed," because such love was the "great center of elaboration of interpersonal relationships."[44]

Lacan reminds us that the interplay between perversion and culture, the latter of which he distinguishes from society, employs a kind of censorship that leads to what he refers to as the "disintegration" that happens in neurosis, which means we can understand perversion as an "elaboration, construction, or even sublimation," the last of which is a cultural product. "The circle closes," Lacan says, as "perversion contributes elements that shape [*travaillent*] society, and neurosis favors the creation of new cultural elements."[45] But homosexuality is still perverse, Lacan claims, because then and now it is essentially a perversion.[46] Lacan differentiates "contemporary homosexuality from Greek perversion" by their relative location in the "quality of objects."

Near the end of the *Symposium*, Socrates' speech comes to the reader through a woman, Diotima, and Lacan distinguishes women in the ancient world from modern women by saying that "women of Antiquity demanded their due" by attacking men.[47] Aristophanes, Lacan says, did not hesitate to depict Greek women as they really were. Lacan implies that the nature of Greek women led to Greek men's love of boys, although he fears some will accuse him of advocating a return to such "Platonic love," and he says that love has long "been disconnected [*désengreneé*] from beauty."[48] Lacan refers to Agathon's speech (187e) when he talks about Polyhymnia, the Muse of sacred poetry, song, and dance, demanding, "that no debauchery [ὂν δεῖ εὐλαβούμενον] be implanted with the reaping of his pleasure [ἡδονὴν], just as in our craft we set high importance on a right use of the appetite [ἀκολασίαν] for dainties of the table, that we may cull the pleasure [ἐπιθυμίαις] without disease [νόσου]." According to Agathon, in other words, seeking pleasure is permissible in moderation.

In his concluding remarks, Lacan notes that the *Symposium* depicts a time when psychoanalysis naturally did not exist and the unconscious was "the most unexpected of dimensions," which he says he had mentioned in *Seminar IV: The Object Relation and Freudian Structures, 1956–1957* and *Seminar VI: Desire and its Interpretation, 1958–1959*. Nevertheless, Lacan reminds us the "desiring subject" possesses some kind of lack.

Session III

Lacan opens the third session, "The Metaphor of Love: Phaedrus," by positing an affinity between love and transference in the context of the dialectic between the ἐραστής (*erastès*, the one who loves) and the ἐρώμενος (*erômenos*, the one who is loved).[49] In this lecture, Lacan analyzes the speech of Phaedrus. According to James Penney, Phaedrus' speech along with the two that follow (Pausanias and Eryximachus) "offer a lofty idealization of love in its putative function as a catalyst for aesthetic, political, and moral virtue. These forms of love qualify as instances of resistance in the Freudian framework, and Lacan argues that Plato's presentation of them is designed to invite ridicule."[50] Like the last chapter, this chapter will focus on the ancient, early modern, and modern authors, figures, and texts to provide context to the ancient material Lacan only mentions in passing.

Lacan on Love and Transference

Lacan asks his audience whether they have held back (emotionally) from someone they cared about, which he says is precisely what the analyst must do. This results in a "fantasy" [*fantasme*] replacing the loved one/analysand.[51] Freud ultimately abandoned the idea that the fantasy of a false memory of seduction or sexual abuse was opposed to reality and therefore resides in the imagination; psychoanalysis does not view reality as a space that can be experienced objectively, however, and must be understood discursively.[52] Lacan focused on what Dylan Evans refers to as the "protective function of fantasy" with a "fixed and immobile quality."[53] Evans refers to *Seminar IV: The Object Relation & Freudian Structures*, in which Lacan opposes the French "object relations" psychoanalytic school that appeared after Freud's death. He had criticized the British object relations analysts in *Seminar I: Freud's Papers on Technique.*

Because the relationship between analyst and analysand must reach transference and counter-transference, the analyst must have what Lacan refers to as the "Freedom to be indifferent [*liberté d'indifférence*],"[54] a concept he borrows from moral philosophy employed by René Descartes and

Gottfried Wilhelm (von) Leibniz. Descartes of course based his conception of subjectivity on the famous phrase *cogito ergo sum*, and he greatly influenced the polymath Leibniz, who, among many other things, was a part of the seventeenth-century universal language movement, which posited the creation of an *a priori*, artificial language (like Esperanto) for scientific purposes.

Lacan recounts a metaphor in the *Symposium* involving statues of a satyr or Silenus within which something was lodged, "assuredly precious objects [*des choses précieuses*]," to which Alcibiades compares Socrates.[55] Alcibiades says (215b) that Socrates,

> is likest to the Silenus-figures that sit in the statuaries' shops; those, I mean, which our craftsmen make with pipes or flutes in their hands: when their two halves are pulled open, they are found to contain images of gods. And I further suggest that he resembles the satyr Marsyas. Now, as to your likeness, Socrates, to these in figure, I do not suppose even you yourself will dispute it; but I have next to tell you that you are like them in every other respect.[56]

> ἐν τοῖς ἑρμογλυφείοις καθημένοις, οὕστινας ἐργάζονται οἱ δημιουργοὶ σύριγγας ἢ αὐλοὺς ἔχοντας, οἳ διχάδε διοιχθέντες φαίνονται ἔνδοθεν ἀγάλματα ἔχοντες θεῶν. καὶ φημὶ αὖ ἐοικέναι αὐτὸν τῷ σατύρῳ τῷ Μαρσύᾳ. ὅτι μὲν οὖν τό γε εἶδος ὅμοιος εἶ τούτοις, ὦ Σώκρατες, οὐδ᾽ αὐτὸς ἄν που ἀμφισβητήσαις: ὡς δὲ καὶ τἆλλα ἔοικας, μετὰ τοῦτο ἄκουε.

Marsyas was a satyr who challenged Apollo musically and lost his life, making him a hubristic figure. Lacan uses the metaphor to represent the "lack" [*manque*] in the analysand that the analyst seeks to uncover through treatment. But, as Ellie Ragland-Sullivan notes, a Lacanian analyst "seeks to imitate lack itself in order to incite an analysand to work with desire, without the analyst's confusing the transference that comes back from the analysand with love to which he or she must respond, or a desire to be satisfied."[57] In other words, the analyst must provoke desire from the analysand to seek to fill his lack through the analyst and the treatment. A. D. C. Cake similarly argues that Socrates is the "cause of desire" for the young Alcibiades because of a "lack," a "withholding that Alcibiades identifies with the *agalma* inside the *silenus*."[58] Because Socrates is the cause of Alcibiades desires, he merely wishes to "point the power of Alcibiades desire beyond himself and to guide Alcibiades on the correct path," which makes Socrates the analyst who needs to employ the "force of desire" directed at himself as analyst while simultaneously rechanneling the desire to the goals of treatment.[59] Lacan then mentions one of Freud's *Papers on Technique*, "Observations on Transference-Love," in which Freud discusses transference manifesting as literal love on the part of the analysand for the analyst, a phenomenon that occurs because of "the analytic situation" and not "the charms" of the analyst.[60]

Lacan explains that an individual who seeks psychoanalytic treatment presumably does not "know what he has, and the whole unconscious, the fundamental 'he doesn't know,' is already implied therein," which Lacan associates with the "know thyself" [γνῶθι σεαυτόν] tradition for which Socrates was known, as in Plato's *Apology* (38a), Socrates says at his trial, "the unexamined life is not worth living" [ὁ δὲ ἀνεξέταστος βίος οὐ βιωτὸς ἀνθρώπῳ]. Lacan says that Freud essentially teaches that an analysand who reaches the completion of analysis finds his own lack, and that psychoanalysis seeks to address this lack, which he suggests might refer to castration or *Penisneid*, "penis envy." Analysis, in other words, reveals the "unconscious Other."[61] Lacan says that analysts must know that the analysand does not know what is lacking (the unconscious Other), which is precisely why someone seeks treatment and which provides what Lacan calls the "inscience that is characteristic of the unconscious," meaning the lack of knowledge constitutive of the unconscious.[62]

Lacan says that in love people encounter the "wrenching and discordance" [*déchirement, la discordance*], whereby people do not need "to dialogue" or "to dialectize" concerning love to experience this discord or gap because they are already "in the thick of it" [*dans le coup*].[63] Ragland-Sullivan argues that in this *Seminar* Lacan reads Plato's depiction of Socrates as a "master teacher" to demonstrate how analysts can employ transference dialectically to get the analysands to "distinguish between desire and love."[64] But being in love comes with the great risk of "exposing" oneself "to the risk of a certain immediate misunderstanding."[65] Lacan then goes further, suggesting "a formulation that takes up anew what is already indicated in the analysis of the creation of meaning in the signifier—signified relation [*sens dans la rapport significant-signifie*], provided we are prepared to see in what follows how it should be handled and its truth" because love is merely a signifier, that is, a metaphor or a substitution.[66] Lacan's complicated syntax here obscures what he means to say, in essence that the love object, the beloved, is only half of the meaning of an analysand's reason for seeking treatment because it includes no signified. In Saussurean linguistics, the relationship between the signifier and signified produces meaning in spite of the arbitrary nature of the relationship between signifier and signified. Lacan suggests that the analyst view love as a signifier without an apparent conscious signified that would have a similarly arbitrary relationship to the love signifier.

Lacan on Love and Religion

In this section, Lacan makes a digression to talk about love in the context of religious thought since the birth of Christ, all of which he claims has mentioned Plato's *Symposium*. Lacan refers to a hypothetical "country bumpkin who leaves his little patch of ground [*lopin*] outside Athens" who would merely view the Symposium as a "gathering of aging faeries [*tantouses*], as people call them, a meeting of old faggots [*lopes*]."[67] Lacan says that the *Symposium* creates an "illusion of authenticity—distance, indications of transmission, of who repeated what another told him," by means of which Plato creates "depth" [*profondeur*] that amplifies what the characters say. Lacan suggests that the *Symposium* can be considered a "eulogy" for love, or perhaps an encomium or praise.[68] Phaedrus provides the first speech in the dialogue.

Phaedrus is of course the title of one of Plato's dialogues from what has become known as his middle period, which also includes the *Republic* and the *Symposium*. The *Phaedrus* addresses the proper way to practice rhetoric before it turns to a discussion of erotic love. The real Phaedrus was an Athenian Socratic philosopher who also appeared in the *Protagoras* as well as the *Symposium*. According to classicist William David Ross, Plato depicts Phaedrus as "enthusiastic and rather naïve."[69] Ragland-Sullivan characterizes Phaedrus as "candid and modest," and Phaedrus' attribution of Love's "power and superiority" to his having no parents suggests "the urge to enshroud questions regarding human origins in mystery and enigma is far from new."[70]

Lacan notes that Phaedrus' task is to focus his speech on "religion, myth, or even ethnography."[71] Lacan says that Phaedrus mentions two "theologians," Hesiod (eighth–seventh century B.C.E.) and Parmenides (sixth or fifth century B.C.E). Hesiod's *Theogony* provided a genealogical account of the Olympian gods, and Parmenides, a pre-Socratic, whose sole surviving work survives only in fragments, had a dialogue by Plato named after him. Parmenides' poem opens (1.1–3) with a description of his allegorical chariot ride from daylight into night and then his meeting a goddess whose speech forms the rest of the poem: "The mares which carry me, as far as ever my heart may desire, were escorting me, when they brought and placed me on the resounding road of the goddess, which carries through all places the man who knows" [῞Ιπποι ταί με φέρουσιν, ὅσον τ' ἐπὶ θυμὸς ἱκάνοι, / πέμπον, ἐπεί μ' ἐς ὁδὸν βῆσαν πολύφημον ἄγουσαι / δαίμονος, ἣ κατὰ πάντ' ἄστη φέρει εἰδότα φῶτα].[72] The poem principally deals with the nature of reality and perception as well as matters of ontology and epistemology. Heidegger gave a lecture course on Parmenides in the early 1940s and Lacan mentions a study of Parmenides by Jean Beaufort, a French philosopher important to the popularization of Heidegger's thought in France.

Lacan anticipates how all of this relates to his tripartite model of subjectivity, the Symbolic, Imaginary, and Real. For Lacan, the Symbolic is the locus of language, which inaugurates the human infant into human subjectivity upon its learning how to use it. The Imaginary in Lacan's formulation refers to a challenge to the Symbolic and the law of language and serves as the site of narcissism. The Real is the pre-linguistic state of the human infant that exists outside of the Symbolic network of language and discourse. The Symbolic introduces a cut in the Real by subjecting purely phenomenological, sensory perception to language and discourse. According to Lorenzo Chiesa, Lacan allows us to understand that "love does *not* belong to the Real but functions as an intermediary between the Real and what in Lacanian theory is opposed to it, that is, everyday reality (in its symbolic and imaginary connotations)."[73]

Lacan says that the Greek gods "are a mode by which the real is revealed," which he says is the reason philosophical developments have attempted to "eliminate them."[74] Bruce Fink argues that Lacan here refers to the "multiplicity of gods associated with nature—immanent in nature and in natural events like storms, lightning, thunder, and wind—that are independent of our will and do with us as they please."[75] This is because the ancient Greeks believed that the gods were constitutive of the very "fabric of the world, coextensive with it, and involved in every facet of it."[76] Ragland-Sullivan argues "Lacan stresses that the gods are of the Real–something more obscured (or repressed) from our knowledge today than from Greek knowledge when the gods were plural and powerful in multiple ways. Yet for Socrates love is not itself a good object."[77] It is also the reason "Christian revelation," as Hegel believed, resides on the same path that eliminates them because it is on the same path from polytheism to atheism. In contrast to the divine as the "height of revelation, of *numen*, as real shining and appearance," revelation in Christianity rests on a "path that leads to the reduction" and "abolition" of the divine. This is because it reduces the Christian God to the word, the λόγος, which resembles the philosopher's destiny to deny the gods.[78] People look for Logos "at the level of signifying articulation" instead of for revelations he has hitherto found only in the Real. As Fink notes, with Christianity we can no longer seek truth in "material signs" but rather in "speech itself," i.e., the "self-consistency of concepts" within the "internal coherence of the signifier" of the entire signifying system.[79] Fink offers the French saying for removing the petals of a flower to illustrate the alternative to the internal/external dichotomy: "*il m'aime, un peu, beaucoup, passionnément, à la folie, pas du tout*," which he says provides five choices to chose from instead of two: "he loves me, a little, a lot, passionately, to madness, not at all."

Lacan is also referring here to the beginning of the New Testament, "In the beginning [ἀρχῆ] was the Word [λόγος], and the Word was with God, and the Word was God," which contrasts with the opening of Genesis, "In the beginning God created the heaven and the earth. And the earth was without form [תֹהוּ], and void [וָבֹהוּ]; and darkness [וְחֹשֶׁךְ] was upon the face of the deep [תְהוֹם]." In other words, Creation provided order and structure to a formless void that resembles the Real. But in the New Testament, we already have form and structure (the Symbolic), and the Word was always already present with and as God. The Old Testament opens with the Pentateuch, the Books of Mosaic Law that outline the strict legislative contract God creates with humankind. The only thing that God can create after this covenant is, therefore, a challenge to that Law (Imaginary) through the introduction of the impossible man-god Christ. By introducing Christ the man-god, God conflates the divine Law into a human form that, according to Lacan, can only lead to the ultimate denial of God's very existence.

Lacan mentions what he has called Plato's *Schwärmerei*, German for "enthusiasm" but with a sense of fanaticism, and says this has attracted mystagogues to Plato's works, which he says are the part of Christianity that have always been gnostic.[80] Phaedrus mentions love as the oldest of the gods, having been born just after Chaos, as well as love being the first goddess mentioned in Parmenides' poem. Phaedrus refers (178b) to Hesiod's *Theogony* (116), saying, "Hesiod says that Chaos came first into being—and thereafter rose Broad-breasted Earth, sure seat of all for aye, And Love" [Ησίοδος πρῶτον μὲν Χάος φησὶ γενέσθαι— ... αὐτὰρ ἔπειτα Γαῖ' εὐρύστερνος, πάντων ἕδος ἀσφαλὲς αἰεί, ἠδ' Ἔρος]. But love transformed over the centuries, and, as Lacan notes, by the seventeenth century, people began speaking of Eros, which Lacan says resided in the courtly love tradition, as in Honoré d'Urfé's pastoral novel *L'Astrée*, published in the early 1600s.

Lacan mentions Plotinus' Second *Ennead*, which he says illustrates what *L'Astrée* echoes, "words with no import" [*des mots sans importance*].[81] The Greek-speaking, Egyptian-born philosopher Plotinus (205–269/270 C.E.) was one of the primary founders of Neo-Platonism and had a profound influence on the development of subsequent Western philosophy. Compiled by his student Porphyry, his *Enneads* in part address the Platonic mind-body problem through the perspective of materialism, and the word Plato and Plotinus use for "Soul" is ψυχή, *psyche*. In the Second *Ennead*, Plotinus in fact mentions Plato several times. Plotinus writes (II.1.2) that Plato believes that "the nature of body [σωμάτως] is in continual flux" and he suggests (II.1.7), "perhaps we should listen more carefully to Plato."[82] Plotinus notes (II.3.9) that in Plato's *Timaeus*, "the God who makes the world gives the 'first principle of the soul,' but the gods who are borne through the heavens 'the terrible and inevitable passions,' 'angers' and desires [ἐπιθυμίας] and 'pleasures [ἡδονὰς] and pains [πάθη],' and the 'other kind of soul,' from which come passions of this kind." Plotinus also claims (II.3.15) that Plato believed in self-determined destiny combined with fate, as "Plato gives the souls lots and choices before the circling of the Spindle."

Plotinus also writes (II.2.1) of matters more relevant to Lacanian psychoanalysis, defining heavenly movement as "A movement of self-concentrated awareness [συναισθητικὴ] and intellection [συννοητικὴ] and of life." Plotinus also discusses (II.2.3) desire: "And in heaven, where the soul is in good and more vividly perceptive, it moves to the good and sets its body moving in space in the manner natural to it there. The perceptive power in its turn receives the good from that which is above and in delight pursues its own and is carried everywhere to the good which is everywhere." Plotinus also refers (II.9.5) to people with a body like men have desire [ἐπιθυμίαν] and griefs [λύπας] and passions [ὀργὰς].

Plotinus discusses (II.4.1–9) the Platonic theory of forms, which Plato had developed in the *Republic*, at one point referring to an ideal form of a couch or chair that has characteristics of "couchness" or "chairness" that define the properties for every real, tangible couch or chair. Socrates asks (*Republic*, 597a), "Were you not just now saying that he does not make the idea or form which we say is the real couch, the couch in itself, but only some particular couch?"[83] Shortly thereafter, Socrates says (*Republic*, 597a), "We must not be surprised, then, if this too is only a dim adumbration [ἀμυδρόν τυγχάνει] in comparison with reality [ἀλήθειαν]." This resembles Saussurean linguistics, in which the sign is an abstract concept that refers to a literal thing through an arbitrary connection within language. Plotinus asks (II.4.16) whether matter is "the same thing as otherness" [Ἆρ' οὖν καὶ ἑτερότητι ταὐτόν;] and answers, "No, rather it is the same thing as the part of otherness which is opposed to the things which in the full and proper sense exist, that is to say rational formative principles. Therefore, though it is nonexistent, it has certain sort of existence in this way, and is the same thing as privation [στέρησις], if privation is opposition to the things that exist in rational form" [Ἢ οὔ, ἀλλὰ μορίῳ ἑτερότητος ἀντιταττομένῳ πρὸς τὰ ὄντα κυρίως, ἃ δὴ λόγοι. Διὸ καὶ μὴ ὂν οὕτω τι ὂν καὶ στερήσει ταὐτόν, εἰ ἡ στέρησις ἀντίθεσις πρὸς τὰ ἐν λόγῳ ὄντα]. Plotinus could just as easily have written that alienation results from inadequate indoctrination into the symbolic order.

Lacan concludes this section by saying that any theological text about the Trinity, which Lacan equates to Zeus, Aphrodite, and Eros as the father, son, and holy spirit, respectively, has its genesis in the ancient understanding of love. Like Lacan's tripartite Symbolic-Imaginary-Real, Plato had a tripartite model of the soul the ψυχή, *psyche*, which included the λογιστικόν (*logistykon*, logical), the θυμοειδές (*thymoeides*, spirited), and the ἐπιθυμητικόν (*epithymetikon*, appetitive). These arguably resemble the Symbolic, the Real, and the Imaginary, respectively.

Lacan on Love and Mythology

Lacan mentions Euripides' tragedy *Alcestis* (first performed 438 B.C.E.) as illustrative of "the between-two-deaths." In Euripides' play, when the Greek King Admetus fails to offer a sacrifice to Artemis on the night he was to wed the Greek princess Alcestis, he finds his bedchamber full of serpents. Apollo coerces the Fates to allow someone to die in place of Admetus for this transgression, and only Alcestis agreed. After she died, her life was transferred to Admetus. The myth demonstrates the popular belief that "a man's truest friend is a good wife."[84] According to Kevin and Elena Corrigan, the clearly homosexual Phaedrus does not understand love only as a "sexual drive," as using Alcestis as an example "speaks of love as related to nobility of spirit" and provides a speech that does not have a clear direction.[85]

Lacan mentions Phaedrus' comments about Orpheus (179d), whom the gods sent

> back with failure from Hades, showing him only a wraith of the woman for whom he came; her real self they would not bestow, for he was accounted to have gone upon a coward's quest, too like the minstrel that he was, and to have lacked the spirit to die as Alcestis did for the sake of love.

> ἐξ Ἅιδου, φάσμα δείξαντες τῆς γυναικὸς ἐφ' ἣν ἧκεν, αὐτὴν δὲ οὐ δόντες, ὅτι μαλθακίζεσθαι ἐδόκει, ἅτε ὢν κιθαρῳδός, καὶ οὐ τολμᾶν ἕνεκα τοῦ ἔρωτος ἀποθνήσκειν ὥσπερ Ἄλκηστις, ἀλλὰ διαμηχανᾶσθαι ζῶν εἰσιέναι εἰς Ἅιδου.

The gods showing Orpheus a "wraith" [φάσμα] instead of a real woman, according to Lacan, call to mind "the difference between the object of our love insofar as our fantasies cover it over, and the other's being, insofar as love wonders whether or not it can reach it."[86] In other words, we do not fall in love with another person for who they really are but rather our projection of what we want or think our beloved to be. This creates an impossible ideal for our beloved to live up to and is often the cause for the failure of love. The gods in other words engender Orpheus with a lack through the introduction of a phantom of a woman.

Lacan then distinguishes between the story of Alcestis and that of Achilles. Achilles has a choice, according to Lacan, of whether or not to kill Hector to avenge the death of his male lover, Patroclus. Achilles' mother Thetis tells him if he chooses not to avenge the death of Patroclus, he will live to an old age, but if he seeks revenge he will follow Patroclus in death. Lacan derides French classicist Mario Meunier's claim that Achilles kills himself in Patroclus' tomb, something Lacan says he has been unable to find in any of the sources.[87] According to Chiesa, "Lacan takes Phaedrus's speech at face value and claims that Achilles is an *eromenos*; and what is more, he sacrifices his life for his lover *in spite of the fact* that Patroclus is already dead. Strictly speaking, he cannot be his substitute."[88]

Phaedrus focuses his speech about Achilles in the context of the erotic connection between Achilles and Patroclus. Lacan says that the gods find it "sublime" and "more marvelous than anything else" when a "beloved behaves as one would expect a lover to behave." This is what contrasts Achilles with Alcestis. Lacan suggests that this story has significance because of the amount of time Phaedrus spends telling it, and he says that Plato in this passage explores *Carte Tendre*, "the Map of the Tender Feelings." Because the gods give the "love prize" to Achilles, according to Lacan, Alcestis becomes the lover, which means that Achilles' sacrifice as the beloved is more "admirable" than that of Alcestis. Lacan says that the "hypochondriac" Phaedrus therefore illustrates what Lacan calls the "signification of love."[89] In his concluding remarks, Lacan says that the Alcestis narrative shows how analysts can discover "what women can experience regarding their own lack." Lacan qualifies this by arguing that Alcestis represents both "lack" and "activity."[90] As Corrigan and Corrigan argue, "the real importance of this speech is Phaedrus's genuine wonder at the effects of love."[91]

Notes

1. Jacques Lacan, *The Seminar of Jacques Lacan, Book VIII: Transference, 1960–1961*, ed. Jacques-Alain Miller and trans. Bruce Fink (Cambridge, UK; Malden, MA: Polity, 2015), p. 19.
2. Lacan (2015, p. 19).
3. French quotations taken from Jacques Lacan, *Le Séminaire de Jacques Lacan, Livre VIII: Le Transfert, 1960–1961*, ed. Jacques-Alain Miller (Paris: Éditions du Seuil, 2001).
4. Lacan (2015, p. 20).
5. Ibid.
6. Lacan (2015, pp. 20–21).
7. Ibid., p. 21.
8. Ibid.
9. Ibid.
10. English translations of Plato taken from Plato, *Lysis. Symposium. Gorgias*, trans. Walter R. M. Lamb (Cambridge: Harvard University Press, 1967).
11. Lacan (2015, p. 21).
12. Ibid., p. 22.
13. English translations of Plutarch taken from Plutarch. *Lives*, trans. Bernadotte Perrin (Harvard University Press, 1916).
14. Lacan (2015, p. 23).
15. Ibid., p. 24.
16. A. D. C. Cake, 'Lacan's Psychoanalysis and Plato's *Symposium*: Desire and the (In)Efficacy of the Signifying Order,' *Analecta Hermeneutica* 1 (2009): 186–187.
17. Lacan (2015, p. 25).
18. Leo Strauss, *Leo Strauss on Plato's "Symposium"* (Chicago: University of Chicago Press, 2001), pp. 155–156.
19. Jacques Lacan, "The Instance of the Letter in the Unconscious, or Reason Since Freud," *Écrits: The First Complete Edition in English*, trans. Bruce Fink (New York: Norton, 2006), p. 423.
20. Lacan (2015, p. 26).
21. Ibid., p. 27.

22. Ibid., p. 28.
23. Ibid.
24. Lacan (2015, p. 28).
25. Dylan Evans, *An Introductory Dictionary of Lacanian Psychoanalysis* (New York: Routledge, 1996), pp. 110–111.
26. Jacques Lacan, *The Seminar of Jacques Lacan, Book III: The Psychoses, 1955–1956*, ed. Russell Grigg, trans. Jacques-Alain Miller (London: Routledge, 2000), p. 152.
27. Jacques Lacan, *The Seminar of Jacques Lacan, Book VII: The Ethics of Psychoanalysis, 1959–1960*, trans. Dennis Porter (New York: Norton, 1992), p. 223.
28. Lacan (2000, p. 212).
29. Ibid.
30. Evans (1996, pp. 187–188).
31. Lacan (2015, p. 29).
32. Ellie Ragland-Sullivan, 'Plato's *Symposium* and the Lacanian Theory of Transference: Or, What Is Love?' *South Atlantic Quarterly* 88 (4) (1989): 735.
33. Lacan (2015, p. 30).
34. Ibid.
35. Ibid.
36. Ibid.
37. Evans (1996, p. 198).
38. Lacan (1992, p. 91).
39. Evans (1996, p. 198).
40. Lacan (1992, p. 293).
41. Evans (1996, p. 199) and Lacan (1992, p. 112).
42. Evans (1996, p. 199).
43. Lorenzo Chiesa, '"Le ressort de l'amour": Lacan's Theory of Love in His Reading of Plato's *Symposium*.' *Angelaki* 11 (3) (2006): 69.
44. Lacan (2015, p. 31).
45. Ibid.
46. Ibid.
47. Ibid., p. 32.
48. Ibid., p. 31.
49. Lacan (2015, p. 36).
50. James Penney, *The Structures of Love: Art and Politics Beyond the Transference* (Albany: State University of New York Press, 2012), p. 56.
51. Lacan (2015, p. 37).

52. Evans (1996, p. 59).
53. Evans (1996, p. 60).
54. Lacan (2015, p. 37).
55. Ibid., p. 38.
56. English translations of Plato's *Symposium* taken from Plato, *Plato in Twelve Volumes*, trans. Harold N. Fowler (Cambridge; London: Harvard University Press; William Heinemann Ltd., 1925).
57. Ellie Ragland-Sullivan, 'Plato's *Symposium* and the Lacanian Theory of Transference: Or, What Is Love?' *South Atlantic Quarterly* 88 (4) (1989): 745.
58. A. D. C. Cake, 'Lacan's Psychoanalysis and Plato's *Symposium*: Desire and the (In)Efficacy of the Signifying Order,' *Analecta Hermeneutica* 1 (2009): 186.
59. Cake (2009, p. 186).
60. Sigmund Freud, 'Observations on Transference-Love (Further Recommendations on the Technique of Psycho-Analysis III' (1915), in *The Standard Edition of the Complete Psychological Works of Sigmund Freud, Volume XII (1911–1913): The Case of Schreber, Papers on Technique and Other Works*, trans. James Strachey (London: Vintage, 2001), p. 160.
61. Lacan (2015, p. 39).
62. Ibid.
63. Ibid., p. 40.
64. Ragland-Sullivan (1989, p. 725).
65. Lacan (2015, p. 40).
66. Ibid.
67. Ibid., p. 41.
68. Ibid., p. 42.
69. William David Ross, 'Phaedrus (1),' in *The Oxford Classical Dictionary*, ed. N. G. L. Hammond and H. H. Scullard (Oxford: Clarendon, 1970), p. 807.
70. Ragland-Sullivan (1989, p. 733).
71. Lacan (2015, p. 43).
72. Parmenides, *Parmenides: A Text with Translation, Commentary, and Critical Essays*, trans. Leonardo Taran (Princeton: Princeton University Press, 1965), pp. 7–8.
73. Lorenzo Chiesa, '"Le Ressort de L'amour": Lacan's Theory of Love in His Reading of Plato's *Symposium*,' *Angelaki* 11 (3) (2006): 61–81, 62.
74. Lacan (2015 p. 44).

75. Bruce Fink, *Lacan on Love: An Exploration of Lacan's Seminar VIII, Transference* (Cambridge, UK; Malden, MA: Polity, 2016), p. 167.
76. Fink (2016, p. 167).
77. Ragland-Sullivan (1989, p. 741).
78. Lacan (2015 p. 44).
79. Fink (2016, p. 167).
80. Lacan (2015, p. 44).
81. Ibid., p. 45.
82. English quotations of Plotinus come from Plotinus, *Ennead II*, trans. A. H. Armstrong (Cambridge: Harvard University Press, 2011).
83. English quotations of Plato's *Republic* come from Plato, *The Republic II: Books VI–X*, trans. Paul Shorey, vol. 1, 2 vols. (Cambridge: Harvard University Press, 1963).
84. Herbert Jennings Rose, 'Alcestis,' in *The Oxford Classical Dictionary*, ed. N. G. L. Hammond, and H. H. Scullard (Oxford: Clarendon, 1970), p. 36.
85. Kevin Corrigan and Elena Corrigan, *Plato's Dialectic at Play: Argument, Structure, and Myth in the 'Symposium'* (University Park: Pennsylvania State University Press, 2004), p. 51.
86. Lacan (2015, p. 47).
87. Ibid., p. 47.
88. Chiesa (2006, p. 63).
89. Lacan (2015, p. 48).
90. Ibid., p. 49.
91. Corrigan and Corrigan (2004, p. 56).

References

Cake, A.D.C. 2009. Lacan's Psychoanalysis and Plato's *Symposium*: Desire and the (In)Efficacy of the Signifying Order. *Analecta Hermeneutica* 1: 178–190.

Chiesa, Lorenzo. 2006. "Le ressort de l'amour": Lacan's Theory of Love in His Reading of Plato's *Symposium*. *Angelaki* 11 (3): 61–81.

Corrigan, Kevin, and Elena Corrigan. 2004. *Plato's Dialectic at Play: Argument, Structure, and Myth in the "Symposium"*. University Park: Pennsylvania State University Press.

Evans, Dylan. 1996. *An Introductory Dictionary of Lacanian Psychoanalysis*. New York: Routledge.
Fink, Bruce. 2016. *Lacan on Love: An Exploration of Lacan's Seminar VIII, Transference*. Cambridge, UK and Malden, MA: Polity Press.
Freud, Sigmund. 2001. Observations on Transference-Love (Further Recommendations on the Technique of Psycho-Analysis III (1915). In *The Standard Edition of the Complete Psychological Works of Sigmund Freud, Volume XII (1911–1913): The Case of Schreber, Papers on Technique and Other Works*. Trans. James Strachey. London: Hogarth Press.
Hammond, N.G.L., and H.H. Scullard (eds.). 1970. *The Oxford Classical Dictionary*. Oxford: Clarendon Press.
Lacan, Jacques. 1992. *The Seminar of Jacques Lacan, Book VII: The Ethics of Psychoanalysis, 1959–1960*. Translated by Dennis Porter. New York: Norton.
———. 2000. *The Seminar of Jacques Lacan, Book III: The Psychoses, 1955–1956*. Translated by Jacques-Alain Miller. London: Routledge.
———. 2001. *Le Séminaire de Jacques Lacan, Livre VIII: Le Transfert, 1960–1961*. Edited by Jacques-Alain Miller. Paris: Éditions du Seuil.
———. 2006a. *Écrits: The First Complete Edition in English*. Translated by Bruce Fink. New York: Norton.
———. 2006b. The Instance of the Letter in the Unconscious, or Reason Since Freud. In *Écrits: The First Complete Edition in English*. Translated by Bruce Fink, 412–441. New York: Norton.
———. 2015. *Transference: The Seminar of Jacques Lacan, Book VIII*. Edited by Jacques-Alain Miller and Translated by Bruce Fink. Cambridge: Polity.
Plato. 1925. *Plato in Twelve Volumes*. Trans. Harold N. Fowler. Cambridge; London: Harvard University Press and William Heinemann.
———. 1963. *The Republic II: Books VI–X*. Trans. Paul Shorey. Cambridge: Harvard University Press.
———. 1967. *Lysis. Symposium. Gorgias*. Trans. Walter R. M. Lamb. Cambridge: Harvard University Press.
Plotinus. 2011. *Ennead II*. Trans. A. H. Armstrong. Cambridge: Harvard University Press.
Plutarch. 1916. *Lives*. Trans. Bernadotte Perrin. Cambridge: Harvard University Press.
Ragland-Sullivan, Ellie. 1989. Plato's *Symposium* and the Lacanian Theory of Transference: Or, What Is Love? *South Atlantic Quarterly* 88 (4): 725–755.
Strauss, Leo. 2001. *Leo Strauss on Plato's "Symposium"*. Chicago: University of Chicago Press.

Rose, Herbert Jennings. 1970. Alcestis. In *The Oxford Classical Dictionary*, ed. Hammond, and H. H. Scullard, 36. Oxford: Clarendon.

Ross, William David. 1970. Phaedrus (1). In *The Oxford Classical Dictionary*, ed. N. G. L. Hammond and H. H. Scullard, 807. Oxford: Clarendon.

3

"The Psychology of the Rich: Pausanias"—Commentary on Session IV

Stephanie Swales

In the beginning of this session, Lacan reviews his earlier formulations on love, including Phaedrus' idea that love is a god and the gods are of the real, and that the "other, insofar as he is aimed at in love, is…aimed at as a beloved object"[1] as opposed to a subject. Next, building off of his comments regarding Phaedrus' encomium, Lacan says that love is something that begins with being loved, with the other reaching toward you as beloved object or *erómenos*. Then, it becomes a more elevated form of love when you become *erastés*, or the one who desires and loves. Love is what occurs with the substitution of *erastés* for *erómenos*. In other words, love, like a symptom—for early Lacan at this time—has the structure of a metaphor. Love is the signification produced by the metaphor.

Lacan's example for the metaphor of love is found in the actions of Achilles, who was said to have been in the position of *erómenos* because he was younger than Patroclus. In Lacan's words, in avenging the death of Patroclus, Achilles "places himself not in the stead of, but rather in

S. Swales (✉)
University of Dallas, Irving, TX, USA

G. Basu Thakur and J. Dickstein (eds.), *Reading Lacan's Seminar VIII*,
The Palgrave Lacan Series, https://doi.org/10.1007/978-3-030-32742-2_3

the wake of Patroclus. He makes of Patroclus' fate the debt he must pay, the debt with which he must come to terms."[2] In so doing, "Achilles the beloved becomes the lover."[3] In this transition, Achilles is not simply switching positions with Patroclus, but is rather taking on his debt or lack. This kind of taking on the other's lack stands in comparison with the sacrifice of Alcestis, in which she is willing to die in the stead of her husband, putting herself in his place. Alcestis' sacrifice is considered "a less radical, total, and brilliant manifestation of love than the switching of roles that takes place in Achilles when he changes from *erómenos* into *erastés.*"[4] Although the sacrifice of Alcestis was admirable, she, as the lover, was only fulfilling her duty as a lover whereas the "miracle"[5] of love was achieved by virtue of Achilles' transformation from beloved into lover.

The Heavenly vs. The Common Aphrodite

Lacan begins his second section by highlighting Pausanias' proclamation that love is not one. Lacan points out that Pausanias speaks of there being not one but two Aphrodites: a Heavenly Aphrodite, born with no mother from "the projection onto Earth of the rain engendered by the primal castration of Uranus by Cronus,"[6] and a Common Aphrodite who resulted from the union of Zeus and the Titaness Dione. Pausanias celebrates the Heavenly Aphrodite and associated form of love and denigrates the Common Aphrodite, who is "the Venus of those who confuse one form of love with the other, who seek it at base levels…"[7]

Lacan comments here that while Phaedrus' speech reflected his love of myth, Pausanias' speech reflects his love of observing societies, rendering it almost "a sociologist's discourse."[8] As such, "[e]verything in it [Pausanias' speech] apparently hinges on the diversity of positions in the Greek world with respect to higher love, the kind of love that develops between those who are both the strongest and the most vigorous, and who are also the most intelligent…: men."[9] In other words, Pausanias' conception of higher love is based on value—a value which might change from society to society. In the Greek world of his time, if the beloved possesses a certain kind of beauty and intelligence, then he is worthy of love.

For Pausanias, the virtuous lover is one who has the good taste to love someone worthy, and he is also virtuous insofar as he seeks to give something worthy to the beloved. For instance, he might contribute to his beloved's education, thus increasing the beloved's value in terms of intelligence and career potential. Since Greek love between men typically involved an older lover and a younger, developing beloved, it would be an expected part of the relationship exchange that the older man would contribute to the younger man's education and career advancement. Even though Pausanias' higher love is based on a meritocracy—one in which it is ignoble to love someone for their money[10]—it is still founded on an exchange at the level of profit. Love, from this perspective, is an investment; as such one must take care to "invest one's psychic funds properly"[11] in young men who are old enough to prove themselves worthy of an investment. In basing love on a person seen as a good investment or a "good fund of capital,"[12] one renders the beloved as comparable and in some sense equivalent to other potential love objects. People are only more or less special, attractive, humorous, and so on. This sounds more like the metonymic operation of desire than love. Lacan proclaims that this kind of love "that presents itself as a love of the Good, love for acquisition of the best goods…is far from being Plato's opinion."[13]

Often interacting with notions of class, such that it would be a waste or a shameful degradation to marry below one's social rank, those operating under Pausanias' theory of love have been found in a myriad of cultures and historical times. In our time, under capitalism, this type of love is thriving. A focus on value and exchange, of course, is part and parcel of capitalism just as much as it is the love which is the subject of Pausanias' encomium. We can clearly see this capitalist form of love thriving via the many dating apps which proliferate. Dating app users see pictures and a brief amount of information about a person, and with a swipe to the left or to the right, users indicate their romantic or sexual interest or disinterest in that person as a potential beloved. The potential beloved of value is typically one who is quantitatively more attractive or in possession of a higher-status career. What is more, users of the app are investing their time and money into those they choose to meet in person for a date, and so happy customers of the app are those who feel they got a return on their investment. Nowadays, people even speak of "putting themselves on the market." In the capitalist discourse of love, the countable is all that counts. This perspective, one in which the question of value is on the forefront of relations with others, is what Lacan calls "the psychology of the rich."[14]

What is the status of what passes for love relations, then, under the discourse of the capitalist? Lacan viewed the capitalist discourse as a contemporary version of the master's discourse such that at its foundation is a foreclosure of symbolic castration.[15] Within capitalism, the lack at the heart of subjectivity is seen as a mere frustration or flaw which can be corrected by a particular object or other—or dating partner—in the market. This idea is also reminiscent of the spherical people mythically invented by Aristophanes as described in the sixth session of the seminar, as what each person is lacking is precisely what the beloved has, thinking that if only they could connect with their other halves they would be whole once again. Even if a sphere can be cut into halves, each half still cannot exactly be said to be castrated. Potential beloveds under the capitalist discourse occupy the status of an object or an S1 which answers the call of the divided subject and functions as its truth. Under the logic of the capitalist discourse, the semblance of dissatisfaction, in other words, can be remedied by a beloved as S1 who, by virtue of being a lawyer or potential trophy wife, seems to promise satisfaction and completeness. We can see then that the capitalist discourse reduces desire to a demand by translating desire into something that can be gratified by a product on the market. A love, then, such as that described by Pausanias which is founded upon the social capital of the beloved, is one which may function to foreclose castration.

Such a love is firmly rooted in the imaginary, when you "love" someone on account of their being similar to you (you're both Red Sox fans, from a Jewish background, etc.) and their beautiful image, smell, etc.. Lacan said that "the phenomenon of passionate love [*amour-passion*] [is] determined by the image of the ideal ego."[16] In some cases of homosexual love, in the *Family Complexes*[17] Lacan theorized that the lover not only loves but also identifies with the beloved, creating a love between two semblables. The lover might see something of his ideal ego in the beloved and identify with him on account of it. Alternatively, Pausanias may be speaking of instances in which the lover puts his beloved in the place of his own ego-ideal, seeing his beloved as a perfect representation of certain ideals (honesty, perhaps) which he himself has failed to live up to. This too is a kind of imaginary order love as it is based on one's own ego-ideal rather than that of the beloved.[18]

Lacan says that where Pausanias goes wrong in his speech is that his ethics in love only corresponds to "what one might call outward signs of value."[19] So what are the inward signs of value upon which an alternative ethics in love might be based? In order to answer this question, Lacan launches upon the story of a rich Calvinist—a man who believed that "it is on Earth that God rewards the people he loves with plentiful goods."[20] The Calvinist accidentally knocked a woman over with the bumper of his car. She was a pretty concierge's daughter, and she "reacted coldly to his apologies, even more coldly to his proposal to indemnify her, and still more coldly to his proposals to go have dinner together."[21]

There are two things about his choice of beloved or *erómenos* that are more striking than the fact that she was pretty. First, even as she refused his offer of money, her status as a concierge's daughter was perhaps attractive because it allowed the rich man to see himself as being able to give to her something in the way of riches that she was lacking and would want. Second, and more importantly, by reacting coldly to his advances, she incited his desire for her as special, as being in a different category than all the other women he encountered who may have reacted more warmly on account of his riches. She was incomparably more valuable than these other women because her value existed outside of the signifying system that considers money to be the ultimate surplus value, in which anything and everything is more or less valuable in monetary terms. The greater her refusal, the more the Calvinist wanted not just to take her to dinner but to marry her. The concierge's daughter thus located her value outside of what could be bought, outside of capitalism and exchange. And this value, that of embodying object *a*, is in a register from which money or any other "outward signs of value"[22] is regarded as worth next to nothing.

The rich Calvinist, then, like many rich people, had likely been used to being able to obtain everything that he wanted, thinking along the logic of capitalist discourse that what he wanted was this or that car, this or that woman—that his lack was easily filled up. The concierge's daughter, by her refusals, brought out the lack in him, enlivening his desire, perhaps even enabling him for once to give not what he had but what he didn't have. This part of the story of the rich Calvinist might therefore meet Lacan's formula for love, given later in the seminar: "love is giving what you don't have."[23] But this kind of love was difficult for the concierge's daughter to perceive, since in her perspective he offered her this and that object of monetary value.

Lacan tells us that the concierge's daughter acquiesced to the marriage and was provided with costly jewels and the like, only to run off with a man of modest means. The moral of the story Lacan points to here is that since the Calvinist was so rich, his lavish presents of jewels so previous they had to be kept in a safe were akin to mere trifles and flattery. His giving what he had—and had lots of—did not elevate him to the signification of love. This story paves the way for his later formulation of love as giving what you don't have. The signification of love is not achieved if you give what you do have, which is what the virtuous lovers in Pausanias' higher love do. As Lacan puts it in the third section of this session, "it is the epitome of the Christian curse that what is most worthwhile is forever refused to the rich."[24]

Pausanias Having Paused

Lacan begins his third section with an exploration into the meaning of Apollodorus' words "*Pausaníou de pausaménou*" or "Pausanias having paused." Lacan mentions a recent talk he had with Alexandre Kojève, who had taught him about Hegel. Kojève had said, "In any case, you will never be able to interpret the *Symposium* if you do not know why Aristophanes had the hiccoughs."[25] When Pausanias finally pauses his speech, it was Aristophanes' turn to speak about love. However, Plato tells us that Aristophanes "had such a bad case of the hiccups—he'd probably stuffed himself again, though, of course, it could have been anything—that making a speech was totally out of the question" (185c–d). If the cause of Aristophanes, hiccoughs had simply been overeating, then Plato would not have added "of course, it could have been anything." We get a clue in Lacan's observation that after the initial mention of "Pausanias having paused," in very short order—in a 16-line conversation about the problem of how to stop Aristophanes' hiccoughs—"paus" is used as a pun a total of seven times. Why all the punning? Well, Lacan reasons, there must have been some sort of joke underlying the discussion. Lacan reflects that "if Aristophanes has the hiccoughs, it's because throughout Pausanias' discourse he's been splitting his sides laughing—and Plato has been doing the same" (62). Pausanias' speech is something about which to laugh.

Notes

1. Jacques Lacan, *Transference: Seminar Book VIII* (1960), trans. B. Fink (Malden, MA: Polity Press, 2015), p. 51.
2. Ibid., p. 53.
3. Ibid., p. 54.
4. Ibid., p. 53.
5. Ibid.
6. Ibid., p. 54.
7. Ibid.
8. Ibid., p. 55.
9. Ibid.
10. Ibid., p. 59.
11. Ibid., p. 56.
12. Ibid., p. 57.
13. Ibid., p. 59.
14. Ibid., p. 50.
15. Jacques Lacan, 'Du discours psychanalytique', in *Lacan in Italia 1953–1978. En Italie Lacan*, ed. G. B. Contri (Milan: La Salamandra, 1972), p. 48.
16. Jacques Lacan, 'Variations on the Standard Treatment' (1955), in *Écrits: The First Complete Edition in English* (2006), trans. B. Fink (New York and London: W. W. Norton, 2006), p. 285.
17. Jacques Lacan, 'The Family Complexes' (1938), in *Critical Texts,* vol. 5, issue 3 (1988), trans. C. Asp.
18. Bruce Fink, *Lacan on Love: An Exploration of Lacan's Seminar VIII, Transference* (Malden, MA: Polity Press, 2016), p. 61.
19. Jacques Lacan, *Transference: Seminar Book VIII* (1960), trans. B. Fink (Malden, MA: Polity Press, 2015), p. 58.
20. Ibid., p. 57.
21. Ibid., p. 58.

22. Ibid.
23. Ibid., p. 129.
24. Ibid., p. 60.
25. Ibid., p. 61.

References

Fink, B. 2016. *Lacan on Love: An Exploration of Lacan's Seminar VIII, Transference*. Malden, MA: Polity Press.

Lacan, J. 1938. "The Family Complexes". In *Critical Texts*, vol. 5, issue 3 (1988), translated by C. Asp.

———. 1955. "Variations on the Standard Treatment". In *Écrits: The First Complete Edition in English* (2006), translated by Bruce Fink. New York and London: W. W. Norton.

———. 1972. "Du discours psychanalytique". In *Lacan in Italia 1953–1978. En Italie Lacan*, edited by G. B. Contri, 32–55. Milan: La Salamandra.

———. 2015. *Transference: Seminar Book VIII* (1960), translated by Bruce Fink. Malden, MA: Polity Press.

4

"Medical Harmony: Eryximachus"—Commentary on Session V

Calum Neill

Lacan begins Session V by reminding us that this discourse, this seminar, concerns the question of transference. Although he is taking Plato's *Symposium* as his starting point, he self-deprecatingly points out that analyzing ancient Greek texts is not his forte. Nonetheless, he also draws our attention to the fact that in providing an interpretation of the text, he is most likely already influencing how we read the text. This is a crucial point concerning interpretation and transference. Already in the reading of the text, which may be read as a text about transference *avant la lettre*, we encounter transference at work. We thus have, from the outset, an entwining of communication, interpretation, and transference.

Implicitly drawing our attention to the link between Socrates and the contemporary figure of the psychoanalyst, Lacan comments that people assume, when they go to see an analyst, that "he" (*sic*) will be able to tell them something about themselves, that the analyst will have some knowledge which they, the analyst, can impart to them, the analysand.

C. Neill (✉)
Edinburgh Napier University, Edinburgh, Scotland, UK
e-mail: c.neill@napier.ac.uk

G. Basu Thakur and J. Dickstein (eds.), *Reading Lacan's Seminar VIII*,
The Palgrave Lacan Series, https://doi.org/10.1007/978-3-030-32742-2_4

Here Lacan uses the French term *science*, rather than the more common term *connaissance.* While both terms translate as "knowledge," there is an obvious invocation of science in the former choice which allows him to immediately open up a double reading. The analyst is assumed to have some particular knowledge (or science) of the subject but he is also assumed to have access to a (scientific) methodology which can function in relation to the analysand.

Lacan underscores that what he is describing here is "simply" the subjective perspective. People think analysts are endowed with special knowledge or abilities. The analysand, at the beginning, knows nothing of the unconscious, both insofar as they are not thinking in terms of psychoanalytic theory and insofar as they are unaware of (their) unconscious thoughts. In what ways then, Lacan asks, is this simple relationship of the naïve analysand with, and their assumptions with regard to, the analyst, like the relationship we would find in love?

As we have known since Freud (1914), transference can simultaneously be understood as a specific mode of love and, through the specificity of this mode, that which brings other more familiar modes of love into question (Lacan 2015: 65). Transference works to bring out the ambivalence in love, the intertwining of love and hate. This is a peculiar insight of psychoanalysis, an insight which is not explicitly voiced in the philosophical tradition but there all the same. Although Socrates may not have overtly brought out the ambivalence buried within love, something of this idea is already there from this beginning. The journey of analysis, while driven by the goal of discovering what is in one without one's knowing it (i.e., the unconscious), is always ultimately a movement toward the encounter with one's lack (desire). Transference, thus, articulates to desire.

"Desire is not a good," Lacan tells us, explicitly emphasizing, "in any sense of the term" (ibid.). Here, we should hear "good" in the sense of an advantage, a benefit, a possession, an object. It is certainly not a good in the sense of a product or something created (*ktesis*). An inversion occurs between the search for what one (unknowingly) has—which marks both the beginning of analysis in the prosaic sense and the beginning of analysis in the logical sense—and the encounter with desire. This inversion marks the emergence of transference. Which would then be to say that transference plays some part in the shift from the aim of uncovering what one has to the encounter with what one does not have.

The status of desire here is crucial and is what appears to have motivated Lacan to choose *The Symposium* as his textual focus. The key passage of *The Symposium* in this regard is the discussion immediately preceding and following Alcibiades' appearance. Lacan characterizes this appearance as doubly strange—strange dramatically and strange formally. Alcibiades bursts in suddenly, drunk. But he also breaks the Form of the discourse by turning it from the general to the specific and personal.

Alcibiades takes umbrage at Socrates' sharing a seat with the most attractive man in the room, Agathon, and then proceeds to eulogize Socrates. In the course of his eulogy, among other things, he confesses his love for Socrates, while also accusing him of being manipulative, insofar as he pretends to be someone's lover but then orchestrates things in such a way that the roles invert. Socrates, in turn, interprets Alcibiades' speech as having a practical aim: to jealously separate him from Agathon.

Lacan asks two questions here. Firstly, why does Alcibiades confess (his love)? And secondly, why does Socrates so immediately point to the eulogy's practical purpose? Lacan draws our attention to the similarity between this scene and something which at times happens in transference. This impression of a similarity, he tells us, will need to be explored in more depth. However, while it may be tempting to read the scene as an adumbration of psychoanalysis, we should resist this temptation. What is important in the scene, for Lacan, is the encounter, which reveals a number of crucial points.

Lacan underscores here the need to understand context. The encounter between Alcibiades and Socrates is core to his reading of *The Symposium*, but it should not be read out of context. Once again, a broader point concerning interpretation seems to be being made here. Transference entails interpretation but there is no interpretation of a text without context.

Lacan now jumps back to an earlier speech that was from Eryximachus, a medical doctor. Lacan emphasizes that he is a doctor and raises the question of the significance of this fact. He dismisses the idea that we should take Plato's writing here as particularly representative of the state of medicine at the time, but he does think the speech brings out something general and important about the field or discourse of medicine.

Socrates categorizes medicine as a technical discipline (*techne*), a delimited field of knowledge with a particular end. Of these arts (*techne*), Eryximachus sees medicine at the greatest and, Lacan points out, Socrates, elsewhere, holds a similar opinion.

Eryximachus begins by complementing Pausanias on starting his speech well but comments that it didn't end so well. Lacan wants to emphasize the apparent consent on this matter, concluding that although Pausanias' speech might not have seemed that bad to us, it obviously would have seemed so to a contemporary audience. Again, context is crucial here. We are more than used to hearing all sorts of flimsy discourses on love, so Pausanias' speech does not leap out as particularly puerile or simplistic. Tone here, Lacan tells us, is important, both in understanding Plato and, more widely, in any act of interpretation, including, then, obviously, the work of the analyst.

Although having previously declined the idea of exploring the history of medicine in relation to this speech, Lacan now announces a departure to look at one specific point—the idea that medicine has always positioned itself as a science. Lacan briefly traces a history of Hellenic medicine, from the well-known school of Hippocrates, back to Cnidus in Rhodes and Alcmaeon in Croton. This latter school is contemporary with Pythagoras and Lacan points to the link between Pythagorean philosophy and Platonic philosophy, although he says that to explore this link in detail would be too complicated. The link does, however, alert us to something of the broader positioning of *The Symposium*. In particular, Lacan wants to draw our attention to the Pythagorean lineage of the term *harmonia*. It is worth noting, given the context of the seminar, that, in Greek mythology, the goddess Harmonia is Eros' sister.

The appeal to Pythagorean harmony, Lacan wants to suggest, indicates that the field of medicine has always positioned itself as scientific. In positioning itself in relation to the science of its time, however, medicine has always risked its value on the relative strength of contemporary science. As science is constantly being denuded and rethought, medicine then constantly shows itself as outmoded and fallible. This might be exemplified in the fact that the soul was considered scientifically in the time of Pythagoras, and even Socrates, but this notion would seem a little ridiculous now.

A core issue here is that medicine concerns the idea of health. Curiously, the term "health" used here in Fink's translation (69) derives from the German for wholeness, while the French term *santé*, which Lacan uses, has its roots in "sanity." The French assumes, more forcefully than the English, a relationship between the mental and the physical and, moreover, might be understood as prioritizing the mental. The English and German, on the other hand, clearly point to an impossibility which would seem rather Lacanian. Indeed, Lacan, here, is indicating the impossibility of being able to pin health/*santé* down. We don't really know what health is. This is evident by the various means with which we attempt to achieve this unknown goal. Medicine predicates itself on a notion of harmony, but this term remains necessarily vague. We are no more advanced in this matter now than in the time of Plato.

Lacan then, following Eryximachus, draws a line from medicine to music. Both rely on a notion of harmony. As noted above, Lacan wants us to appreciate the importance of tone in the processes of understanding and interpretation which are core to the analytic setting. It is apposite, then, to emphasize the conjunction of medicine and music in the notion of harmony. The music of speech is crucial in a clinical setting, in that the analyst must tune in to the harmonic (and disharmonic) tone of the analysand's speech, just as we must here tune in to Eryximachus.

Again, Lacan draws our attention to context. While we have access to the words spoken (or written by Plato), we cannot access everything of the context in which the words were produced. Neither can we access beyond the text in the sense of what happened off stage, nor the thought processes or internal context of the speakers. This seems very pointed in the psychoanalytic context, particularly given some of the definitions of transference we find in other schools of psychoanalysis, where it is very much presented as a special access to the analysand's thought or affect.

Lacan points out that the period in which Plato was writing was particularly fertile, before making a curious and seemingly facetious sales pitch for Russell's *Wisdom of the West*. The salient point here is perhaps his statement that the most important things are those that are unknown. The West is perhaps not as wise as Russell would have us believe.

Although the people of Plato's time are faced with the same problems as we are, they, so Lacan thinks, discerned more immediately an essential antinomy, contradiction, or disharmony in the nature of the harmonious. In experience, all harmony appears to hide some disharmony. This would then suggest that the very notion of harmony cannot be derived from experience. It is an *a priori* concept.

We are then faced with the paradoxical question: Does harmony itself have to be harmonious? Lacan asks this in a number of ways, pointing already to the disharmony, or disunity in the very question. Does harmony (*accord*) suppose a principle of harmony? This would suggest the conclusion Lacan brings us to, that it is not something drawn from experience. He also asks, can harmony arise from disharmony? Which raises a different issue—that of causation. While this might bring Freud to mind, for Lacan, it is clear that these questions were raised long before.

Lacan quotes Eryximachus' argument that the love manifest in health is distinct from the love manifest in disease. The idea here, in Plato, seems to be that the love of the healthy would reflect a certain health in the lover insofar as a healthy person would love a healthy person and this might then be categorized as a healthy love. An unhealthy lover, on the other hand, would choose an unhealthy love object and would therefore display an unhealthy love. It is important to pay attention to the logic implicit here. The mode, manner, or definition of love is the denominator which connects the lover to the beloved and the love. This points to a virtue in health and in love.

Lacan then offers a direct translation of Plato, stating that "medicine concerns the knowledge of bodily erotics" (Plato, 186c). Hijacking this claim, Lacan says "no better definition, can … be given of psychoanalysis" (71).

Not only is medicine concerned with the knowledge of bodily erotics, this concern is formulated in terms of fullness and emptiness. The French terms used here, *la réplétion* and *la vacuité*, have a more active sense than the English, rendering them closer to "making" or "becoming full or empty." Lacan takes us back to an earlier passage from *The Symposium* and, in particular, a comment regarding the transmission of knowledge. Agathon uses the metaphor of the transportation of liquid from one vessel to another, suggesting an idea of knowledge or wisdom being passed from one interiority to another. Again, this is clearly alluding to the idea of communication and transference.

Lacan refers again to Eryximachus' comments on music and, particularly, on the above-mentioned opposition of harmony and disharmony. Eryximachus refers to Heraclitus' idea that unity or harmony arises from disharmony, thus positing disharmony as original. Eryximachus' explanation of this point is that the work of the musician is to bring distinct notes into harmony with each other. Disharmony in itself cannot lead to harmony. Lacan struggles to see where this notion, which is apparently so obvious for Eryximachus, finds its ground. He describes Heraclitus' perspective as seeing conflict as potentially creative and Eryximachus as unable to discern this. Here, Lacan sees a stark disjunction between contemporary and Platonic thought, citing modern physics to support this.

Lacan refers us again to Plato's *Phaedo* and, in particular, to Simmias and Cebes' discussion of the soul and its relation to harmony. When Simmias and Cebes' each in turn debate the possibility of the persistence of the soul after death, Socrates rejoinders with what Lacan characterizes as a sophism. The doctrinal starting point for the interlocutors in *Phaedo* is the belief that the soul partakes in the ideal of harmony. Socrates' argument appears to be no more, or no less, than that the soul cannot perish because the soul will always retreat from that which would perish.

The imperishable nature of the soul, tangled in this circular logic, leads Lacan to confront the core Platonic notion of the Forms. Here, Lacan says, "The idea that anything whatsoever that exists could participate in the Platonic idea as incorporeal essence proves to be fictional in nature, an illusion" (74). The core point here is the separation between Platonic ideas or Forms and incorporeal essences. For Plato, the corporeal world maintains its consistency through participation in the Forms. All horses, in order to be and to be understood as horses, must reflect or partake in the idea or Form of horse. What is not clear is how this theory applies to the non-corporeal—e.g. the soul, in the example of *Phaedo,* or love, in the example of *The Symposium*. Both the soul and love are abstract, non-corporeal concepts. In this sense, they are rooted in ideas and usage rather than in some higher Form.

The point Lacan wants to make here concerns whether or not Plato would himself have been aware of the logic here. Arguing that he would have, on the possibly spurious grounds that it would be arrogant to assume we knew better than Plato, Lacan is able to suggest that the logic at work on the surface in *The Symposium* should not be read literally. Rather, so Lacan claims, we should, in order to maintain consistency in our reading, see it as comic or ironic. Once again, Lacan is foregrounding the act of interpretation.

Jumping back to *The Symposium*, Lacan raises the idea that it is the Form (in the structuralist sense, not the Platonic sense) of the dialogue which is important. We have already seen that Pausanias' speech is ridiculous. Now, we realize that there is a comedic core to the structure of the whole dialogue, which brings us back to Alcibiades, the true comedic figure, and the question of why Plato brings him in at all. Lacan notes that there is something scandalous in Plato's inclusion of this character, insofar as he was implicated in Socrates' trial, as one of the youths Socrates had allegedly corrupted. Where *The Phaedo* is properly tragic in tone, Lacan asserts, *The Symposium* is never not comedic.

Lacan refers to an interlocutor who had thought he had taken Phaedrus' speech too literally. Lacan corrects this, stressing that Phaedrus' speech is just as ironic as Pausanias'. The idea that the Gods could say anything sensible about love is clearly ironic insofar as the Gods know nothing of love. When Eryximachus comes to talk of the Gods, he seems to see them in, at least structurally, the same way as he sees men. He talks of communication between them and of astronomy as the science which facilitates this communication in such a way as to maintain harmony. It is this maintenance of harmony which is the essence of love. For Lacan, rather than demonstrating anything firm about the cosmos, what this tells us is something about the modes of identification in which people engage. Man posits himself in the version of reality he encounters. Which is to say, we forge an idea of ourselves, our identity, on the basis of our mistaking of the world around us. This seems a basic echo of the mirror stage. If science can be understood as an expedition into the real, wherein what is encountered is given symbolic Form, then it is always on the edge of this "progress" that we find our idea of ourselves. Thus, Eryximachus naturally explains things in terms of the current understanding of the world. It is self-evident to the Greeks that man is concomitant with nature, that man is nature, and, thus, that all that is in man would be reflective of nature. Lacan wants to suggest that, despite our apparent progress, we haven't entirely left this idea behind.

Even analysts aren't immune to this archaic thinking. When we invoke Freud's death drive, we are drawing on a pre-Socratic notion, that of *nikos* or strife, one of Empedocles' two divine powers and the other being *philos*, love.

The next time, Lacan promises us, he will focus on Aristophanes' speech, emphasizing the comedic element and the idea of man as consisting in the cosmos. This will bring our attention to the "opening" Plato leaves in his conception of love. This idea of opening suggests an entry point as well as an incompletion. It could also suggest something unhealthy. Lacan boldly suggests that what we will find here is a ridiculing of the very conceptual basis of Plato's world, the realm of Forms ... although this ridiculing itself may be ironic. This leaves us once again with Lacan pointing to the difficulty, the impossibility, of interpretation. How should we understand a philosopher producing a possibly ironic ridiculing of the basis of his own philosophy?

References

Freud, S. 1914. Remembering, Repeating and Working-Through (Further Recommendations on the Technique of Psycho-Analysis II)—Strachey, J. 1958. *The Standard Edition of the Complete Psychological Works of Sigmund Freud, Volume XII (1911–1913): The Case of Schreber, Papers on Technique and Other Works.*

Lacan, J. 2015. *Transference: The Seminar of Jacques Lacan, Book VIII.* Edited by Jacques-Alain Miller and Translated by Bruce Fink. Cambridge: Polity.

5

First as Comedy, Then as Tragicomedy: Castration, Atopia, and Ab-Sex Sense—Commentary on Sessions VI and VII

Anthony Ballas

Toward the end of his reading of Agathon's speech, Lacan reminds those attending his seminar that his goal in examining Plato's *Symposium* is "less in order to provide you with an elegant commentary, than to lead you to what the *Symposium* can or should provide us."[1] Lacan's qualifying statement will serve as an unofficial guide for the following commentary on Lacan's analysis of both Aristophanes and Agathon from Seminar VIII; the goal here is not elegance, but rather to seek an understanding of what Lacan's reading of the comic poet and the tragedian can or should provide for us today, toward the contemporary coordinates of Lacanian psychoanalytic theory: the real of sexual difference and its function in knowledge.

There are two major questions that need to be addressed apropos of Lacan's readings of Aristophanes and Agathon; first, what is the status of castration—namely the relocation of the genitals that preoccupies a few lines of Aristophanes' speech, and, second, precisely what (or where) is the *atopia*—the no-place—that Lacan assigns to *eros* through the tragedian

A. Ballas (✉)
University of Colorado Denver, Denver, CO, USA

G. Basu Thakur and J. Dickstein (eds.), *Reading Lacan's Seminar VIII*,
The Palgrave Lacan Series, https://doi.org/10.1007/978-3-030-32742-2_5

Agathon's speech? It is from these two instances of negativity (castration and *atopia*) that Lacan develops a crucial backdrop attending to his formulations of sexual difference, the real and knowledge which are the subject matter of his late seminars, particularly XIX and XX.

Before turning to these questions, it is important first to address one of the more prominent and yet under-theorized elements of *Symposium* operative in Seminar VIII—how the tragic and the comic relate to *eros*. Although these dimensions of Plato's text are not lost on Lacan (love, as Lacan tells us, "is a comical feeling,"[2] and "people who love each other have a funny, seriousness about them")[3] they are not as central as they perhaps should be; after all, Lacan himself claims that these two characters, "certainly occupy the central place [in *Symposium*], since everything that was demonstrated before turns out, apparently, to be already remote and devalued when their turns come, and what comes afterward is no other than Socrates' speech."[4] Aristophanes and Agathon, the comic poet and the award-winning tragedian, occupy not only the center of the narrative, but as well—and more crucially—come to occupy the structural centerpiece of Lacan's topology of desire through which he develops the negative logics of castration and *atopia*: two fundamental aspects of the desiring subject.

It is through Aristophanes' famous speech[5] on the *sphairos kukloteres*—the perfect spherical beings which have been split in two by the gods and thereby forced, tragically, to search for their missing half—that Lacan understands a comical aspect of *eros* to present itself. Despite being known for his comic plays—for instance, *Clouds,* his biting, satirical caricature of Socrates—Aristophanes is able to capture the tragic desperation of human longing, through which *eros* is said to intervene in order "to make one out of two and heal the wound of human nature," acting as "the name for our pursuit of wholeness, for our desire to be complete."[6] The *sphairos kukloteres,* having once been whole and engaged in a kind of fully automated incestuous enjoyment (having all the necessary appendages internally, enjoying a full range of motion, etc.), are also found in Plato's *Timaeus,* being described therein as "a figure the most perfect and uniform of all… it had no need of eyes, for nothing visible was left outside; nor of hearing, for there was nothing outside to be heard… for nothing went out or came into it from anywhere, since there was nothing...needing no other acquaintance or friend but sufficient unto itself."[7] The sphere is essentially a figure which is uncontaminated by the outside; devoid of all drives (anal, oral, invocatory, scopic, etc.) and is as well without an other, it is fully self-sufficient, locked in a pure state of solipsistic enjoyment with itself.[8]

"Nowhere," contends Lacan, "not at any moment of the other speeches in the *Symposium*, is love ever taken as seriously or as tragically as it is by Aristophanes."[9] What Lacan here is referring to is the tragic desperation of longing for one's missing half, which is interrupted by the comical appearance of the phallus—arguably the most strange instance of castration in the history of western literature. Lacan sees this castration as confirming what he believes to be "essential to the mainspring of comedy, which is always, in the end, a reference to the phallus."[10] This reference to the castrated organ, which is intended as an ameliorative gesture from the gods in order to remedy the beings tragic pursuit of their missing halves, results, says Lacan, in the derision of the sphere: "what is derided here, what is cast in this ridiculous form, is the sphere itself."[11]

For Lacan, "Aristophanes' discourse derides Plato's *sphairos* as it is articulated in the *Timaeus*,"[12] emphasizing how, "the text stresses the shift of the genitalia to the front side."[13] The duplicitous nature of this gesture, simultaneously a cut and a remedy (a veritable *pharmakon* of erotic proportions), captures the dualistic nature of the phallus: The paradox of the phallus is that its appearance is simultaneously, and consequently, its disappearance—it participates in its own dissolution as it is an organ which is simultaneously lacking and too much. The phallus, says Lacan, "is the signifier that is excluded from the signifying system... it can only enter the signifying system by artifice, contraband, and degradation, which is why we never see it except as a function of the imaginary φ."[14] Thus, this "sign of desire" marks the imaginary point of inscription of fantasy into the symbolic register, which is why Aristophanes' mythical discourse is perturbed by the phallic appearance: The myth of the perfectly self-sufficient and fully enjoying spherical beings is derided by the relocation of the genitals, by the appearance of the phallus which simultaneously de-completes the sanctity and perfection of the One and also functions as its supplement, its point of abundance or excess.

It is important to note that Lacan does not view the phallus as providing the ameliorative faculty that the gods in Aristophanes' discourse profess it to have: "this does not merely mean that the genital organ now has the possibility of serving as a copula, allowing junction with the beloved object, but that it is literally printed over [*en surimpression*] this object, almost superimposed on it."[15] The phallus, as castrated organ, an organ which is too much and too little, marks the point where *eros* "make[s] a sign of someone—to make the sign assimilate the someone to whom the sign designates something, such that this someone also becomes this signifier."[16] Thus the phallus, although a point of failure, functions as the condition of possibility for the shift from *erastes* to *eromenos*—from lover to beloved.

Through this moment of failure, what is bestowed to humanity is the satisfaction of sexual intercourse to fill in the gap of the two longings to fuse into one. Aristophanes here stumbles inadvertently upon a formulation of desire as supplement—desire as that which ultimately serves no other function than the by-product of the satisfaction of intercourse. For Zupančič, this action of relocating the genitals generates a "purposeless purpose… a supplement that brings with it a logic of its own."[17] This logic functions in the following way for Zupančič, who explains that "not only do we not get what we are searching and longing for [our desperate search for our other half to complete us], *on top of that* we get something we haven't even asked for (and something which only further complicates things)."[18] This supplement, intended as a gift from the gods to remedy the tragedy of longing, functions instead—rather comically—as the very obstacle ironically complicating the desire to unite and fuse with the lost half.[19] Aristophanes, by illustrating the disequilibrium of human desire is this way, marked as it is by the paradox of castration, arrives at "the linchpin that shifts the entire discourse that is to follow into another register."[20] Here Lacan inches toward one of the definitions of love that we find in Seminar XX, that "love is a sign that one is changing discourses."[21] Castration, via the derision of perfection—this loss which is simultaneously a gain—indicates not only the shift from the dimension of tragedy to the comical, but functions as a sign that the subject is changing discourses.

Desire as a supplemental excess delivers the subject beyond the strict needs of reproduction, demonstrating how these driveless, otherless *sphairos kukloteres* become "sexuated" by simultaneously receiving an organ and a beloved partner in which object *a* is housed. This is why, for Lacan, "desire is not a life function"—it has no place (*atopia*) in the fulfillment of evolutionary, biological need.[22] Lacan goes on to locate how what he dubs "the transgressive character" of desire, and the state of "permanent disorder" it engenders in the words of Agathon, the tragedian.[23] In Agathon's speech, it is in his ridiculous platitudes to *eros*—"violence never touches love," and, "once Love touches him, *anyone* becomes a poet"[24]—that Lacan understands *atopia* to operate: Lacan explains how in "the tragedian's macaronic discourse… the point is always to produce an ironic effect, and even a disorientation."[25] "This," continues Lacan, "for a tragic poet, has no other meaning than to stress that love is what is truly unclassifiable, blocking every important situation. Love is what is never in its place and is always inopportune."[26] Agathon's ridiculous speech in praise of love indicates the essence of Hegel's notion of the comical; insofar as Agathon *qua* subject comes to embody the alienated substance. The comical comes into being precisely in Agathon's stubborn belief in his own "elevated" subject position: As though he is not simply playing the *role* of award-winning tragedian, but that he in fact *is* in actuality the award-winning tragedian. Through his vapid and ridiculous praise of love, Agathon ultimately dilutes the potency of *eros* while in the midst of elevating and honoring what he deems to be its special attributes. In sum, he inadvertently produces a caricature which displaces desire—and thus the *atopia* of *eros* that Lacan speaks of. Agathon's "macaronic discourse" shows us how comedy is "not the story of the alienation of the subject, [but] it is the story of the alienation of the substance, which has become the subject."[27] The comical comes into being—indeed, the phallus makes another, albeit more implicit, appearance—when Agathon's sophistic and rhetorical account of love is rendered impotent by Socrates' questioning.[28] Through Socrates' ridicule, we come to understand that it is desire itself which is lacking, indicating that, far from imaginary impotence (Agathon's vain attempt to honor *eros* poetically) we are in actuality at the level of real impossibility: Desire is already split from within—a "split in relation to oneself."[29]

Agathon, the tragedian *cum* accidental comic poet, shows us how *eros* is itself lacking in its formulation as concrete universality.[30] Lacan concludes his reading of Agathon in the following way, asserting how, "in short, we find ourselves at a crossroads at which, as will be recalled in the final conclusions of *Symposium*, it is not enough, in speaking of love, to be a tragic poet. One must also be a comic poet."[31] Through this crossroads, the chiasmatic merger of the tragic and the comic—the infernal appearing and disappearing act of the phallus via castration and *atopia*—we arrive at one of the fundamental characteristics of transference, namely the explosion of the truth where the desiring subject falters. Plato, seemingly anticipating the psychoanalytic conception of the subject, is aware that the process through which the subject emerges is marked by a series of failures: Through an incessant array of breaks and ruptures, (castration and *atopia* among others), the "basic topology of desire" and "its rational ethics" can be understood.[32] Lacan insists that it is Socrates who marks such a break or opposition in the text—even describing at one point the *atopia* of Socrates himself, likening it to "the *atopia* that is demanded of us as analysts."[33]

It is no wonder that Socrates intervenes in *Symposium* as the "subject supposed to know" after the cut of castration and the *atopia* of desire are produced through the tragicomic chiasm. This indicates what Zupančič refers to as "the comical aspect of transference in psychoanalysis," and, "the peculiar emergence of the 'subject supposed to know,' this presupposition that the Other knows the truth about the subject's unconscious desire."[34] For Bruce Fink, analysts are "placeholders of the knowledge inscribed in the analysand's own unconscious and/or placeholders of object *a* — that shiny, glittering, quintessentially fascinating thing Alcibiades saw in Socrates that raised the latter to the position of dignity above all other potential partners."[35] For Zupančič, "it is precisely this treasure, situated in the Other, that activates the transference of knowledge."[36] Socrates, just as the figure of the analyst, comes to represent "'blind faith' in the object-cause of the subject's desire, which is situated in the Other." "In spite of… its blindness," Zupančič continues, "it functions in such a way that it produces, in analysis, real effects of knowledge and truth."[37] Zupančič's notion of the subject's "blind-faith" demonstrates the negativity part and parcel to the process of knowledge itself, or, as Badiou puts it, the "function of the real in knowledge," through what Lacan calls in L'Étourdit "ab-sex sense."[38] The analyst, through transference, protreptically turns the analysand toward the cut between sense and nonsense, or ab-sex sense, just as Socrates turns his interlocutors toward a point of *aporia* through *elenchus*.[39] This is perhaps why, as Alan Pero notes, "for Badiou, love, like revolution, is an event in the sense that it disrupts the situation of the Two who find themselves in this singular edge-of-the-void evental site. Love prompts a shift in the discursive formation of the Subject."[40] It is through castration and *atopia* that *eros* comes to function as a medium of the truth (a truth procedure), permitting the transmission of knowledge of the truth, embodied through a figure like Socrates or the analyst as *agalma* or object *a* respectively.

This process of knowledge transmission indicates why, for Lacan, *There's No Such Thing as a Sexual Relationship*, insofar as jouissance "is always inadequate — perverse, on the one hand, insofar as the Other is reduced to object *a*, and crazy and enigmatic, on the other." Lacan formulates a question as to the relation of this inadequacy to the real and love, asking, "isn't it on the basis of the confrontation with this impasse, with this impossibility by which a real is defined, that love is put to the test?"[41] In Badiou's terms, love is put to the test through fidelity to the event; through a kind of negative "interval of suspense"[42] which presents itself as ab-sex sense in the process of transference, we arrive at "a point," which, for Badiou, "is a transcendental testing-ground for the appearing of a truth."[43] And is this not precisely what Lacan attempts to highlight in his reading of *Symposium*? Namely, the specific capacity of discourse operative in the way in which "Socrates brings truth to the level of discourse," allowing for this turn toward the truth?[44] One of Lacan's major innovations in analyzing *Symposium* is to demonstrate "how history itself arises from a certain way that discourse enters into reality [*reel*]."[45] What Lacan zeros in on, what he places the most emphasis on—particularly on his reading of Aristophanes—is precisely how with Plato, "a discourse developed that deliberately targeted the universe, aiming to render it discursive."[46]

We find an interesting parallel in Lacan's emphasis on the theory of discourse employed here by Plato and what Badiou describes as the Greek event: By isolating a subtractive point against the poetic shape afforded to nature by the pre-Socratics, Plato "*interrupted* the poem with the matheme," and, "in so doing... opened up the infinite possibility of an ontological text," writes Badiou.[47] In *Symposium*, it is not so simple as to say that through the tragicomic discourses of Aristophanes and Agathon a view of reality from the vantage point of reality comes to light, but rather that through the particular ways in which their discourses fail—through castration and *atopia*—a hole is punctured through the real via the appearance of the phallus as missing signifier.[48] As Lacan explains, "what Plato wants... is the Thing, *to pragmá*," as a isolatable point, and thus not the imitative tendency of poetry, which is why he famously bans poetry in Seminar X of the republic.[49] *To pragmá* is not to be found in the poetic, but rather in what occurs in the changing of discourses ushered in precisely where the poetic fails: at the point where castration and *atopia must* intervene in order to give consistency to reality itself, or, what Badiou describes as "the function of the real in knowledge": the incompleteness of reality—the fact that the sexual relationship does not exist—negatively inscribed into knowledge.[50]

What Lacan finds in Plato is not the "Thing, *to pragmá*, the main concern" as rendered accessible through the discourse of the poets, but a certain characteristic operative at the level of discourse which subtractively opens up the cut of the real, which, in turn, "commands transmissible thinking."[51] It is only through the subtractive point ushered in through the Greek event that the possibility of unequivocal knowledge (i.e., knowledge which breaks free of the circuit of *lalangue*) as a point in which affect and matheme (as Badiou puts it, "the place and the formula") are superimposed and truth is rendered tenable for the desiring subject.[52] In sum, Lacan sees something like the matheme operating in Plato's discursive ontology, as he indicates how:

> It is Socrates who comes up with the new and essential idea that one must first guarantee knowledge. To show everyone that they know nothing is a path that is in itself revealing — it reveals a virtue which, in in its finest successes, does not always succeed. In what Socrates calls *epistéme*, science, what he finds, in the end, what he brings out or detaches, is that discourse engenders the dimension of the truth. Discourse, which is ensured by a

> certainty inherent in its very action, ensures truth as such wherever it can. It is nothing but this practice of discourse.[53]

It is through Lacan's insistence on sexuation, structure, and logic in his late seminars (what Badiou refers to as Lacan's anti-philosophy) that the categories of truth and the real become available and accessible to knowledge. The superimposition of affect and matheme enables "the production of transmissible knowledge," or what Lacan would call the analytic Pass.[54]

Whereas philosophy espouses the coincidence of the "two," the couplet of truth and knowledge, thereof psychoanalytic theory (or perhaps more accurately, Lacan's anti-philosophy) maintains a third element of crucial import, argues Badiou. Badiou posits a Lacanian formula for philosophy as "a subversion of the three by the two."[55] This is why for Badiou and Lacan, the two of truth-knowledge *must* be supplemented by the real, or truth-knowledge-real, or that which is made possible through ab-sex sense. As well, it is through the imposition of this third element that the tragic and the comic become "negatively" sutured to one another: castration and *atopia*, operating as this third, are located at the border between the comic and the tragic, where one discourse bleeds into another—where the dialectical movement from one to two is supplemented by the third.[56]

The dimension of the tragicomic operative in *Symposium*, far from being a simple Janus-like dyad, is, rather, best conceived of as a triad: an instance of three, the vital element of the cut itself being the third which holds together the tragic and the comic, permitting the shift from one discourse to another as signaled by castration and *atopia*. Tragicomic space is not to be conceived of as a whole, but rather a series of incomplete and unresolved tensions wherein the subject fails to maintain (even the semblance of) unity with itself, and where the real impossibility of the One is inscribed in reality itself through concrete universality, as the self-split inherent to substance as subject.[57]

This is why, in the end, "love is giving what you don't have": The *eromenos*, in which the *agalma qua* object *a* is embodied, has *nothing*—has the *nothing* precisely that the *erastes* seeks—and it is through the signification of love which fills in for the cut of castration and *atopia* that this *nothing* can be transmitted without remainder.[58] According to Lacan, what such a view "allows is to go beyond, and to grasp the moment at which a shift or reversal occurs in which, from the conjunction of desire with its object qua inadequate, the signification called love *must* arise."[59] Transference love is, ultimately, the method of the transmission of unequivocal knowledge via the medium of ab-sex sense.

Notes

1. Jacques Lacan, *Transference: Seminar Book VIII* (1960–1961), trans. B. Fink (Cambridge, UK: Polity, 2015), p. 105.
2. Ibid., p. 33.
3. Ibid., p. 86.
4. Ibid., p. 105.
5. The December 21, 1960 session on Aristophanes entitled "Deriding the Sphere" from Seminar VIII is most certainly an allusion to Freud's early text on impotence, "The Universal Tendency to Debasement in the Sphere of Love," written in 1912. See Sigmund Freud, "On the Universal Tendency to Debasement in the Sphere of Love," *The Complete Psychological Works of Sigmund Freud*, vol. XI. trans. J. Strachey (London: Hogarth and Institute of Psycho-Analysis, 2001), pp. 177–190.
6. C.D.C. Reeve, *Plato On Love* (Indianapolis: Hackett Publishing, 2006), pp. 49 and 50.
7. Plato, *Timaeus*, trans. F.M. Crawford (New York: Macmillan, 1959), pp. 23–24.
8. It is in this image that two characters emerge simultaneously: the asexual *l'etre-ange*, and the fully enjoying father. As Lorenzo Chiesa summarizes nicely early on in *The Not-Two*, "man unsuccessfully aims at totalizing structure by reifying the feminine Other, whom he can love only as the other One, and with whom he attempts to establish a fusional two-as-One that would obliterate woman's phallic incompleteness just as much as sexual difference" (Chiesa, *The Not-Two*, p. xix).
9. Lacan, *Transference*, p. 87.
10. Ibid., p. 94.
11. Ibid., p. 88. Lacan continues, "Since we know that Plato's grasp of tragedy… did not go much further than [the death of] Socrates, how can we fail to be struck by the fact that here, for the first and only time, he brings into play the genital organ as such in a discourse concerning a serious

manner, that of love?" Although Lacan fails to mention it, *Timaeus* contains another reference to the genitals: in "Differentiation of the Sexes," at the very end of the work, the phallus makes an appearance in the description of the "*eros* of begetting," the male genitalia as "disobedient and self-willed, like a creature that will not listen to reason" (Plato, *Timaeus*, p. 115). One wonders if this is the source of St. Augustine's famously disobedient phallus? It is also worth mentioning another fascinating passage from *Timaeus* in which Plato subtly "derides the sphere" in his description of how "the god set water and air between fire and earth, and made them, *so far as was possible*, proportional to one another" (Plato, *Timaeus*, p. 22, my emphasis). Here it would seem that Plato inscribes a kind of resistance into the objects generated by the god, as though the god has created something that pushes back minimally against him—as though the god lacks a bit of knowledge as to what he has himself generated.

12. Lacan, *Transference*, p. 93.
13. Ibid., p. 94.
14. Ibid., p. 260.
15. Ibid., p. 94.
16. Ibid., p. 261.
17. Alenka Zupančič, *The Odd One In* (Cambridge, MA: MIT Press, 2008), p. 189.
18. Ibid., emphasis original.
19. As Zupančič puts it, the genital object is "superimposed" on the beloved [*eromenos*], and in this dimension, "love itself emerges *inside* this very incongruity" (Zupančič, *The Odd One In*, p. 190). The maneuvering of the genitals from the side to the front of the entity gives a whole new twist on the colloquial notion of a "side-splitting" comedy; in *Symposium*, a literal splitting of the side occurs, perhaps indicating the possibility that Aristophanes' *sphairos kukloteres* are simply in the throes of violent laughter...
20. Lacan, *Transference*, p. 94.
21. Jacques Lacan, *Encore, Seminar Book XX* (1972–1973), trans. B. Fink (New York: W. W. Norton, 1998), p. 16.
22. Lacan, *Transference*, p. 95.
23. Ibid., p. 97.
24. Reeve, *Plato on Love*, pp. 54–55.
25. Lacan, *Transference*, p. 106.
26. Ibid., p. 108.

27. Zupančič, *The Odd One In*, p. 28. Zupančič goes on to write how, in these moments, "the concrete and the universal coexist, the concrete being the indispensable grounding of the universal" (ibid., p. 30).
28. Socrates immediately pokes a hole in Agathon's discourse, summarizing his ridiculous attempt "to apply to the object the grandest and most beautiful qualities, whether he actually has them or not" (Reeve, *Plato on Love*, p. 57).
29. Ibid., p. 191. As Hegel puts it apropos of comedy, "the *individual self* is the negative power through which and in which the Gods, as also their movement, vanish." Quoted in Zupančič, *The Odd One In*, p. 26.
30. In brief, Lacan writes, "it is… the 'he did not know' that I wrote for you at the top of the Graph of Desire, on the enunciation line that is fundamental to the topology of the unconscious" (99). The comic import of Agathon's speech may very well lie in the fact that, similar to Oedipus, Agathon does not know of his own failure. This is a reference to what Oedipus himself did not know, which Lacan isolates as the most important lesson of Freud's Oedipus Complex: "[m]any heroes other than Oedipus kill their fathers and want to sleep with their mothers. The reason Freud found his fundamental figure in the tragedy of Oedipus lies in the fact that 'he did not know' he had killed his father and was sleeping with his mother" (Lacan, *Transference*, pp. 99–100).
31. Lacan, *Transference*, p. 109.
32. Lacan, *Transference*, p. 97. Bruce Fink recounts several such instances in *Symposium*: Aristophanes' hiccups, Alcibiades' drunken intrusion into the scene, Agathon being interrupted by Socrates, and the breakdown of Socrates' *elenchus* and resorting to the mythos provided by Diotima (Bruce Fink, *Lacan on Love* [Cambridge, UK: Polity, 2016], p. 34). Todd McGowan as well observes how in *Symposium* "the dissymmetry of love leaves the loving subject in a permanent condition of disruption, and yet this disruption is the source of the satisfaction that love provides," calling *Symposium*, "the first great treatise of love because it is the first great treatise of disruption." See Todd McGowan, *Capitalism and Desire* (New York: Columbia University Press, 2016), p. 183.
33. Lacan, *Transference*, p. 80. Colette Soler provides a nice formulation of Socrates' *atopia*, noting how Socrates, as a kind of hysterical figure, "becomes the active agent of the Other's castration" (*Reading Seminar* XX, p. 53).
34. Zupančič, *The Odd One In*, p. 86.
35. Fink, *Lacan on Love*, p. 47.

36. Zupančič, *The Odd One In*, p. 86.
37. Zupančič continues, "this automatic love for the analyst, is certainly not without its comic dimension" (ibid.).
38. Badiou and Cassin, *There's No Such Thing as a Sexual Relationship*, p. 55.
39. One should contrast Platonic *eros* and its relation to the real to the Stoic conception thereof: In Seminar VI of *Meditations*, Marcus Aurelius describes sexual intercourse as "the friction of a piece of gut and, following a sort of convulsion, the expulsion of some mucus," a view, so wrote the Emperor, which is intended to "reach through to the things themselves and strike the heart of them, allowing us to see them as they truly are." For thinkers like Hegel and Lacan, such a view of reality paradoxically always distorts reality further, representing not the direct access to the thing-in-itself, but a further distantiation between reality and the subject. The lesson is that there is no possible "naked" view of the real unmediated by fantasy (Marcus Aurelius, *Meditations*, trans. R. Hard [Oxford: Oxford University Press, 2011], p. 47).
40. Alan Pero, "The Chiasm of Revolution: Badiou, Lacan, and Lefèbvre," *The Symptom*, 10 (2016). We must keep in mind, however, that this figure, "the subject supposed to know," does not actually possess the knowledge the *erastes* or analysand believes them to. Rather, as Lacan points out in Seminar VII, "from a certain point of view, the analyst is fully aware that he cannot know what he is doing in psychoanalysis. Part of this action remains hidden even to him" (Jacques Lacan, *The Ethics of Psychoanalysis, Seminar Book VII*, trans. B. Fink [New York: W. W. Norton], p. 291).
41. Lacan, *Encore*, p. 144.
42. Badiou, *Being and Event*, p. 207.
43. Badiou, *Logics of Worlds*, p. 399.
44. Lacan, *Transference*, p. 80. Lacan even goes out of way to stress that the point that for Plato, "the universe appears as a universe of discourse…there will never be any universe other than a universe of discourse…the universe must give itself over to the signifying order" (ibid., p. 78).
45. Ibid.
46. Ibid.
47. For Badiou, Plato "originally *untied* the thought of being from its poetic enchainment to natural appearing" (Badiou, *Being and Event*, p. 126).
48. The missing signifier is precisely what Lacan later in Seminar VIII describes as what indexes "real presence."
49. Lacan, *Transference*, p. 84. As Plato writes, "it appears to me that [the poet's] art corrupts the minds of all who hearken to them, save only those

whose knowledge of reality provides an antidote" (Plato, *The Republic*, p. 285). Poetry oscillates between the tragic and the comic, functioning as a kind of mechanism of phallic jouissance, whereas a break in the cycle of repetition—a suspense interval to use Badiou's language—is what is made possible through the matheme. For Plato, "the poet will use meter, rhythm, and harmony; and no matter whether his subject matter concerns generals or shoemakers, his hearers will call everything praiseworthy" (ibid., p. 291). The latter directly recalls Agathon's ridiculous display mid-speech in which he claims to be "suddenly struck by a need to say something in poetic meter" (Reeve, *Plato on Love*, p. 106).

50. Badiou and Cassin, *There's No Such Thing as a Sexual Relationship*, p. 55.
51. Badiou, *Being and Event*, p. 126.
52. Badiou and Cassin, *There's No Such Thing as a Sexual Relationship*, p. 45. Badiou here borrows from Rimbaud's "Vagabonds," "*moi, presse de trouver le lieu et la formule*" [I, impatient to find the place and the formula].
53. Lacan, *Transference*, p. 80.
54. Badiou and Cassin, *There's No Such Thing as a Sexual Relationship*, p. 53.
55. Ibid., p. 56.
56. In *Timaeus*, Plato seems to understand the crucial function of third as well: "Now that which comes to be must be bodily, and so visible and tangible; and nothing can be visible without fire, or tangible without something solid, and nothing solid without earth. Hence the god, when he began to put together the body of the universe, set about making it of fire and earth. But two things alone cannot be satisfactorily united without a third; for there must be a body between them drawing them together" (Plato, *Timaeus*, p. 21).
57. This explains why, for both Badiou and Lacan, the choice is for Plato over Aristotle (the latter of whom becomes Lacan's great interlocutor in Seminar XX), shifting from philosophy to anti-philosophy, from "the One is" to "there is something of the One" [Y a d'l'Un], or "the One ex-sists."
58. Lacan insists that the beloved is "the only one in the couple who has something" (Lacan, *Transference*, p. 34).
59. Ibid (my emphasis).

References

Badiou, Alain. 2013. *Logic of Worlds: Being and Event II.* Trans. Alberto Toscano. London: Bloomsbury.

———. 2015. *Being and Event.* Trans. Oliver Feltham. London: Bloomsbury.

Badiou, Alain, and Barbara Cassin. 2017. *There's No Such Thing as a Sexual Relationship.* Trans. S. Spitzer and Kenneth Reinhard. New York: Columbia University Press.

Barnard, Suzanne, and Bruce Fink. 2002. *Reading Seminar XX: Lacan's Major Work on Love, Knowledge, and Feminine Sexuality.* New York: State University of New York Press.

Chiesa, Lorenzo. 2016. *The Not-Two: Logic and God in Lacan.* Cambridge, MA: MIT Press.

Fink, Bruce. 2016. *Lacan on Love.* Cambridge, UK: Polity Press.

Freud, Sigmund. 1986. "On the Universal Tendency to Debasement in the Sphere of Love." In *The Complete Psychological Works of Sigmund Freud,* vol. XI. Trans. J. Strachey. London: Hogarth and Institute of Psycho-Analysis.

Lacan, Jacques. 1998. *The Seminar of Jacques Lacan, Book XX: Encore (1972–1973).* Translated by Bruce Fink. New York: W.W. Norton.

———. 2015. *Transference: The Seminar of Jacques Lacan, Book VIII.* Edited by Jacques-Alain Miller and Translated by Bruce Fink. Cambridge: Polity.

McGowan, Todd. 2016. *Capitalism and Desire: The Psychic Cost of Free Markets.* New York: Columbia University Press.

Pero, Allan. "The Chiasm of Revolution: Badiou, Lacan, and Lefèbvre." The Symptom, Lacan.com, 29 April 2016. www.lacan.com/symptom10a/the-chiasm.html.

Plato. 1959. *Timaeus.* Trans. F.M. Crawford. New York: Macmillan.

———. 1985. *The Republic.* Trans. R.W. Sterling and William C. Scott. New York: W. W. Norton.

Reeve, C. D. C. 2006. *Plato One Love.* Indianapolis: Hackett Publishing.

Zupančič, Alenka. 2008. *The Odd One In: On Comedy.* Cambridge, MA: MIT Press.

6

Hypothesizing Love: Lacan and Plato's *Symposium*—Commentary on Session VII

Cindy Zeiher

Seminar VIII, on the subject of transference, commences with a long section consisting of a detailed reading of Plato's *Symposium*. However, this response to Seminar VIII begins not with Lacan but with Catherine Millot, his lover and analysand. Her memoir of him eloquently captures what it was like to be in love with a man who kept her in continual suspense. She writes "Lacan was very generous with his women. And when he gave one a present, he did not forget the others. He covered them with jewels and foliage. It was his way of paying them homage and his homage was long-lasting. Foliage plants flocked to my house."[1] From reading Millot it is obvious that she and Lacan were *in love,* notwithstanding that he was also in love with or loved other women. However, according to Millot at least, it seems that they shared something sublime beyond the pragmatics of everyday life, beyond the usual constructs of love, such as marriage, shared resources, children, history-building, and so on. Lacan and Millot shared

C. Zeiher (✉)
School of Language, Social and Political Sciences; Sociology and Anthropology, University of Canterbury, Christchurch, New Zealand
e-mail: cindy.zeiher@canterbury.ac.nz

G. Basu Thakur and J. Dickstein (eds.), *Reading Lacan's Seminar VIII*,
The Palgrave Lacan Series, https://doi.org/10.1007/978-3-030-32742-2_6

an idealized love, the stuff of dreams. What makes Millot's reflections so captivating is that in recounting their time together as an almost mystical experience, she at the same time addresses the very task Lacan sets out for us: What does love do to the subject? Notwithstanding Lacan's comment that love is a signifier which spirals the subject into imbecility, Millot is anything but stupid. In her memoir, she ponders *Encore*, his seminal work on feminine *jouissance*, also his claim of the impossible relationship between the sexes, his typologies and the nuanced expression of his flow of thought. She does not hold back from harsh criticism, saying at one time of his *Encore* sessions, "the way he linked mysticism with feminine *jouissance* that year left me unenlightened…".[2] Millot's memoir of love is neither imbecilic nor pessimistic. It refuses to alienate self-hood in the quest for love, on the contrary, it perceives love as the strangest transference to which we are beholden.

In his work, Lacan mentions love again and again, thereby ensuring that the correlation of love with desire remains the core vocabulary of his psychoanalysis. For example, in Session VII of Seminar VIII, *Atopia of Eros*, Lacan continues with his reading of Plato's *Symposium* as a way of handling the complexities of love in terms of a specific transference, akin to what he calls "the tragic poet" which is also necessarily "the comic poet." Certainly, Plato held that love should be left to the poets as philosophy was ill-equipped to address it, a provocation which Lacan takes seriously, albeit with some skepticism. He begins by claiming that the dialectic of desire is both formed by and constitutive of the subject via metonymy, a process which leaves a trace, this being the trace of desire which is constituted externally and fixated. Such fixation is strange because although we can't really recognize love itself, we can recognize its trace as something definable. Lacan refers to this ideogram as signifying in terms both of recognition and function. That is, it is both the signification of love and its signifying effects which allow us to grasp love, albeit clumsily. The signifying chain which forms repetition is attributed by Lacan to Freud's constitution of the *Id* in the death drive. Lacan says in Seminar VIII[3]:

> No doubt there are explorers, like Socrates or the die-hards or the saints [who] give us some indications about the field that is in question [love], and

> not just some indications, but precisely this [...] that on reflection, we refer to it [love], for our part [as] our science, I mean experimental science...

Lacan is certainly having some fun. Love as an experimental science? On the face of it, this is absurd. But what he is getting at is that love is something which we can not only think about but also seriously undertake. When interrogating love, what we are really asking concerns *l'homme du désir.* What is the will of my desire? Is the will of your desire, me? How can I be the object of your will to desire? Socrates can be seen as Lacan's interlocutor concerning love, perhaps even as his Other, because for Lacan the question of love is more than just a question of knowing that one knows nothing (as is the case for the subject of science), it is also discovering what the knowledge one does have consists of and how this substantiates the object of one's will. At the same time, through invoking *l'homme du désir* Lacan is rebelling against the Socratic position that there is nothing to know: "Truth is nothing but what knowledge can learn that it knows merely by putting its ignorance to work."[4] The question of knowing seductively contends with the passivity of not knowing and in this way it is the best question to ask about love because it highlights love's ultimate contradiction: that during the love relationship crises will occur. In *Atopia of Eros*, Lacan asserts passivity to be a feature of love in that one is the lover and the other, the beloved. It is within the relation between the lover and the beloved that one realizes that the notion of overcoming potential crises is already intrinsic within the characterization of love. This is eloquently put by Millot as she recounts her anger at discovering Lacan's infidelity[5]:

> On these occasions my anger erupted; he endured it patiently. His ability to endure feminine wrath was remarkable, and left me thinking that passivity, sometimes, is a sign of virility.

Lacan's attention to desire maintains an ethical stance and traces both as a manifestation of the body as well as how, as an effect of the *Id*, it must be constituted so as to appear but without necessarily being regulatory of the subject. Thus the *Id*, although for the most part hidden and notwithstanding its domestication by the super-ego, remains a powerful drive because it motivates and propels the subject. In this regard, Lacan states that the function of the *Id* is "to save appearances" and is moreover a topology which defines images of desire, one which "signifies nothing [other] than wanting to reduce to forms that are supposedly perfect…".[6] Lacan is here reading Freud's anguish of identification robustly: The subject struggles with inserting itself into the relationship between its identification with the object of love and the very concept of identification which itself contradicts identification with the love object. The upshot of this is that in order to identify with the love object, that is, to preserve its appearance, one also needs to remain individuated from it. We could conclude that according to Freud, the destiny of love is no more than a libidinal catharsis in which the love object is a projection of the ego. Lacan repeatedly speaks of the appearance of love inevitably dissolving into pseudo-appearances. For Lacan, here love can only be a metaphor, namely, its ambiguity transcends the Symbolic in order to obey the rule of repetition rather than that which appoints *point de capiton* for the purpose of marking differences. Thus for early Lacan, love *per se* is merely a sort of procrastination, a retention of narcissistic self-deception of the ideal-ego. Love is imposed on *objet a* through recognition of the thing itself (e.g. beauty) and further, such recognition relies on participation with such notion (e.g. the notion that beautiful things are in actuality) as a consolidation of love, notwithstanding that this is a masquerade.

Love can never be satiated because of the lovers' unending craving to be loved. This reversal of the dyadic relation between subject and object in reality leads to the subject's (the lover's) attempt to grasp even more from the object (the beloved). Love is a fantasy game which at the same time pierces the narcissistic bubble thereby revealing love to be a masquerade. This is the crux of identification and is what Millot constantly evokes in her memoir. Lacan states that love is "a ceremony, with rules, a sort of ritual, intimate contest among the elite, or parlour game"[7] which is certainly the impression one gets through reading Millot. However, like Socrates is to Lacan, she is something of an analyst of love, one who as Lacan states, is positioned "at the beginning of analytic practice."[8] How is this relevant as an elaboration of reading *Transference*? Analysis offers no final truth on the matter of love as a actuality, but rather functions inevitably as self-referral to the signifier upon which the love relationship pivots. The signifier, as Lacan rightly asserts, is propped up by the subject[9] but is also temporarily suspended by the subject, when momentarily retreating from the love relationship in order to analyze it. The signifying chain does not cease but is simply resumed once a new hypothesis about love arises. The break in love produces an unwinding effect which propels it toward resumption, thus the signifier of love as transference continues. This is the dialectical nature of the love relationship: Love is always re-starting and each re-start is a gradual accumulation of existing love. Here Lacan speaks of the miracle (and fiction) of love as always being recognition consisting of the lover's hand extending to the beloved.[10] In this way, authentic love is never unreciprocated, but is rather a metaphor or "substitution of the lover [*erastés*] for the loved one [*erómenos*]."[11] As Bruce Fink puts it, love is the process of becoming two within the Symbolic order.[12] For the lovers, the rest of the world becomes a strange contradiction in which there is both indifference and the need for this indifference to recognize their love so that it becomes a worthy hypothesis to which both lovers subscribe and belong.

Indeed, Lacan later states that identification is "the transformation that takes place in the subject - when he assumes an image."[13] Identification is the interpellation of the image, its assumption whereby the subject appropriates itself. In Seminar VIII, Lacan destabilizes the relation between love and desire, by moving from the "one-ness" of love into a transferential modality where love manifests from and cohabits with transference. Dylan Evans provides the background to this[14]:

> One of the most complex areas of Lacan's work concerns the relationship between love and desire. On the one hand, the two terms are diametrically opposed. On the other hand, this opposition is problematised by certain similarities between the two:
>
> 1. As an imaginary phenomenon which belongs to the field of the ego, love is clearly opposed to desire, which is inscribed in the symbolic order, the field of the Other (Seminar XI, pp. 189–191).
>
> 2. On the other hand, there are elements in Lacan's work which destabilise the neat opposition between love and desire.

In Seminar VIII, Lacan returns to the *Symposium* as a starting point in pondering the metaphysics of love. In the *Symposium*, tragedy plays out as a distinctly Christian phenomenon which is comedic in its relationship with death. For Plato, the problem of love begins with a discussion on the morality of sex. Those before Socrates speak of love as an exquisite elevation: beauty, praise, a desire for excellence. Sexual love by contrast was not as good, worthy, beautiful, or notable. Socrates says that love cannot simply be beauty because in possessing love, one already possesses beauty which is inherent in true love. The *Symposium* then suggests that the goal of love is to possess beauty, to "give birth to it" no less. Here love is beginning to take a particular turn, away from the subjective and toward the love of knowledge. In spite of Lacan's linking of love with imbecility, everyone praises love as something to which we should be beholden because in our pursuit of knowledge it offers us truth.

Lacan maintains that to inhabit the space of tragedy is also to occupy the space of concealment and lack. He cites Oedipus as an example of this topology, as "the locus of this fundamental conjecture"[15] insofar as the tragedy of Oedipus is his somewhat risible lack of recognition. Such a tragi-comedic dialectic is often played out in love for the study of which Lacan uses *Symposium* as an episteme. Here love is elevated to the conscious position of a Socratic science, to "the dignity of something absolute or the position of absolute dignity."[16] This resonates with Alenka Zupančič's theorization of love, in which love is elevated to the status of "das ding" despite it never having ever been a thing.[17]

For Lacan, love is transmitted as Socratian insofar as it is transformed by the tragic "fear and trembling"[18] of a total presence preceding the first (physical) death, as distinct from the second death which offers the much greater significatory coherence of finality and "absolute power."[19] Something similar to the second death occurs once one has fallen in love, when there is something both lost and found for the subject who is simultaneously individuated from and bound to the love object who is another subject. This power of the second death in which the lover leaves one life for a "truer life, an immortal life"[20] is attributed by Lacan to the desire for a metonymic discourse and in passing he refers to Platonic love as an eternal conception of the justice of friendship. This brings to mind Socrates's elevation of the lover to an intellectual level in order to locate love beyond the *objet a*. However, Lacan's position is precisely the opposite: be faithful to the *objet a* and thereby enable love to apprehend desire. Millot speaks to this phenomena when she recounts her realization that her own desire to be a mother eclipses that of being with Lacan[21]:

> The ground was cleared for a new and immediate desire to raise its head with all the force of an imperative: the question of having a child, a question that was all the more urgent because of my age. And it was too late to have a child with Lacan. This was a desire analysis with him had freed from all its intensity, and I did not want it to remain a dead letter, for in my eyes this would have invalidated all the progress of my analysis. In the name of this desire, I cruelly separated from him as to have a chance of fulfilling it. It was a wrench for me, and an earthquake for him.

During Seminar VIII, Lacan goes on to consider the problematic positing of the soul as a way of avoiding the finality of the second death's prevention of regeneration, by actually equating this second death with "the notion of the soul, the figure of the soul,"[22] thereby implying that the soul, in harboring a materiality which can be recognized, allows for some sort of regeneration after the first physical death. For Lacan, the mortality/immortality issue is a rejoinder to the illusion of an allegorical framework which escapes meaning. Likening belief one way or another to the temperament of a scale, Lacan turns instead to the more important question of desire as a precise articulation: What is his desire for Socrates?

For Lacan, the articulation of his desire for Socrates is the platform from which his topology of Socrotarian loves springs. He calls this an *atopia* of desire. This is an imprecise discourse in a number of ways, yet it does provide a central point from which desire pivots the subject, the *place* of desire from which love might spring. Lacan claims that the dialectic between love and desire is purely propositional because once it is introduced via enunciation into the complexity of transference then desire becomes a desire for discourse. Here Lacan echoes Plato's ridiculing of Pausanias's claim that love is a neutral value determined by the intention to produce virtue. Allegedly Aristophanes too thought this so preposterous that in between eating and drinking, he developed hiccups from laughing so hard, a somewhat comical interruption to an otherwise grave discussion on the nature of love which inevitably signaled love between the gods. Lacan however takes note of what might be behind this interruption.

Love makes one self-conscious: If I want the other, what does the other want? And do I want the same? Here the disjuncture is between me and the other is what provides an intersubjective relation which entangles the subject who does not want to lose either the other or the self. However, for Lacan the dialectic of love always remains because there is a third presence, the fantasy of the fullness of love. Such a mythology is the very thing, the essence of love. Here mythology is Hegelian in that love is a struggle toward recognition embracing contradiction. This is the true fiction of love. Although not directly referenced, Hegel provides Lacan with a strategy to reveal that the intersubjective relationship is necessarily never equal because for love to endure it must be complicit in securing a fantasy third presence. Thus, love provides no miracle to behold, merely one to imagine.

For Lacan, the analyst's desire for insight begins with questions posed by another (the Other) concerning the fundamental fantasy and its effects. What mark does the analyst bear when delving into desire? The typology of desire is, for Lacan, the desire of the analyst who is distinctive for the analysand in standing in for the latter's *objet a*. This is the starting point from where love can be tolerable rather than thought. Might it be here that toleration of love as a discourse can be seriously considered as part of the clinic? Whereas for the Greeks, love is a signifying discourse between the gods, in the clinic, it is one between consciousnesses and unconsciousnesses of both analyst and analysand. This is a tricky situation as Bruce Fink points out[23]:

> In most instances, we do not even want to know our own unconscious 'conditions of love' – that is, what makes us tick, what makes us love one person instead of another, or what makes us love in one particular way rather than in another – we wish to ignore all of that. Some people worry that if they knew the unconscious determinants of their love, their love would dissipate; if they realised they had fallen in love with someone because of that person's similarities to a parent, they might stop loving him or her. Love, in such cases, does its job: it conveys its message without revealing to consciousness anything that is unconscious.

This is both the miracle and the frustration of love in which we all participate. For the analysand, the analyst is not just another subject, but one who in standing in for the *objet a* is positioned to enforce the analysand's acceptance of castration. The will to fall in love is always already there and the analysand knows full well that that it is exactly what the analyst will keep at bay. This poignant aspect of transference is the unavoidable result of perverse love in the praxis of psychoanalysis in which the analysand submits to misery in the quest of handling the symptom. Resultant alienation is noted by Freud when he remarks that when the analysand is confronted with the analyst not returning love, the analysand becomes disenchanted and tempted to end analysis as a procedure which fails to give love a go.

In Seminar VIII, Lacan contends with the impossibility of actualizing the sublime *objet a* when he refers to Aristotle's concept of recognition as a reciprocity which, although circumscribed in the Symbolic, is still not a rational process[24]:

> What Aristotle evokes with the term φιλία, namely, what represents the possibility of a bond (*lien*) of love between two of these beings, can also, manifesting the tension toward the Supreme Being, be reversed in the way in which I expressed it—it is in their courage in bearing the intolerable relationship to the Supreme Being that friends, recognize and choose each other.

For Lacan, love is inscribed in the Real, an investable yet impenetrable location where love is realized. This dilemma presents both the comedy and the tragedy of love and is thrown open when Lacan takes seriously Agathon's revalorization of love as *kedos*, a worthy relationship that invites, to some degree at least, pleasure as a necessary condition of love. In the transferential relationship, the analysand trusts that in his or her contention with lack the analyst is able to bridge the gap, the analyst providing a much-needed counterpart which reveals the fantasy of and desire for love. From this position, Lacan deliberates the distinction between courtly and passionate love as a response to Robin's, *Théorie platonicienne de l'Amour*,[25] in which *Eros* is more tragic than comic. He then jokingly considers the trouble love brings, to be a symptom of love's disorder, yet insofar as the discourse of love is a comedy transmitted as "someone who wishes to amuse,"[26] the joke is on those who take love too seriously. Lacan observes that one cannot ignore the context of speaking about love because although somewhat peripheral, context orients the event of love while remaining basically disorienting in its function. He offers jealousy as an example of the tragic purity of love in that jealousy functions as comic relief to the intensity and confusion of love and desire.

Although the jury is still out concerning the matter of love in the *Symposium*, what does Lacan glean from it? He accepts the appearance of love to be a timeless and profound experience. This vision or image of love is implicitly linked to satisfaction, yet it must also traverse rationality and cognition. On this, the *Symposium* is clear: In order to release oneself from the power of an idea [*idée*], one must have had an experience of love. Freud later seized upon this as transference, a particular transference which is recognition of oneself through the love of another. We are stabilized and credible to one another as subjects when the other acknowledges love for us. Love both transfers and mediates this declaration founding the encounter of love, becoming a very different idea [*pensée*] which includes both the body and desire. Love removes oneness in terms of its pragmatics because it requires at least two to embark on love; it further removes the oneness of demand because love includes but is not dependent on desire. The oneness of love is simply not an inevitability, as Lacan points out in *Encore*[27]:

> In truth, we will see that we must turn things around, and instead of investigating a signifier (*un signifiant*), we must investigate the signifier One(Un), but we haven't reached that point yet…

Love is a desire for recognition and this is what is at stake in the struggle for love. However, being the killer of desire sometimes gives love a bad name because, as Dylan Evans contends, whereas love fantasizes an ideal, desire not only gives rise to differences, but thrives on them.[28] In considering Lacan's reading of the *Symposium*, love and desire are in a dialectic: love is comparable to desire in that both can never be satisfied yet both are based on an eagerness to be the object of another's love and desire.

In the *Symposium*, Aristophanes offers a harmonious structure of love, a form of oneness made of two. However there is a third term here, *Eros*, which provides the intervention which in a loving experience one has to navigate. Lacan notes how Socrates parallels the task of philosophy with that of *Eros*—in the viability of plurality and also in the disrupting of the notion that love is essentially a "beautiful thing", a position one should perhaps not unquestioningly adopt. At the same time, prior to Socrates, five speakers shape the scope of thinking about love as *being with* another, an approach which fixates on satisfaction obtained from one's lover. *Eros* is the satisfaction rather than the mediator between lovers. As Socrates points out, there is always detachment and asymmetry between lovers, between the lover and beloved. This asymmetry is marked by *Eros* and maintains the love relationship. In contending with this, Lacan concludes that transference—arguably the most transcendent Hegelian "misfortune of consciousness"—requires striving to be in the position of the beloved who is always worthy of being loved.

Notes

1. Catherine Millot, *Life with Lacan* (Cambridge: Polity Press, 2018), p. 28.
2. Ibid., p. 49.
3. Jacques Lacan, *Le transfert* (Paris: Seuil, 1960 [2001]), p. 95.
4. Jacques Lacan, The Subversion of the Subject and the Dialectic of Desire in the Freudian Unconscious, in *Écrits: The First Complete Edition in English* (1961), p. 675.
5. Catherine Millot, *Life with Lacan* (Cambridge: Polity Press, 2018), p. 93.
6. Jacques Lacan, *Le transfert* (Paris: Seuil, 1960 [2001]), p. 87.
7. Ibid., pp. 20–21.
8. Ibid., p. 4.
9. Ibid., p. 169.
10. Ibid., p. 52.
11. Ibid., p. 40.
12. Bruce Fink, *Lacan on Love* (Hoboken, NJ: Wiley, 2015).
13. Jacques Lacan, *Encore: On Feminine Sexuality, the Limits of Love and Knowledge* (1972), p. 2.
14. Dylan Evans, *An Introductory Dictionary of Lacanian Psychoanalysis* (London and New York: Routledge, 1996), p. 106.
15. Jacques Lacan, *Le transfert* (Paris: Seuil, 1960 [2001]), p. 5.
16. Ibid., p. 6.

17. Alenka Zupančič, On Love as Comedy. *Journal of Gender, Politics and Culture* 2 (1) (2003).
18. Jacques Lacan, *Le transfert* (Paris: Seuil, 1960 [2001]), p. 91.
19. Ibid., p. 91.
20. Ibid., p. 92.
21. Millot (2018, p. 118).
22. Jacques Lacan, *Le transfert* (Paris: Seuil, 1960 [2001]), p. 93.
23. Bruce Fink, *Lacan on Love* (Hoboken, NJ: Wiley), p. 176.
24. Jacques Lacan, *Le transfert* (Paris: Seuil, 1960 [2001]), p. 85.
25. Léon Robin, *Théorie platonicienne de l'Amour* (Paris: Alcan, 1908).
26. Jacques Lacan, *Le transfert* (Paris: Seuil, 1960 [2001]), p. 98.
27. *Encore: On Feminine Sexuality, the Limits of Love and Knowledge*, trans. B. Fink (New York and London: W. W. Norton, 1972 [1999]), p. 20.
28. Dylan Evans, *An Introductory Dictionary of Lacanian Psychoanalysis* (London and New York: Routledge, 1996).

References

Badiou, Alain. 2009. *In Praise of Love*. New York: New Press.

Evans, Dylan. 1996. *An Introductory Dictionary of Lacanian Psychoanalysis*. London and New York: Routledge.

Fink, Bruce. 2015. *Lacan on Love*. Hoboken, NJ: Wiley.

Lacan, Jacques. 1960. *Le transfert*. Paris: Seuil [2001].

———. 1972. *Encore: On Feminine Sexuality, the Limits of Love and Knowledge*. Translated by Bruce Fink, New York and London: W. W. Norton [1999].

———. 2006. The Subversion of the Subject and the Dialectic of Desire in the Freudian Unconscious. In *Écrits: The First Complete Edition in English*, translated by Bruce Fink in collaboration with H. Fink and R. Grigg. New York and London: W. W. Norton [1961].

Millot, Catherine. 2018. *Life with Lacan*. Cambridge: Polity Press.

Robin, Léon. 1908. *Théorie platonicienne de l'Amour*. Paris: Alcan.

Zupančič, Alenka. 2003. On Love as Comedy. *Journal of Gender, Politics and Culture* 2 (1): 61–80.

7

"From *Episteme* to *Mythous*": Commentary on Session VIII

Owen Hewitson

We reach the point in the Seminar where Lacan turns to Socrates' speech on the nature of love in *The Symposium*, and its strange relation to Agathon's preceding contribution to the assembled guests. In this session, Lacan will approach transference by showing how myth and stories take over where knowledge and discourse fail; how love occupies the shadowy space between them; and how lack itself is the key to being able to love.

Lacan opens by asking his audience to remember one thing: Socrates' claim that if he knows anything it is about love. But Socrates appears to have a hard act to follow. Plato's text tells us that when Agathon concludes his own speech on love there are shouts of admiration, with Socrates praising its beautiful phrasing to such an extent that he nearly runs away in shame.[1] Lacan's reading is a little more cautious. He too notes that Socrates appears enthralled but wonders why he commends it only as a

O. Hewitson (✉)
London, UK
URL: http://LacanOnline.com

G. Basu Thakur and J. Dickstein (eds.), *Reading Lacan's Seminar VIII*,
The Palgrave Lacan Series, https://doi.org/10.1007/978-3-030-32742-2_7

"fine speech."[2] Agathon's contribution is, after all, verbose but simultaneously somewhat half-hearted, a triumph of style over substance. Lacan even labels it "derisory."[3] The tone shifts when Socrates begins his response, pursuing the sharp and rigorous questioning synonymous with his style to reveal what has "dialectically exploded" in Agathon's highfalutin words.[4] When it comes time for his own speech on love, Socrates tells Phaedrus he will offer not a eulogy but the truth.

Yet despite his claim to be ignorant of everything but love, Socrates' approach is curious. He defers wisdom—the place of knowledge—to Diotima, telling his story through the tale she told him. This, Lacan believes, changes the game:

> Socrates' intervention comes as a kind of rupture or break…. At the very moment at which he introduces the wedge that his dialectic rams into the topic to contribute what one expects from the Socratic light, we have the sense of a discordance, and not of a comparison.[5]

While other authors had viewed this shift as a sign of Socrates' wish to avoid humiliating Agathon with further questioning, Lacan does not agree. He is more interested in why Plato put these two very different speeches side by side in the progression of the text. Lacan detects something hidden in the extravagant style of Agathon's speech that "was simply asking to be heard,"[6] something that allows it to be "situated in another register"[7] compared to Socrates' speech. What then are these two different registers and what place does Socrates' speech have in *The Symposium*? If Agathon's speech is pure style, florid, and wordy, Socrates' contribution has three interesting nuances:

1. Its *content*—the story itself, which we will come to examine.
2. Its *medium*—the deferral to Diotima, which we can see as a way to "triangulate" the response to Agathon, avoiding both a simple rebuttal and the offer of a speech in kind.
3. Its *function*—not the functioning of the Socratic method for its own sake, but insofar as it brings out what Lacan calls the "function of lack."[8]

The precision of these nuances becomes evident if we see Socrates as attempting to navigate two roles: Socrates-the-questioner and Socrates-the-storyteller. As Lacan puts it, what should interest us in the text is, on the one hand, "the testimony that constitutes the essence of Socrates' questioning," and on the other, "what Socrates introduces, wants to produce, and conventionally speaks about."[9] This distinction also separates the approach of the Socratic method from that of the Sophists. The aim is not the demonstration or transmission of knowledge by Socrates as orator, but the emergence of knowledge from within his interlocutor. Knowledge is embedded in the soul, and it requires only the skill and precision demanded by the Socratic method to liberate it from its "infinite anteriority" there.[10] The parallels with the psychoanalytic process—which isolates alternative significations arising from the formal properties of the analysands' signifiers to reveal how they exceed his or her conscious intention—are tempting. Indeed, Lacan draws the parallel himself in describing "the effect of his [Socrates'] questioning on what I call the coherence of the signifier."[11]

Take, for example, the phrasing that interests Lacan in Socrates' question to Agathon: "Is Love such as to be love of something or of nothing?".[12] The "of" here could refer to its origin (as in the expression, "son of…," referencing the story of the progeny of Eros)[13] or "to what love as a signifier is correlated with" (for instance, Socrates' love of knowledge, or his knowledge of love).[14] It is through such ambiguity that the signifier operates—something that again Socrates and psychoanalysis share in their methods—as demonstrated by the fact that it allows Socrates to bring out the internal contradictions of Agathon's own words.

Lacan is quick to notice another tactic of Socrates, however. He points to a sudden substitution in the dialogue with Agathon of love for desire:

> We can point in the text to the moment at which, asking Agathon whether he thinks love is or is not the love of something, he substitutes the term "desire" for the term "love".[15]

These two categories are bridged by a third—"the function of lack"—insofar as, for Socrates, it allows "a return to the desiring function of love."[16] As Lacan's commentary presents it, we therefore have a function of lack, and a function of love, both of which are to desire. The substitution, it seems, would appear to be between love and lack, rather than between love and desire. To prise these apart, we should recognize that two separate things are at work: a conceptual substitution (Lacan) and a terminological conflation (Socrates). For Lacan, to lack something is not simply to desire it—we do not automatically desire everything that we lack. The object of desire, that to which desire tends, is not a bodily or material object but *lack itself.* The "positivization" of a lack is therefore what remains of desire even when an object of satisfaction is at hand. It is this that allows Lacan to say that "Loving is to give what one does not have."[17] On Socrates' part, the terminological conflation becomes clear when we remember that the true subject of the speeches in *The Symposium* is Eros, the god of ancient Greece, conflating *both* love and desire as we understand them today. This subtle shift allows for a further differentiation of Socrates' speech from that of his predecessor. As Lacan comments:

> It is clearly around the articulation of love-Eros and desire-Eros that the entire dialectic developed in the dialogue as a whole in fact revolves.[18]

Taking Lacan's conceptual substitution and Socrates' terminological conflation together we can perhaps detect the wider maneuver, Lacan is trying to execute over the course of this Seminar: a reframing that would move us from Eros to love/desire; from love/desire to object; and finally, from object to lack.

For Lacan, the goal of the dialogue with Agathon which forms the prelude to Socrates' own speech is not to transmit a knowledge but to question or interrogate a knowledge that is supposed. As a practice based on speech, the Socratic method shares with psychoanalysis the premise that knowledge depends on,

> … The coherence of discourse that involves dialogue and that revolves around the apprehension of the necessity of the law of the signifier.[19]

Contrary to the highfalutin discourse of Agathon, the Socratic method entails that "knowledge resides within the play of the signifier," and that its practice—like psychoanalysis—brings out "the autonomy of the law of the signifier."[20]

And yet, why isn't this enough? Socrates has not yet said anything himself about love and to do so, Lacan believes, he needs more than just a semi-pedantic mode of interrogation. He needs to introduce Diotima.

It is at this point that Lacan can specify the difference between the Socratic and psychoanalytic methods. What is new about psychoanalysis is the contention that "something can find sustenance in the law of the signifier, not only without involving knowledge but *by explicitly excluding it*."[21] Psychoanalysis is about the unconscious and if, as Lacan claims, the unconscious is independent of the subject insofar as it subsists and is transmitted in the signifying chain, then the subject no longer needs to be posited as the seat of this knowledge. The implication for how we think about transference is obvious: The transferential relationship, a relationship of love, is identified and developed not through a supplementation of knowledge (by simply pointing out the transference in an attempt to dissolve it, for instance) but by following the path of the signifier, even if this path may appear circuitous and unrelated to the object at stake (that the person of the analyst cannot easily be equated to the mother or father, for instance).

In a similar way, Socrates' tactic of speaking through Diotima is not simply a way of subtly distance himself from the story he relays from her, even if—as Lacan notes—Socrates is not entirely convinced by it.[22] Instead, Lacan introduces the term *dioecisme* here, which refers to the partitioning of a population from a defeated enemy city. Lacan contends that a similar partitioning is employed by Socrates in the appeal to Diotima, and—perhaps somewhat tenuously—he also links it to Freud's *Spaltung*, which he liberally interprets as the division of the subject. In choosing to use Diotima to speak in his stead, Socrates reveals this gap in the speaking subject. Whatever we might think of Lacan's interpretation, it is the *form* of the story that Socrates relates through Diotima that is worth noting. It marks, for Lacan, a limit point in speaking about love:

> When one arrives… at a certain terminus regarding what can be obtained at the level of *episteme* or knowledge, myth is necessary in order to go further.[23]

Myth takes over where knowledge reaches its limit. Here we see once again the contrast between function and form that first interested Lacan in the abrupt shift from Agathon's contribution to that of Socrates. The appeal to myth might appear somewhat odd however, given that—to return to Lacan's opening framing—if Socrates knows anything it is about love.[24] Perhaps it is insofar as love itself is a product of this gap, split, or lack that his recourse to Diotima's story can make sense. The story itself is, after all, a myth about the birth of love (Eros) from two unlikely parents. As Diotima tells Socrates in *The Symposium*, the object of love is not beauty, as he had supposed, but reproduction and birth in beauty as the path to pure immortality.

These unlikely parents, Poros and Penia, are the embodiment of sharply contrasting backgrounds. Penia, the mother, stands for Poverty, or even destitution (read: lack, in Lacanian terms). She is an orphan. She is also, Plato tells us, *aporia*, meaning that she is without resources. Poros, the father, stands for the exact opposite of *aporia*—he embodies Resource, and is himself is the son of Metis, which in turn Lacan translates as invention. The two are at the birthday party of Aphrodite. Penia is not of a high enough status to be allowed in, so instead waits outside, and when Poros becomes drunk and falls asleep she takes advantage.[25] Two things immediately stand out in this story. First, that the date of Love's conception is the same as the birthday of Aphrodite. Hence Lacan claims that "Love will always have some obscure relationship with beauty."[26] Second, that Love will inherit a mixture of his parents' characteristics. This prompts Lacan to return to his oft-repeated maxim that "love is giving what you don't have."[27] It is Penia who instigates the drunken copulation which leads to the birth of Love because "she has nothing to give above and beyond her constitutive lack or aporia."[28] She gives what she does *not* have and this, for Lacan, is the essence of loving. We find here a recurrent theme of this Seminar. Discussing the myth later in the year, he repeats that the key to love, to being able to love, is to accept one's lack:

> One cannot love without presenting oneself as if one does not have, even if one does. Love as a response implies the domain of not having.[29]

How do we connect this ancient story to Lacan's broader psychoanalytic theory? One possible reading, using Lacanian terminology, is that the story demonstrates the move from the imaginary phallus (the presumed object of the mother's desire) to the symbolic phallus (a pure signifier of a plus or minus in symbolic relations). The castration complex, on Lacan's reading, involves nothing more than the assumption of lack. "Loving is to give what one does not have" means to offer or locate your castration in an other. Lacan expresses this idea neatly in Seminar X:

> … Real love, the central question of transference is established [through] what he lacks, because he loves with this lack. It is not for nothing that I'm always drumming it into you that to love is to give what one hasn't got. This is even the principle behind the castration complex. To have the phallus, to be able to make use of it, [one] must not *be* it.[30]

This is not so abstract. We can think of the countless stories—from *Titanic* to *Beauty and the Beast*—where love arises on condition of a materialized lack on the part of the protagonist, just as we find here in *The Symposium* where only Poverty (Penia) can conceive Love. Love hangs on nothing, as it were, a refrain Lacan had been repeating for several years already:

> There is no support for love… as I have told you: to give one's love, is very precisely and essentially to give as such nothing of what one has, because it is precisely in so far as one does not have it that there is question of love.[31]

If love is sustained by a something which is nothing, we get a sense of why throughout his work Lacan felt the need to turn to myth and storytelling to convey the nature of love. Yet for love to be produced, the way in which a lack is manifested is crucial. It should be presented not as a deficiency (the man or woman is a loser, hopeless, pathetic) but as a "positivized" lack: a loss or limitation that is used to one's advantage, something missing that has been produced, as if from nothing. The status of love, as Lacan concludes in his commentary on Socrates' story, thus resides in an "in-betweenness": in between the beautiful and the ugly; in between *episteme* (knowledge) and *doxa* (discourse); in between the gods and the mortals.[32]

Lacan will go on, in the next session of this Seminar, to discuss Diotima's myth in more detail. But it is immediately after Socrates concludes his speech that Plato reports a knock on the door and the sound of the drunken Aristophanes outside demanding to enter. This is where Lacan locates the turning point in *The Symposium*, and which, he promises, will allow us to see how the experience of the transference unfolds dialectically.[33]

Notes

1. Plato, *The Symposium*, trans. C. Gill and D. Lee (London: Penguin, 2005), p. 39.
2. Jacques Lacan, *Transference: The Seminar of Jacques Lacan, Book VIII* (2015), trans. B. Fink (Cambridge: Polity, 2015), p. 113.
3. Ibid., p. 110.
4. Ibid., p. 111.
5. Ibid., p. 112.
6. Ibid.
7. Ibid., p. 113.
8. Ibid.
9. Ibid., p. 114.
10. Ibid.
11. Ibid., p. 115.
12. Ibid.
13. Ibid., p. 116.
14. Ibid., p. 110.
15. Ibid., p. 115.
16. Ibid.
17. A formula repeated many times across his work. See, for instance, in perhaps its first use, Jacques Lacan, 1957/1958. Unpublished, May 7, 1958, from Seminar V: The Formations of the Unconscious. In this Seminar, p. 121.
18. Jacques Lacan, *Transference: The Seminar of Jacques Lacan, Book VIII* (2015), trans. B. Fink (Cambridge: Polity, 2015), p. 115.
19. Ibid., p. 116.
20. Ibid., p. 117.

21. Ibid., emphasis added.
22. Ibid., p. 118.
23. Ibid.
24. Ibid., p. 110.
25. Ibid., pp. 120–121.
26. Ibid., p. 121.
27. Ibid.
28. Ibid.
29. Ibid., p. 357.
30. Jacques Lacan, *Anxiety: The Seminar of Jacques Lacan, Book X* (2014), trans. A.R. Price (Cambridge: Polity, 2015), p. 108. Emphasis in original.
31. Jacques Lacan, 1957/1958. Unpublished, May 7, 1958, from Seminar V: The Formations of the Unconscious.
32. Jacques Lacan, *Transference: The Seminar of Jacques Lacan, Book VIII* (2015), trans. B. Fink (Cambridge: Polity, 2015), p.122.
33. Ibid., pp. 122–123.

References

Lacan, Jacques. 1957/1958. Unpublished, May 7, 1958, from Seminar V: The Formations of the Unconscious.

———. 2014. *Anxiety: The Seminar of Jacques Lacan, Book VX (1962–1963).* Translated by A.R. Price. Cambridge: Polity Press.

———. 2015. *Transference: The Seminar of Jacques Lacan, Book VIII.* Edited by Jacques-Alain Miller and Translated by Bruce Fink. Cambridge: Polity.

Plato. 2005. *The Symposium.* Trans. C. Gill and D. Lee. London: Penguin.

8

The Question of the Meaning of *Ágalma*: Between Hermeneutics, Topology, and Unconcealment—Commentary on Sessions IX and X

Hue Woodson

At the close of Session VIII of the *Transference* seminar, after Jacques Lacan describes the relationship between *epistéme* and *mýthous* in Plato's *Symposium*, he suggests that "the only field in which the elucidation of its truth can develop is the one that follow Alcibiades' entrance."[1] For Lacan, following the speeches delivered by Phaedrus, Pausanias, Eryximachus, and Aristophanes culminating in the epistemological and mythological expressions of the meaning of love, followed by speeches by Agathon and Socrates focused respectively on the rhetorical and philosophical expressions of the meaning of love, Alcibiades' speech provides a unique elucidation that brings Lacan to argue that "Alcibiades' entrance is essential."[2] What makes this entrance "essential" is that, on one hand, Alcibiades' lateness and drunkenness inject an unconcealedness into what he says in *Symposium*, while, on the other hand, the fact that he physically seats himself on a couch with Socrates and Agathon provides a similar unconcealment to the meaning of love.[3] Lacan certainly recognizes this, viewing

H. Woodson (✉)
Tarrant County College, Fort Worth, TX, USA
e-mail: HUBERT.WOODSON@tccd.edu

G. Basu Thakur and J. Dickstein (eds.), *Reading Lacan's Seminar VIII*,
The Palgrave Lacan Series, https://doi.org/10.1007/978-3-030-32742-2_8

each of the speeches before Alcibiades' entrance as concealing the meaning of love much more than the intention of each to unconceal it. In an effort to unconceal the meaning of love, Lacan asserts the following:

> It is only the action that develops afterward between Alcibiades, Agathon, and Socrates that we can effectively delineate the structural relationship in which we can recognize what the discovery of the unconscious and the practice of psychoanalysis—namely, the experience of transference—finally allow us as analysts to be able to express dialectically.[4]

This "experience of transference," as a form of unconcealment, is embodied in the relationship between Alcibiades, Agathon, and Socrates. Yet, even as a structural relationship that unconceals the individualized roles of the unconscious for each, and to the extent that what is "express[ed] dialectically" between Agathon and Socrates, Socrates and Alcibiades, and Alcibiades and Agathon are each isolated experiences of transference, Lacan enters Session IX by focusing on the uniqueness of Socrates' speech and how "Socrates has Diotima speak in his stead."[5]

* * *

Following a preliminary recapitulation of the previous session, Session IX entitled "Exit from the Ultra-World" revisits an analysis of Socrates' speech as marked with a line of questioning that demonstrates "lack to be at the heart of the question of what love is."[6] For Lacan, through the constitution of substitution, "love can, in effect, only be articulated around lack, owning to the fact that love can but lack what it desires."[7] Not only does Lacan view that the problem in the dialectic Socrates describes is ultimately between *what love lacks* and *what love desires*—or how love constitutes through the substitution of what it lacks—but Lacan also concedes that "[Socrates] brings [this dialectic] to bear on the coherence of the signifier."[8] That is to say, Socrates' questioning into the meaning of love is predominantly about interrogating the signification of the signifier "love." This allows Socrates, as Lacan notes, to distinguish the meaning of love as *epistéme* from the meaning of love as *mýthous*—with respect to the latter, "[Socrates] ambiguously yields the floor to she who, in his stead, expresses herself through myth."[9]

This ambiguity has significant implications for Lacan's reading of Socrates' Diomita's speech. Here, in one sense, Lacan recognizes that there is always-already an ambiguity in what Socrates says, when considering that the Socrates–Plato relationship creates an impossibility in determining where the dividing line is between what Socrates says and what Plato says. To be sure, we know that, in *Symposium*, as well as other Platonic dialogues in which Socrates is a main or central character, there remains the inability to measure Socrates' words as his alone and not simply as a mouthpiece for Plato's philosophy. In this way, if utilizing Lacan's words, Plato, too, "ambiguously yields the floor to [Socrates] who, in [Plato's] stead, expresses himself through myth"—to this extent, there is often a mythology to what Socrates expresses generally the Platonic dialogues, which, by attempting to locate where Socrates can be separated from Plato, the need for demythologizing Socrates becomes all the more important. In *Symposium*, in particular, the fact that Lacan points out this similar ambiguity in how Socrates "yields the floor to [Diotima], in his stead," suggests a similar demythologizing task through the very contextualization of Diotima "express[ing] herself through myth." Nevertheless, because the implications of Diotima upon Socrates are analogous to Socrates upon Plato, Lacan's demythologizing task toward Diotima over Socrates has a similar imperative toward understanding how Socrates speaks for Plato. In fact, Diotima's role in *Symposium* is to speak for Socrates on the meaning of love as a *mýthous*—since *mýthous* "is what people say," Lacan concludes that "this is what Socrates defers to in letting Diotima speak."[10]

Diotima's speech—which is just as deferred to by Socrates as Socrates is deferred to by Plato—does not maintain Socrates' meaning of love being grounded on the notion of lacking. Instead, Lacan points out that "we see something develop in it that makes us slip further and further away from the original notion Socrates introduced in his dialectic," such that Diotima's speech interprets the meaning of love as not having a dialectic with lacking, but a dialectic with good things.[11] In other words, rather than the meaning of love being defined by searching what is lacking, Diotima's definition of love is predicated on searching for good things—in this case, according to Lacan, "every aspiration towards good things is a sort of love."[12] However, Lacan finds that "in order for us to speak of love, strictly speaking, something must be made more specific." What this means, in Lacan's view, is that simply referring to love in terms of its directedness toward "good things" does not actually nor completely unconceal the meaning of love—instead, "good things," as a generality, merely conceals love. It is this regard that, as Lacan points out, "[Diotima] introduces the theme of love of beauty."[13] Lacan continues by positing that "beauty specifies the direction in which the call or attraction to possession, to the enjoyment of possessing, to the constitution of a κτῆμα (*ktéma*) arises."[14] Not only does Lacan highlight this as "the point to which Diotima leads us in order to define love," but we also find that this definition poses a problem. As much as "beauty specifies the direction in which the call or attraction to possession," beauty itself is not defined solely by what is possessed. Essentially, beauty, the directedness of attraction, and what is possessed are three very different elements. Each certainly shares a relatedness in the question of the meaning of love, but, as Lacan would likely agree, there is no strict contingency nor dependency from one to another—for example, though beauty may allow for the directedness of attraction, neither hold a special or inevitable contingency over what is possessed. Lacan describes this problem in the following: "What [Diotima] presents is the following: beauty has nothing to do with having, with anything that can be possessed, but rather with being, and specifically with mortal being."[15] If we follow Lacan here, it becomes evident that, if "beauty has nothing to do with having," beauty has an independence in its dialectic with "having." From this, if we trace the meaning of love to a dialectic with beauty, we find that, though love and beauty share this dialectic, the meaning of love is not contingent on nor regulated by the meaning of "having." When we approach the question of the meaning of love, it is not a question that is associated, as Lacan argues, "with anything that can be possessed."

What this means, too, is, if reminding ourselves of Socrates' notion that love has a dialectic with lacking, Lacan's disagreement with this is all the more important—if the meaning of love was grounded on a dialectic of lacking, this means that, when one loves someone, the directedness of that love is always-already about unfulfillment. We can certainly think of this unfulfillment in terms of the possibility (or impossibility) of "having." In effect, love sharing a dialectic with lacking is a love that is always-already unrequited. This cannot be so, especially if "beauty has nothing to do with having, with anything that can be possessed." As Lacan suggests, if beauty has more to do "with being, and specifically with mortal being," the question of the meaning of love and the dialectic between love and beauty has a directedness toward existence, especially coming to bear on mortality. It is in light of this morality that Lacan views "beauty [as] the mode of a kind of giving birth."[16] In Lacan's view, this birth "is not painless, but [is one] which involves the least pain possible."[17] Beauty, as "giving birth," becomes a "painful escape route" that carries all that is mortal "toward what [beauty] aspires to: immortality."[18] This immortality that beauty "aspires to" is, by way of beauty's dialectic with love, a kind of immortality that love "aspires to" as well—what love "aspires to," when considering the question of the meaning of love, is directed towards immortality by way of the meaning of beauty.

Despite this directedness and aspiration, Lacan is careful to conclude that:

> Diotima's whole speech articulates the function of beauty as being first and foremost an illusion, a fundamental mirage, by which perishable and fragile beings are sustained in their quest for permanence, which is their essential aspiration.[19]

Here, Lacan points to an ongoing problem when addressing the meaning of beauty in relation to the meaning of love. It is a problem that occurs in the dialectic between the two, grounded in the groundlessness of what immortality holds for either side of the dialectic in the structural relationship between love and beauty. The crux of the problem, in Lacan's view, is that, in the directedness with which the meaning of love moves toward the meaning of beauty, there exists an inevitable duplicity in what the former "aspires to" through the latter. To "aspire to" points to a limitation or an apex—the meaning of love and the meaning of beauty, in what they respectively "aspire to," become two horizons that are never ultimately unified in the fulfillment of what either "aspires to."

For the function of beauty to be, according to Lacan, "first and foremost an illusion, a fundamental mirage," this functionality situates beauty more on the side of mortality than immortality. That is to say, the meaning of beauty, at its very functionality, is to depict the aspiration of immortality as more than an aspiration—the function of beauty as being partly about what is aspired to give the "illusion" or the "mirage" that it can be completely unconcealed. We find that what is concealed is actually a further but necessary unconcealment. What makes the function of beauty "first and foremost an illusion, a fundamental mirage" is that the meaning of beauty seems meaningful enough to be authenticated—to be unconcealed in its complete unconcealment—to the extent that what is aspired to is never anything more than an aspiration. As lamentable as this seems, Lacan considers this false unconcealment as "fundamental," in the sense that what becomes concealed is something "by which perishable and fragile beings are sustained in their quest for permanence." I take this to mean that what "perishable and fragile beings" seek in their aspiration for beauty is a meaning that is not in the total unconcealment of the meaning of beauty and the constitution of immortality—instead, it is in the limitations in the interplay between partial concealment and partial unconcealment, which becomes "sustain[ing] in their quest for permanence." The meaning of beauty and the underlying meaning of love do not sustain "perishable and fragile beings" in the realms of themselves alone, within the total unconcealment of both. What sustains these "perishable and fragile beings" is the desire for beauty as that which is fundamentally "aspired to"—the sustainment is not in the function of beauty as "an illusion, a fundamental mirage," but, rather, it is a sustainment in the desire of beauty as what is possibly beyond the illusion or, essentially, fundamentally undergirding the "fundamental mirage." This is what Lacan calls the "quest for permanence," which arises from the "fundamental mirage" of the meaning of beauty fundamentally tethering "perishable and fragile beings" to an inauthentic immortality. The grounding groundlessness of this "quest for permanence" is predicated on the meaning of desire—for Lacan, desire calibrates the meaning of beauty, the meaning of the illusion or fundamental mirage, and the meaning of the quest for permanence for the perishable and fragile beings. Lacan describes this calibration as the following:

> The desire for beauty [*désir de beau*]—desire insofar as it attaches itself to this mirage and gets caught up in it—is what corresponds to the hidden presence of the desire for death. The desire that comes from beauty [*désir du

> *beau*] is what, reversing this function, makes the subject choose the trace or appeals [*appels*] of what the object offers him, or at least certain objects.[20]

Notice, here, that Lacan draws a careful distinction between "the desire for beauty" and "the desire from beauty." This points to, in one sense, the grounding groundlessness of desire itself. In short, it is the extent at which desire can serve as the ground for "perishable and fragile beings," while, simultaneously, desire offers a groundlessness. If we think of this in terms of the meaning of the illusion or fundamental mirage, it is possible to say that the difference between "the desire for" and "the desire from" hinges on beauty's functionality as the ambiguity of the authenticity/inauthenticity of the illusion/mirage. A turn that is made from encountering what is thought to be unconcealment by way of how "[*the desire for*] attaches itself to the mirage and gets caught up in it" toward finding what is encountered is really concealment, so that *the desire from* "makes the subject choose the trace [...] of what the object offers him."

The turn, as I have termed it, is what Lacan refers to as the "reversing" of the function of beauty. Lacan views the "reversing [of] this function" as bringing the meaning of beauty into a Hegelian reflective self-consciousness of sorts.[21] It is particularly because of this reversal that Lacan finds that:

> It is here that the slippage occurs in Diotima's speech that turns beauty—which was not, strictly speaking, a medium, but rather a transition or passageway—into the very goal that is sought. In remaining, so to speak, the guide, the guide becomes the object(ive) or rather takes the place of the objects that can be its prop. And this transition is explicitly indicated in her speech.[22]

"The slippage," as Lacan calls it, is represented in the reversal that "turns beauty [...] into the very goal that is sought." This "slippage," then, arises from Diotima's speech engaging in the hermeneutical activity of translating beauty "into the very goal that is sought." Viewed this way, the hermeneutics of Diotima, as "the guide," becomes ultimately directed toward interpreting how "the guide becomes the object(ive)."

What this means is that "the slippage" that occurs in Diotima's speech allows for the guide to become the object, such that it eventually opens up the possibility for the guide to become the objective. The fact that this slippage occurs at all suggests that, when Diotima's role as the guide "takes the place of objects that can be its prop," this "slippage" is always-already wired into the dialectical definition of love itself as it is predicated on the function of desire.

Accordingly, Lacan concludes that:

> [...] one might say that the dialectical definition of love, as it is developed by Diotima, intersects with what I have tried to define as the metronymic function in desire. What is at issue in her speech is something beyond all objects that resides in the movement of a certain aim and a certain relation—that of desire—through all objects and toward an unlimited perspective.[23]

As much as Diotima's speech cultivates a "metronymic function of desire," Lacan points out that this metronymity becomes fundamental to "something [that is] beyond all objects." This certain something acts as a regulatory entity, which "resides in the movement of a certain aim and a certain relation [...] through all objects and toward an unlimited perspective." Lacan's yet-to-be-defined "something beyond all objects" directly affects the relationship between the meaning of its movement and the meanings of its "certain aim" and "certain relation." The movement initiated by this certain "something beyond all objects" becomes the means by which we can trace what this "something beyond all objects" is—to bring this certain "something beyond all objects" in view, Lacan systematically delineates this movement, with its "certain aim" and "certain relation," in the following way:

> *Erastés*, *erón*, the lover, is led toward a distant *erómenos*, by all the *erómenoi*, all that is lovable, all that is worthy of being loved. It is a distant *erómenos* or *erómenon*, for his quest can also have a neuter goal. The problem then is what is signified by and what can continue to signify—beyond this outstripping, this marked jump—that which presented itself at the beginning of the dialectic as *ktéma*, the goal of possessing.[24]

With the movement defined as possibly having a "neuter goal," Lacan denotes a problem that must be unavoidably addressed in "what is signified by and what can continue to signify." The problem, here, is not with the goal itself—even when "[the lover's] quest can also have a neuter goal"—but, rather, it is in what Lacan singles out as "the goal of processing" or the "*ktéma.*" Lacan further expounds on "*ktéma*" as:

> In short, the further the subject goes in his aim, the more he is within his rights to love himself, so to speak, via his ideal ego. The more he desires, the more he himself becomes desirable [...] insomuch as in Platonic Eros, the loving person aims only at his own perfection—love aims only at its own perfection.[25]

In light of this recapitulation, and being especially mindful of the implications served upon the meaning of Platonic Eros in the assertion that "love aims only at its own perfection," Lacan carefully notes that:

> This is not where Plato leaves off, on the condition that we are willing to look beyond the immediate terrain and ask ourselves, first, what is signified by the fact that Socrates has Diotima speak in his stead and, second, what happens once Alcibiades arrives on the scene.[26]

Here, Lacan revisits two essential questions that must be addressed when "we are willing to look beyond the immediate terrain" of the meaning of *love aims only at its own perfection.* Lacan's two questions involve, on one hand, "what is signified by the fact that Socrates has Diotima speak in his stead," and, on the other, "what happens once Alcibiades arrives on the scene." Both of these questions pertain to Socrates. While it is clear that Diotima "speak[s] in his stead," we see, too, that "what happens once Alcibiades arrives on the scene" is that Alcibiades also speaks, merely by way of his presence, in Socrates' stead.

Because both Diotima and Alcibiades act as stand-ins for Socrates, the suggestion is that they—either by speaking or arriving in Socrates' stead—express what Socrates cannot. In turn, they respectively root what they express, in Socrates' stead, in a knowability that Socrates does not have. Socrates' knowability into what Diotima and Alcibiades express in his stead becomes an issue of the meaning of what Socrates knows when confronting the meaning of what Socrates does not know. It is with this in mind that Lacan, too, acknowledges that there is a difference between what Socrates knows and does not know, when it comes to matters of love—there is a fundamental situatedness to Socrates' epistemology of love.

Lacan's understanding of this epistemology of love is particularly argued in the following:

> Even though it is posited at the outset that the only matters about which Socrates knows anything are matters of love, he can only speak of them by remaining in the zone of the "he did not know." Even when knowledgeable, he himself cannot speak of what he knows and must have someone else speak who speaks without knowing.[27]

It is "by remaining in the zone of the 'he did not know'" that Socrates defines his epistemology of love as epistemologically disposed toward a negation, which dialectically brings the abstraction of love to it concreteness.[28] Because Socrates "himself cannot speak of what he knows," his epistemology of love remains an abstraction, such that, once he has "someone else speak who speaks without knowing," the Other becomes a negation, through which Socrates is able to concretize his epistemology of love. Still, it is only "by remaining in the zone of the 'he did not know'" that an epistemology of love is even possible for Socrates, since, as Lacan describes:

> Socrates can only locate himself in his knowledge here by showing that there can be no discourse on love but from the point at which he did not know. This is the mainspring of what is signified by Socrates' choice of [allowing Diotima's speech to speak in his stead].[29]

From the "mainspring of what is signified by Socrates' choice," as well as "from the point at which [Socrates] did not know," Lacan finds a transcendence that occurs, which is "played out, in a ghost-like way, [in] the substitution of one for another."[30] The dialectical comportment of Socrates, someone else speaking for him in his stead, and the individual which Socrates loves suggest that, as Lacan argues, "it takes three to love, not just two."[31] For this to be so, Lacan questions whether there is a competition, "by which the object is constituted, insofar as it institutes communication between two subjects"—Lacan answers, no.[32] Instead, Lacan believes that "something of a different order is introduced here."[33] What is introduced is "the object of unique covetousness [which] is constituted as such as the heart of love's action."[34] From this, Lacan eventually arrives at the question: "what kind of object is there behind all of this that leads to such a vacillation in the subject himself."[35] It is at this point, with having introduced the question into the meaning of "the object of unique covetousness," when Lacan concludes the session with:

> I will leave you today with the function of the object, insofar as it is specifically indicated in the whole of [*Symposium*]. What I will tell you will revolve around a word that is found in [*Symposium*], and whose use in Greek allows us to glimpse the history and function, which I believe I have refound, of the object at stake here. This word is ἄγαλμα (*ágalma*), which, we are told, is what is hidden within the disheveled Silenus known as Socrates.[36]

Here, upon introducing the word ἄγαλμα (*ágalma*), Lacan carries forward this idea into the next session, after he considers *ágalma* as "what is hidden within the disheveled Silenus known as Socrates." For Lacan, *ágalma* is concealed, though the function of the object itself "is specifically indicated in the whole of [*Symposium*]." In order to unconceal *ágalma*—and bring it into the clearing to be "refound," as Lacan calls it—Lacan enters the next session working through the "unexplored enigma" of *ágalma.*

* * *

In Session X entitled *Ágalma*, Lacan begins by providing an etymology of *ágalma*, which involves considering its meaning as situated between "ornament" and "jewelry." From here, Lacan considers another word that is etymologically related to *ágalma*: αγάλλω (*agállo*), which can be interpreted as "bejewel" or "adorn." In either case, though *ágalma* and *agállo* signify meanings that are relatively opaque for the purposes of Lacan's limited use of them, they provide contextualization to the importance that Lacan places on the entrance of Alcibiades in *Symposium*. Lacan suggests that "the word *ágalma* appears at the very moment at which I told you the scene changes completely."[37] The fact that, as Lacan continues, "after the eulogistic games regulated up until then by the topic of love, Alcibiades, the actor who changed everything enters," Lacan brings us to a means of understanding his specialized meaning of *ágalma*.[38] That meaning, for Lacan, hinges on the idea that Alcibiades, as "the actor who changed everything," enters, which becomes an entering that is, in itself, an act of unconcealment. In other words, when entering the scene as he does, Alcibiades enters into the clearing—he represents an unconcealment that has yet to be unconcealed "after the eulogistic games regulated up until [his entrance]."

Once in the clearing, it stands to reason that Lacan's assertion that, once becoming the embodiment of unconcealment, "the proof that [Alcibiades] changes everything is that he himself modifies the rules of the game, assigning himself the place of he who presides over the symposium."[39] What Alcibiades unconceals, then, is that "eulogies of love" are nothing more than mere concealments. Lacan notes this, by finding that "[Alcibiades] says, we are no longer going to provide eulogies of love, but of the other, and namely, of the person to our right."[40] If, in fact, as Alcibiades says, we are to provide eulogies "of the other" or "of the person to our right," it is clear that eulogies of love conceal the meaning of love itself—it is only through making eulogies "of the other" or "of the person to our right" that the meaning of love, at its most authentic, is truly unconcealed. Though, to even make such a claim, we are, as Lacan proposes, "already going very far," we still have not fully unconcealed the unconcealment of *ágalma*,[41] which must be accomplished by drawing a distinction between what Alcibiades means by "eulogies of love" and *eulogies of the other* or *eulogies of the person to [the] right*. It is this difference, which Lacan focuses his attention. More precisely, Lacan finds that this difference is based on the unconcealment of the meaning of love as something contingent on the meaning of action. For Lacan, when considering this relationship between love and action, "if love is to be involved here, it's love in action, and it is the relation of the one to the other that will have to manifest itself here."[42]

The unconcealment of *ágalma* is love in action. If we repurpose Lacan's assertion about love and action, it becomes possible to consider how *ágalma* and action necessarily unconceal "the relation of the one to the other." Both similarly are "eulogies of love" in the sense that, as embodiments, they are concealments of love—in fact, they are ontological objectifications of the meaning of love.[43] However, when considering the meaning that can be made from *ágalma* and action, they become "eulogies of the other"—they refer to the metaphysical subjectivities of "the other" or "the person to [the] right."[44] This can only be represented by the meaningfulness of how *ágalma* and action stand out from their ontological objectifications to bring "the other" or "the person to [the] right" out of abstract consciousness and into reflective consciousness.[45] The meaningfulness of *ágalma* and action does not come in-themselves. What is made meaningful arises in the manner in which they stand out from themselves,[46] within the meaning-making confines of "the relation of the one to the other." What "manifest[s] itself here," as Lacan proposes, is more than just the meanings of *ágalma* and action toward "the relation of the one to the other"—what unconceals itself, so to speak, is another "relation of one to the other," which is grounded in *ágalma* and action's "relation of one to the other." Through the possibility of this other unconcealment, according to Lacan:

> This allows us to realize that we are shifting to another register than the one I pointed out in Diotima's speech. What was at stake there was a dyadic relation. He who begins to climb towards love proceeds by the path of identification and of production, as it were, aided by the marvel of beauty. He finds in beauty his terminus and identifies it with the perfection of the labor of love.[47]

The "dyadic relation" of Lacan's ultimate concern is not strictly what exists between *ágalma* and action, nor even between the dyadic separately shared between love and *ágalma* or love and action. We need not even view the dyadic relations beauty has respectively with *ágalma* and beauty as being of our primary concern either. Though, clearly, all of these dyadic relations exist in Diotima's speech, "what was at stake there," in Lacan's words, is the "dyadic relation" between love and beauty. This love-beauty "dyadic relation," as a Master-Signifier to the dyadic relations in the interrelationships between love, *ágalma*, action, and beauty, "proceeds by the path of identification and of production"—what is identified and what is produced along this "path" is *ágalma* and action. When "he who begins to climb towards loves proceeds by [this] path," Lacan posits that love does so, through acts of identifying and producing, by being "aided by the marvel of beauty." This stands to suggest, then, that *the marvel of beauty* allows "he who begins to climb towards love," in order to identify *ágalma* and produce action that fundamentally guides in a directedness toward *the marvel of beauty*—in this sense, "he who climbs towards love" is one who is also climbing toward *the marvel of beauty*, with *ágalma* and action as necessary footholds or guardrails align *he who climbs towards love* with *the marvel of beauty*. The directedness toward *the marvel of beauty* is a directedness toward what Lacan calls a "terminus," such that "[the one who climbs towards love] finds in beauty his terminus and identifies it with the perfection of the labor of love."

If we return, in particular, to what arises between *he who climbs towards love* and *the marvel of beauty*, what remains clear, according to Lacan, is that:

> We see there a twofold relationship whose goal is identification with the Sovereign Good [...] the complexity or, more precisely, the triplicity that proposes to provide us with what I consider essential in the psychoanalytic discovery: the topology from which the subject's relation to the symbolic results at its core, insofar as the symbolic is essentially distinct from the imaginary and its capture.[48]

Here, Lacan undoubtedly aligns *the marvel of beauty* as "terminus" with a "goal" as "identification with the Sovereign Good." It is out of this alignment that Lacan argues that, by way of a "twofold relationship," there exists a "complexity or, more precisely, the triplicity"—a recapitulation from Session IX about "it takes three to love, not just two"—which "provides us with what I consider essential in the psychoanalytic discovery." What makes this especially "essential" for Lacan is that "the path of identification and of production" is most certainly about "psychoanalytic discovery." As we have seen with Lacan's notion about *he who climbs towards love*, the act of climbing toward love and the directedness toward *the marvel of beauty* as "the terminus" are both constituted by a "psychoanalytic discovery."

The path that *he who climbs towards love* takes does contain a topology, which is measured along "identification" and "production," but it is also, as Lacan believes, "from which the subject's relation to the symbolic results at its core." These "symbolic results" are the goal invested in an "identification with the Sovereign Good." This invocation of the symbolic is immediately contrasted with the imaginary, whereby the former, in Lacan's view, is constituted in identifying "with the Sovereign Good" over the illusiveness of the latter. Considered this way, though the symbolic and the imaginary certainly have specific and equally necessary roles in the topology that Lacan ascribes to *he who climbs towards love*, the symbolic provides more sustenance as "the terminus" than the imaginary. Accordingly, Lacan suggests that, because "the symbolic is essentially distinct from the imaginary and its capture," the topology that exists between the two is traversed, navigated, and negotiated by *he who climbs towards love*. This is what leads Lacan to conclude:

> What I am pointing out today is essential if we are to intersect that topology, in the sense that we have to intersect it regarding the topic of love. In question here is the nature of love and a position, an essential but forgotten or elided connection, of which we analysts have nevertheless provided the lynchpin that allows us to bring out its problematic.[49]

If Lacan's intent to "intersect [this] topology" is about interrogating the meaning of it, precisely, as he suggests, "regarding the topic of love," the manner in which this intersection occurs is through questioning "the nature of love and a position."

At this point of intersection—one that is, in Lacan's words, "an essential but forgotten or elided connection"—Lacan points to a "lynchpin" that, in "allow[ing] us to bring out [this lynchpin's] problematic," is able to unconceal "the topic of love" through the unconcealment of itself. What unconceals "this lynchpin" as "the topic of love" and, in turn, unconceals "the topic of love" as a question of the meaning of "the nature of love and a position" denotes that there is a twofold unconcealment. Lacan explains this in the relationship between Alcibiades and Socrates, with the following:

> Alcibiades speaks of Socrates and says that he is going to unmask him. [...] What did Alcibiades try to do? I would say that he tried to get Socrates to manifest his desire to him. He knows that Socrates has some desire for him, but what he wanted was a sign thereof.[50]

To "unmask" Socrates means unconcealing the nature of Socrates' love in terms of manifesting Socrates' desire to Alcibiades, but it also means unconcealing Socrates' position with "a sign thereof." Together, these two forms of unconcealing, for Alcibiades, represent a goal of "identification with the Sovereign Good" at the very end of "the path of identification and of production."

Because Alcibiades becomes the *he who climbs towards love*, this directedness, though aided by *the marvel of beauty*, requires signification of desire by way of desire's manifestation. Alcibiades "knows Socrates has some desire for him" and this is what guides Alcibiades' directedness towards the meaning of love guided by *the marvel of beauty* expressed in the personage of Socrates. Yet, if it is clear that Socrates is not physically beautiful and to say that his representation of *the marvel of beauty* does not have anything to do with his appearance, it stands to reason that Socrates has a loveability to him. If he can be loved by someone as beautifully–handsome as Alcibiades, this suggests that there is something about Socrates that is, in fact, beautiful and desirable to Alcibiades. When considering this difference between what we see of Socrates and what is beautiful/desirable about Socrates, Lacan delineates this dichotomy for Alcibiades in the following:

> This topological indication is essential. What is important is what is inside. *Ágalma* may well mean ornamentation or ornament, but here it means above all gem or precious object—something that is inside. And it is with this that Alcibiades rips us away from the dialectic of beauty that had, up until then, served as the pathway, guide, or mode of capture along the pathway of the desirable. He makes the scales fall from our eyes regarding Socrates himself.[51]

Though Lacan is careful to note that *ágalma* "cannot be translated in any way, shape, or form by 'ornament' or 'jewelry'"—even if his first instinct is to do so—he recognizes that, in the instances in which the term appears in *Symposium*, "it seems to have to do with statues of the gods."[52]

Rather than it referring to ornamentation, in the sense that it points to "what is inside" and is concealed by Socrates' lack of attractiveness, Lacan uses the term's more appropriate translation to confirm that the term "always has to do with something else."[53]

To this end, Lacan narrows the meaning of *ágalma* to "always emphasiz[ing] the fetishistic function of the object."[54] In this kind of function, Lacan recognizes that *ágalma*, as *ágalmata*, exert a controlling influence over those that encounter them, to the extent that we can say that the "fetishistic function" suggests that there exists an irrational, abnormal fixation to how *ágalma* treats objects—perhaps, it is possible to say that this obsessive preoccupation with objects is rooted in spiritual or magical powers contained in them, which causes a phenomenological awareness of *ágalma*. Nevertheless, Lacan defines this fetishization not as "the phenomenology of fetishes, but to show [...] the function this serves in its place."[55] What serves in place of phenomenology is how *ágalma* becomes what Lacan calls "the golden ornament itself"—as ornamentation, *ágalma* has theological ramifications to how it "emphasizes the fetishistic function of the object." Lacan describes this theological comportment as "appear[ing] as a kind of god trap [wherein] there are things that attract the eyes of those real beings known as the gods."[56]

Since *ágalma* has theologically construed function, in Lacan's view, it "attracts divine attention."[57] When viewed this way, Lacan finds that *ágalma* is grounded in the function of the partial object, which is "that of the fundamentally partial nature of the object insofar as it is the pivotal point, crux, or key of human desire."[58] Later, in his *Anxiety* seminar—catalogued as Seminar X, delivered from November 14, 1962 to July 3, 1963—Lacan explains the function of the partial object in the following way:

> [...] in speaking to you about transference, I designated by way of a metaphor, which seems fairly clear to me, of a hand reaching over to a log. Just as the hand is about to reach the log, the log catches light, and in the flame another hand appears, reaching back to the first.[59]

Here, in Lacan's metaphor about transference, he offers, essentially, the notion of what he calls a "transference effect," which he expresses more explicitly in *The Four Fundamental Concepts of Psycho-Analysis*, catalogued as Seminar XI, delivered from January 15, 1964 to June 24, 1964. In this transference effect, as Lacan suggests in "From Interpretation to Transference," a session dated to June 17, 1964, there is "this effect of love [such that] it is clear that, like all love, it can be mapped."[60] From here, as this idea of how love is mapped and unconceals itself in the end of Session X, Lacan introduces the situatedness of *ágalma* as "the threefold topology of the subject, the other with a lowercase *o*, and the Other with a capital *O*."[61]

Notes

1. Jacques Lacan, *Transference: The Seminar of Jacques Lacan, Book VIII*. Translated by Bruce Fink (Malden, MA: Polity Press, 2015), 122.
2. Ibid., 123.
3. I have used the terms "unconcealedness" and "unconcealment" (as well as "unconceal") as synonymous expressions of truth, particularly in the manner that Martin Heidegger uses variants of the term in his *Parmenides* lecture from the Winter 1942–1943.
4. Jacques Lacan, *Transference: The Seminar of Jacques Lacan, Book VIII*, 123.
5. Ibid., 124
6. Ibid.
7. Ibid.
8. Ibid.
9. Ibid.
10. Ibid., 123.
11. Ibid., 125.
12. Ibid.
13. Ibid.
14. Ibid.
15. Ibid.
16. Ibid., 126.
17. Ibid.
18. Ibid.
19. Ibid.
20. Ibid., 127.

21. In *Phänomenologie des Geistes* (1807), often translated as *Phenomenology of Spirit*, Georg W. F. Hegel describes the reflectiveness of self-consciousness in terms of "self-consciousness exist[ing] in and for itself when, and by the fact that, it so exists for another." This occurs in the section entitled "Independence and Dependence of Self-Consciousness: Lordship and Bondage." In it, the meaning of self-consciousness is grounded in a sort of reflectiveness, which is predicated on a twofold significance, a spiritual unity, and the process of recognition. Georg W. F. Hegel, *Phenomenology of Spirit*. Translated by A. V. Miller (Oxford, UK: Clarendon Press, 1977), 111.
22. Jacques Lacan, *Transference: The Seminar of Jacques Lacan, Book VIII*, 127.
23. Ibid., 128.
24. Ibid.
25. Ibid.
26. Ibid., 129.
27. Ibid.
28. The term "abstraction" of used by Hegel to describe how "the other is an immediate consciousness entangled in a variety of relationships," such that its "otherness" is embodied as a "pure being-for-self." Hegel sees this "absolute negation" as something that engages abstraction and becomes the means by which abstraction becomes concrete. See Georg W. F. Hegel, *Phenomenology of Spirit*. Translated by A. V. Miller (Oxford, UK: Clarendon Press, 1977), 114.
29. Jacques Lacan, *Transference: The Seminar of Jacques Lacan; Book VIII*, 131.
30. Ibid., 132
31. Ibid.
32. Ibid., 134.
33. Ibid.
34. Ibid.
35. Ibid.
36. Ibid.
37. Ibid., 136
38. Ibid.
39. Ibid.
40. Ibid.
41. Ibid.
42. Ibid.
43. I have used the term "ontological" to refer to being-ness that can be objectified, or placed in a position of otherness.

44. "Metaphysical subjectivities" draws both a contrast with the "ontological" and "objectification." As a modified term, it refers to how meaning is made beyond what stands out ontologically or can be objectified. "Eulogies of the other," in this regard, point to a metaphysicality or even a subjectivity that allows a eulogy to take place for the other.
45. Georg W. F. Hegel, *Phenomenology of Spirit.* Translated by A. V. Miller (Oxford, UK: Clarendon Press, 1977), 111.
46. "Stand-out from themselves" refers to Heidegger's term "ek-sistence" in his *Letter on Humanism*, written in December 1946. It points to the manner in which being projects itself, or discloses itself, so that it can stand in the clearing of Being. See Martin Heidegger, *Letter on Humanism* (1947).
47. Jacques Lacan, *Transference: The Seminar of Jacques Lacan, Book VIII*, 136.
48. Ibid.
49. Ibid., 137.
50. Ibid.
51. Ibid., 137–138.
52. Ibid., 140.
53. Ibid.
54. Ibid.
55. Ibid., 141.
56. Ibid., 142.
57. Ibid.
58. Ibid., 143.
59. Jacques Lacan, *Anxiety: The Seminar of Jacques Lacan, Book X.* Translated by A. R. Price (Malden, MA: Polity Press, 2014), 94.
60. Jacques Lacan, *The Four Fundamental Concepts of Psycho-Analysis.* Translated by Alan Sheridan (New York, NY: W. W. Norton, 1977), 253.
61. Jacques Lacan, *Transference: The Seminar of Jacques Lacan, Book VIII*, 148.

References

Hegel, Georg W. F. 1977. *Phenomenology of Spirit.* Translated by A. V. Miller. Oxford, UK: Clarendon Press.

Heidegger, Martin. 2007. "Letter on Humanism." In *Pathmarks*, edited by William McNeill. New York, NY: Cambridge UP.

———. 1998. *Parmenides.* Translated by André Schuwer and Richard Rojcewicz. Bloomington, IN: Indiana UP.

Lacan, Jacques. 2014. *Anxiety: The Seminar of Jacques Lacan, Book X.* Translated by A. R. Price. Malden, MA: Polity Press.

———. 1977. *The Four Fundamental Concepts of Psycho-Analysis.* Translated by Alan Sheridan. New York, NY: W. W. Norton.

———. 2015. *Transference: The Seminar of Jacques Lacan, Book VIII.* Edited by Jacques-Alain Miller and Translated by Bruce Fink. Cambridge: Polity.

9

Agalma: Commentary on Session X

Ed Pluth

Lacan begins the session right where he ended the last session, with the word "agalma," which many in his audience apparently didn't quite catch. Someone in his household (his daughter Judith?) knew what it meant: an ornament or a piece of jewelry. While this is technically correct, Lacan thinks it only scratches the surface of what the Greek word is expressing. For him, it seems to be a topological concept (more on this to come), and he suggests that we should think a bit more about why one would ever want to "bejewel" oneself in the first place.

The appearance or use of this word marks a pivotal point in *The Symposium*, for it appears when Alcibiades, "the actor who changes everything" emerges.[1] Recall that the "game" of the night had been to take turns praising love. Alcibiades says: With that finished, why don't we praise the person sitting to our right? The person sitting to his right happens to be Socrates himself. Lacan notes: The topic of the symposium changes from

E. Pluth (✉)
California State University, Chico, Chico, CA, USA
e-mail: EPluth@csuchico.edu

G. Basu Thakur and J. Dickstein (eds.), *Reading Lacan's Seminar VIII*,
The Palgrave Lacan Series, https://doi.org/10.1007/978-3-030-32742-2_9

praising love to praising the other. He reminds us at this point of what Socrates's quasi-analytic interpretation of Alcibiades's praise of him will be at the end of Alcibiades's speech: Alcibiades says what he says about Socrates in order to make an impression on Agathon, who was at the time the true object of Alcibiades' desire.

The function or role of the other in the speech by Alcibiades is very different from what is found in the speech Socrates gave (with Diotima). There, Lacan notes, it was all about love as a "dyadic relation"—one proceeds "toward love" through a series of different identifications, driven by beauty, ultimately up to the Sovereign Good itself.[2] (This point will be important for his critique of "oblativity" and "genital love" later in this session.) In Alcibiades's speech, we see a more symbolic, triple relationship at work—either because of the Alcibiades/Socrates/Agathon triangle or the one involving Alcibiades/Socrates/Socrates's agalma). Again, the concept of "agalma" is key.

Lacan claims that Alcibiades is going to try to "unmask" Socrates and basically obtain from him a sign of his desire (what Lacan will discuss in a later session of the seminar as the "real presence" of desire—an erection). Recall the speech by Pausanius in which it was asked what we seek in love: The claim was that what we look for is that which is desirable. Well, we get a rather different, more graphic take on that question from Alcibiades!

As Alcibiades describes him, Socrates is a Silenus-like figure, ugly on the outside, but he contains riches. And this "topology" of Socrates (inside/outside) is crucial for understanding what the agalma is about. Lacan notes the extreme passion of Alcibiades's speech: Alcibiades doubts that anyone has any idea what is at stake in desire. But he has seen what Socrates has—the "agalmata," the little statues that are described as divine, golden, and totally beautiful, and he says that once one has seen them one can only do everything that Socrates orders!

Lacan makes a couple of notes here: No one tells us what the agalmata are exactly. They're supposed to be little statues of the gods, but this is obviously a metaphor. What is it that Socrates has, really, that causes such desire in others? And two, why do they have the effect that they do? Here Lacan reminds us of his "Che Vuoi?"—a sort of magical, imposing speech by the Other that puts us under its terrifying spell.

At this point, Lacan breaks off his commentary on Alcibiades's speech to explore the concept of agalma in more detail, looking at how it was used in other ancient Greek texts. In the play *Hecuba* by Euripides, Lacan argues that the word "agalma" cannot correctly be translated as jewelry or ornament, for it is about "the agalma" of a god's pain. What is called an "agalma" here is in fact a palm tree that was planted and grown as a testament to this. And indeed we should think of this as a phallic object, Lacan says. Very much playing the role of a Heidegger with Greek words here, Lacan is trying to point out a "hidden accent" in the word "agalma" that is missed when it translated, even "correctly" as jewelry or as statues of gods. Lacan wants to say that the term "always emphasizes the fetishistic function of the object" in question.[3] This is indeed something we would not think if we came across it as "ornament" in a translation. Then Lacan discusses fetish objects in religions and how they differ from icons or images, which are mere "copies" of the god. A fetish object, however—for example, one upon which one pours all sorts of liquids—is an object with special power.

In his exploration of the etymology of the word "agalma" Lacan highlights things such as admiration, envy, pain, seeing, and even a link to the good (agathon) which, in Plato's *Cratylus* (a dialogue dedicated to word origins) is linked to what is admirable. But despite all this, Lacan focuses our attention back to how the agalma is linked to images, and to a specific type of image described in Homer, in whose work "agalma" is used as a word for a statue that is meant to attract the eye of the goddess Athena. Lacan: "Agalma appears as a kind of god trap. There are things that attract the eyes of those real beings known as the gods."[4] Or as a "charm"—the Trojan Horse in the Iliad was considered one as well. Lacan says he could give us a thousand examples of such uses of the term "agalma."

What is at stake, what is being thought here, is, Lacan announces, the function of the partial object. This was one of psychoanalysis' great discoveries, but too quickly psychoanalysts wrapped it up or distorted it into a "dialectic" in which it was supposed to develop into a "total" object: a desire or love for the whole person. Lacan is referring here, critically, to the idea that we should understand the oral, anal, and genital "stages" as a progressive series of stops on the way to normalization. Lacan points out that even a total other, the goal of "oblativity" (giving to the other, selflessly), the ideal and normative object of desire, is maybe just a bundle of partial objects in truth. This is rather different from being a truly "total" (integrated, well-formed, distinct) object! Lacan reminds us here of his criticisms of the "genital ideal" or type. In particular, he wonders: If the genital type, the ideal of "genital love" is somehow modeled after the genital act, does this mean that in love we are trying to bring or give the other satisfaction? Do we care about the other's satisfaction, or are we (rather dubiously) trying to perfect the other?

Lacan is suspicious of the idea that it is better that our beloved be treated as a subject rather than an object. He makes a rather good joke here: If it is bad to consider the other as an object, it is even worse to consider the other to be a subject! The point is maybe a bit dense, but Lacan is saying that among objects, one can be compared to another, and could be considered as good as another… but when it comes to subjects, the problem is that other subjects are not sufficiently other for us. We presume they possess the same "combinatory" as we do, that they express themselves in "articulated language" and that the other-subject can "respond to our combinatory with its own combinations."[5] In other words, as subjects we take others to be part of our symbolic system: They speak like us, they are split by language as we are. And so, as a result, they are subject to the same conditions we are, insofar as we are split subjects.

What does this mean for love, then? What does it mean that such others are ones we love and also objects of our desire? It means that the object of desire in this case is not an object like those that can be put in a series of equivalences, in which one is as good as another, etc. "The psychoanalytic object is the something that is the aim of desire as such, the something that emphasizes one object among all the others as incommensurate with the others."[6] This is also what is called the partial object. So is Lacan saying that what is lost when we treat others as subjects in love is their potential incommensurability?

An interesting aside follows, in which Lacan rants a bit about philosophy and psychoanalysis—however, I think he would also include the "genital love" enthusiasts in psychoanalysis in the former camp. His point is that such metaphysical and moral discourses about other-directed love and behavior seem "weighty and noteworthy" because of the ambiguity of the terms they use, in contrast to mathematics and by implication the sciences (and perhaps Lacan's own version of psychoanalytic theory) which can use "signs with an unequivocal meaning because they don't have any meaning" (consider barred-S, a, i(a), A, etc. etc.).[7] The metaphysicians in philosophy and psychoanalysis get tripped up when talking about relations between subjects and objects because of ambiguities, because of a lack of precision.

But if there is a special partial object at stake in desire, and it impassions us in a particular, incommensurable way, it is because "hidden inside it is agalma, the object of desire." And it is the role of this object in desire and fantasy that Lacan will continue to focus on.

Lacan closes with a reminder of the issues he has with oblativity, as well as how objects have been conceived of generally in psychoanalysis. The function of the object is clearly important for psychoanalysts, especially in the work of Melanie Klein. She and her followers can even be seen to correctly have articulated the function of the agalma at the beginning of things, "before any dialectical development" (of desire/love into a love of a true, whole other, etc.) with their good/bad object split. But what often follows from this is a sort of theoretical temptation to develop one object in particular into a sort of sovereign Good Object, neglecting the persistent role of the agalma: an object beyond compare, something "we find in a being only when we truly love."[8] And thus, getting something fundamental about desire wrong.

Notes

1. Jacques Lacan, *Transference: The Seminar of Jacques Lacan, Book VIII*. ed. Jacques-Alain Miller and trans. Bruce Fink (Cambridge: Polity, 2015), p. 136.
2. Ibid.
3. Ibid., p. 140.
4. Ibid., p. 142.
5. Ibid., p. 145.
6. Ibid., p. 146.
7. Ibid.
8. Ibid., p. 148.

Reference

Lacan, Jacques. 2015. *Transference: The Seminar of Jacques Lacan, Book VIII*. Edited by Jacques-Alain Miller and Translated by Bruce Fink. Cambridge: Polity.

10

Between Socrates and Alcibiades: Commentary on Session XI

Zachary Tavlin

One should be excused for thinking (as many of my more mythologically attuned students do) that Alcibiades, making noise in the courtyard and rapping on the front door, is less a drunken interloper than a *Gott betrunkene Mensch*. Late in Chapter 11, Lacan speaks of "the scandalous objects that the gods of ancient mythology were," especially "when they take it into their heads to love a mortal."[1] Alcibiades, unlike nearly all of the preceding speechmakers of the *Symposium*, cares not a whit for "the Good" (and neither do the gods, especially on Plato's account against the poets). Alcibiades brings to the dinner party something of the sublime, "in any case absolute and impassioned, that verges on an entirely different character with another message…This is the distance that separates Socrates' position from Alcibiades." Alcibiades is a man imbued with desire [*l'homme du désir*].[2] He is, perhaps, the dialogue's resolute

Z. Tavlin (✉)
Department of Liberal Arts, School of the Art Institute of Chicago, Chicago, IL, USA
e-mail: ztavlin@saic.edu

G. Basu Thakur and J. Dickstein (eds.), *Reading Lacan's Seminar VIII*,
The Palgrave Lacan Series, https://doi.org/10.1007/978-3-030-32742-2_10

pervert, at least as much so as Zeus himself, one who epitomizes (as Lacan elsewhere writes) the "[pursuit of] jouissance as far as possible."[3]

The fundamental question of this chapter is the following: What is the *ágalma* Alcibiades recognizes in Socrates? Lacan marks the difference between Alcibiades' speech and all that preceded his entrance (not to mention much that would follow in the Neoplatonist tradition): "It is neither beauty, nor ascesis, nor identification with God that Alcibiades desires, but rather this unique object, this special something he saw in Socrates and which Socrates turns him away from, because Socrates knows that he does not have it."[4] In a dramatic reversal of the hierarchal ladder of Eros that characterizes proper Platonic love, Alcibiades—as Lacan writes in the previous chapter—"rips us away from the dialectic of beauty that had, up until then, served as the pathway, guide, or mode of capture along the pathway of the desirable."[5] It is what's inside the other that matters, not what presses in from the great beyond, which Alcibiades believes is precisely Socrates' confusion and even inhibition, as he always moves from the singular to the general, from the hidden gem to the big idea, from passionate attachment to reasonable affection.

Another term for *ágalma* is *objet a* (a comparison I will make provisionally, and pick up later); it is uncanny, brilliant, disturbing, charming, and ornamental all at once. Alcibiades compares Socrates to the satyr Marsyas, whose musical charms provoked the fatal jealousy of Apollo. Surely, to Socrates, Alcibiades' passion for him is just as violent, and he perhaps feels skinned alive by his encomium ("the satyr's crude and derisory outer crust or envelope" must be opened up "to see inside what Alcibiades calls, the first time, *agálmata theón*, translated as the 'statues of the gods' [215b]"[6]). The eulogy aims at Socrates' singularity, his godlike bizarreness (*atopia*). And it is precisely this singularity—"this unique object, this special something"[7]—that constructs the fetish, that provides the immensely fragile gilding on the idol. As fetishist, then, Alcibiades demands something more than he already has, for as Lacan acknowledges, he "already knows that he has captivated Socrates' desire."[8] But Socrates "knows the score" in the game of love.

Love, like all other games, has a scoreboard. If this is what Socrates *knows*, then he responds to Alcibiades' desire by playing defense: "If I really have in me the power to make you a better man, then you can see in me a beauty that is really beyond description and makes your own remarkable good looks pale in comparison. But, then, is this a fair exchange that you propose?" In other words, is giving beauty to receive truth not "gold in exchange for bronze"? [218d–e] And yet Lacan asks us not to be fooled by Socrates' question. "[P]ay attention," Lacan demands, for Socrates tells Alcibiades that he "should think twice," for "[t]he mind's sight becomes sharp only when the body's eyes go past their prime" [219a]. Alcibiades' youthful eyes see all too well, that is, they see something where there is nothing. Socrates, as wise and crafty as the gods of Antiquity, will not deign to "enter into the scale of the desirable" and thereby reveal for good the very thing he suggests to Alcibiades here, that he is empty or hollow, his essence *kenosis*.[9]

Lacan's dialectic of fullness and emptiness—read as an initial distinction between Agathon and Socrates—appears to turn on the phallus (or, more specifically, the erection) as the ultimate signifier–signified of desire. "Agathon, you are the one who is full, and just as one makes a liquid move from a full vase to an empty one using a wick along which it flows, similarly I'm going to fill myself up" [175d–e]. Experienced readers of Plato might associate the vase with Gorgias' jar, the leaky vessel of the (sexual) appetites. Lacan notes Socrates' ironical usage of the metaphor, since to fill himself up in the form of sexual arousal would be to substitute his position as *erastés* for *erómenos*, the beloved for the lover in the philosophical-pederastic relationship. To do so would mean already accepting "the idea that he himself is, in any way, an object worthy of Alcibiades' desire, or of anyone else's for that matter."[10] And when Alcibiades demands that Socrates put an end to the metaphorical discourse and either give a sign of desire or disavow it—"I really have nothing more to say" [219a]—Socrates defers, situating the previous metaphor as a continual discursive relay: "See you tomorrow. We still have a lot to say about it."

Alcibiades, of course, was hoping to smoke out something more than a temporal deferral. At this point, as the session appears to be coming to an inconclusive end, Lacan-via-Socrates characteristically latches on to an incidental remark, making of Alcibiades-Socrates-Lacan an analytic chain (certainly, in the *Symposium*, couches abound). Alcibiades says to

Agathon, "I warn you, don't let Socrates fool you! Remember my torments; be on your guard!" [222b] "How casually you let it drop," Socrates intervenes, "almost like an afterthought, at the very end of your speech!" [222c]. Agathon was, supposedly, the sideways aim of Alcibiades' speech all along. His speech's for-the-sake-of-which, to adopt a Heideggerianism, was "to enunciate that I should be in love with you and no one else, and that for his part, Agathon should let himself be loved by you and by no one else" [222c–d]. Socrates uncovers a circuit of mimetic desire. And regardless of which of Alcibiades' desires is primary (for Socrates or Agathon), this mimetic relationship allows Socrates to transfer the *ágalmata* he knows he does not possess onto Agathon (as if *he* were the one who has it). As the analytic chain grows so does the complexity of transference and counter-transference involved. Socrates' eulogy of Agathon is a performative "respon[se] to Alcibiades" demand.'[11]

Triangular desire, already articulated early in his career as the product of the subject's entrance into the symbolic order—and perhaps the theoretical product of Lacan's entrance into the order of Kojèvian philosophical analysis—is hardly limited to but is nonetheless clearly operative in the psychoanalytic situation. One might recall Lacan's claim, in Chapter 7, that the analyst need not be a Socrates, but that "[e]xplorers like Socrates, the virtuous, and saints can, no doubt, give us several indications concerning our field."[12] "[I]t is precisely because they are the ones who do the exploring that we can perhaps define, in terms of longitude and latitude, the coordinates the analyst must be able to attain simply in order to occupy the place that is his, defined as the place he must offer up as vacant to the patient's desire in order for the latter to be realized as the Other's desire."[13] Such is Lacan's *post hoc* justification to his auditors of their painstaking exploration of the *Symposium*. And such a task reveals the significance, to Lacan, of Socrates' unmovable choice to remain *erastés* and to thereby preserve the "vacant" place of desire that Alcibiades must recognize as his own.

Rhetorically, Lacan circles around this empty place in a form wholly suitable to Platonic dialogue (or, to the *Symposium*'s unique transformation of dialectic into seminar). The reason, as Bruce Fink has recently suggested, may be that Lacan "has not yet fully formulated the concept of object *a* as we see it in his subsequent work. Although the letter *a* is present in Lacan's work from early on, it refers there exclusively to the imaginary other (or other with a lowercase *o*)."[14] My earlier provisional definition of *ágalma* as *objet a* here deserves more comment, for Seminars VII and VIII mark the place in Lacan's *oeuvre* where *a* gains its consistency in the domain of the Real (as "the Thing" and *ágalma*, respectively). No wonder, then, that he returns to the site of Western thought's primal scenes—*Antigone* and the *Symposium*—to start over in this fashion. No wonder that the true formulation of the Real is marked by a return to the primal site of language's failure: Socrates.

If for Lacan *ágalma* is in fact nothing, as we have seen, it is (almost) always a determinate nothing. We see in the drama of transference the dogged influence of Hegel's master–slave dialectic, a struggle for recognition that masks the subject's concrete negativity. The negativity that can be either offered or withdrawn, revealed or concealed in the game of love, is the *nachträglich* mystery of absolute self-proximity. And *absolute* self-proximity is the center not of love but death. Another reason, then, why Lacan bypasses *agape* for Socratic hesitation and the neurotic's "not *this*": "the Socratic message, if it contains something that refers to love, certainly does not fundamentally begin from a center of love…nothing is further from his image than the radiant love which, for example, stems from Christ's message."[15] Recall, in the Gospel of John, Christ's formulation according to the King James translation, "And the glory which thou gavest me I have given them; that they may be one, even as we are one" (17:22). That is even stronger than Lacan's quotation, "Love thy neighbor as thyself," and better articulates Christ's distance from Socrates's (and the analyst's) refusal to give what it is he does not possess.

Nearing the end of the third section of the chapter, Lacan references "the little schema of the spherical mirror I drew for you in the past," the optical scenario established in his first seminar.[16] By bringing up the illusion of a bouquet in a vase established by the interplay of plane and concave mirrors, he reinforces the interrelation between *ágalma*, *objet a*, and *das Ding* as analytic concepts constituted (like the illusion) "at the end of the Socratic dialectic." The optical object does not exist as such but *as* (a stand-in for) the emptiness at the center of the Real. The image is phantasmatic, and one is here asked to recognize the "narcissistic image" of the vase wrapped around the flowers as a falling in love, as a Socratic *lure*

Lacan now esoterically associates with "the lure of the gods."[17] How to, in the end, reconcile all these commitments as a lesson of the *Symposium*?

Unfortunately, at this point Lacan announces that he will be gone for two weeks. He leaves his audience with a reading assignment, Cicero's *On the Nature of the Gods* (*De Natura Deorum*), one that I will refuse to take up here, for fear of remaining too much in the sway of the general. Instead, it is worth leaving antiquity proper to examine (in keeping with the analyst-philosopher's quickened attention to casual references) Lacan's brief mention of Jean Giraudoux's retelling of the myth of Amphitryon. Here, he marks a difference between the ancient and the contemporary: "For those who know how to hear, this myth remains the height of blasphemy, one might say, and nevertheless this was not at all how it was understood in Antiquity."[18] Giraudoux's title, *Amphitryon 38*, already marks a serial distance between the present retelling and the mythic origin, though the number is somewhat arbitrary; one could continue to infinity. If the myth is "the height of blasphemy," it has only become so in its reinterpretation. Indeed, as the subject of a lost Sophoclean tragedy, we encounter its dramatic origin as *empty*, as the vacant site of hermeneutic desire.

Like the *Symposium* itself, the play is hard to characterize generically (neither dialogue nor public oration; neither tragedy nor comedy). The basics of the myth are thus: after killing his uncle Electryon, Amphitryon flees to Thebes with the former's daughter Alcmena. She refuses to consummate her marriage until Amphitryon avenges her brothers' wartime deaths, and so he joins forces with Creon, the king of Thebes, to battle the offending Taphians under the condition that he first kills the nearly uncatchable and highly destructive Teumessian fox. After seducing the Taphian king's daughter—who out of love for him cuts her father's immortalizing hair, rendering them beatable—Amphitryon defeats the army, returns to Thebes, and marries Alcmena. She gives birth to twins, one of whom is the great child Heracles (whose real father, Zeus, impregnated Alcmena in Amphitryon's absence).

In Giraudoux's version, Lacan opines, "[d]ivine debauchery disguises itself as human virtue."[19] We can easily see what he means, for in this treatment the entire drama centers on Jupiter (Zeus) and Alcmena, *erastés* and *erómenos*, with the latter unsatisfied with her condition and desirous of, among other things, an immortal child. She claims utter faithfulness to Amphitryon but fantasizes about Jupiter, and Jupiter plays the part of a modern pickup artist, caught between asserting his divine superiority and engaging in cloying flattery (going as far as comparing Alcmena to Prometheus, bringing the metaphysical-spiritual fight to the gods through her sexual allure). Lewis Leadbeater shrewdly acknowledges the link Lacan has made but not fully explained:

> What Giraudoux is describing, of course, is that great gap that exists between the knowledge and being of the divine level and the existence of the mortal level, a gap or gulf bridged only by desire—the desire of Jupiter for the consent of Alcmena and the fantasy desire of Alcmena for the beauty of Jupiter and the immortal product he might give her. All of this is quite consonant with Giraudoux' brand of Platonism and the type of eroticism he sees inherent in the relationship between archetype and particular. That is, the eroticism of Acts I and II, based as it is on the physical desires of Alcmena and Jupiter, evolves into a more metaphysical eroticism in Act III, as friendship and mutual understanding replace the earlier emphasis on sensuality. In short, a page, it seems, has been taken from Plato's *Symposium*.[20]

Lacan and Leadbeater only disagree, it seems to me, on *which* page has been taken from the dialogue.

Socrates (via the priestess Diotima) has already located Eros between mortals and the gods, falling short of the latter because it lacks the very thing it aims at. Love requires contact between mortals and the gods, indeed *is itself* defined as a "great spirit" that brings mortals into contact with the divine (hence, in *Amphitryon 38*, the key role of Mercury). And, as Diotima continues, defining Eros as go-between gives it the status of the daemon, hence Lacan's comment about "the daemonic incarnation of [the gods'] scandalous exploits."[21] But most importantly, he claims that in *this very sense* "Alcibiades was Socrates' daemon." What could he mean by this? First consider, in the context of Giraudoux's play, how Alcmena questions Leda about the god's visitation in the form of a Swan: "Was it real down?" she asks of his feathers. "Did he sing?" "Did he overwhelm you?" "And how did he leave you?"[22] If Alcmena's *daemon* is the Eros through which divine messages pass, then is Zeus/Jupiter's *ágalma* the fantasy form through which he incarnates his phallic presence? His mythic figure is the stand-in for transferential knowledge. And so if Alcibiades is

Socrates' *daemon*, then *we* are the philosopher's true patients. The gods were not scandalous for the Greeks, but Socratic philosophy was. Socratic philosophy is not scandalous for us anymore, but psychoanalysis still is. Lacan needs it to remain so: "Don't believe that she who was placed at the beginning of this dialogue, Aphrodite, is a goddess who smiles."[23]

Notes

1. Jacques Lacan, *Transference: Seminar Book VIII* (1961), trans. B. Fink (Cambridge, UK: Polity Press, 2017), p. 161.
2. Lacan (2015, p. 157).
3. Jacques Lacan, 'The Subversion of the Subject and the Dialectic of Desire' (1960), in *Écrits: The First Complete Edition in English* (2006), trans. B. Fink (New York and London: W. W. Norton, 2006), p. 700.
4. Lacan (2015, p. 159).
5. Ibid., p. 138.
6. Ibid., p. 151; for the purposes of consistency, I follow Lacan exactly in all quotes from Plato.
7. Lacan (2015, p. 159).
8. Ibid., p. 153.
9. Ibid., p. 161.
10. Ibid., p. 155.
11. Ibid., p. 159.
12. Ibid., p. 104.
13. Ibid., pp. 104–105.
14. Bruce Fink, *Lacan on Love: An Exploration of Lacan's Seminar VIII, Transference* (Cambridge, UK: Polity Press, 2016), p. 194.
15. Lacan (2015, p. 155).
16. Ibid., p. 159.
17. Ibid., pp. 159, 160.
18. Ibid., p. 161.
19. Ibid.
20. Lewis W. Leadbeater, 'Classical Themes in Giraudoux' *Amphitryon 38*,' *Rocky Mountain Review of Language and Literature* 32.4 (1978), p. 228.
21. Lacan (2015, p. 162).
22. Jean Giraudoux, *Amphitryon 38* (1929), trans. S.N. Behrman (New York: Random House, 1938), pp. 121–122.
23. Lacan (2015, p. 163).

References

Fink, Bruce. 2016. *Lacan on Love: An Exploration of Lacan's Seminar VIII, Transference.* Cambridge, UK: Polity Press.

Giraudoux, Jean. 1938. *Amphitryon 38* (1929). Trans. S.N. Behrman. New York: Random House.

Lacan, Jacques. 2006. The Subversion of the Subject and the Dialectic of Desire. In *Écrits: The First Complete Edition in English* (2006), translated by Bruce Fink. New York: W. W. Norton.

———. 2015. *Transference: The Seminar of Jacques Lacan, Book VIII.* Edited by Jacques-Alain Miller and Translated by Bruce Fink. Cambridge: Polity.

Leadbeater, Lewis W. 1978. Classical Themes in Giraudoux' *Amphitryon 38. Rocky Mountain Review of Language and Literature* 32.4: 222–233.

11

Socrates as an Analyst: A Reading of "Transference in the Present" Commentary on Session XII

Frederic C. Baitinger

The Enigma of Plato's *Symposium*

In the first part of *Seminar VIII*, "A commentary on Plato's *Symposium*," Lacan argued that Plato's last word on love was not revealed, as it is often suggested, in the different philosophical discourses that compose the dialogue, not even in the one of Socrates, but in the enigma that poses the final scene of the text.[1] To support his reading, Lacan proposed approaching the meaning of this enigma by structuring it around the position of two desires: the desire of the analysand Alcibiades and the desire of the analyst Socrates.[2] On the side of the desire of the analysand, Lacan focused on the comparison that Alcibiades made between Socrates and a *sileni* (Plato, 215a–215e), in order to build from it his concept of the object *agalma*, which defines the idealized loved object.[3] On the side of the desire of the analyst, Lacan isolated Socrates' final interpretation of Alcibiades' speech,

F. C. Baitinger (✉)
Department of Romance Languages at Hunter College, The City University of New York, New York, NY, USA

G. Basu Thakur and J. Dickstein (eds.), *Reading Lacan's Seminar VIII*,
The Palgrave Lacan Series, https://doi.org/10.1007/978-3-030-32742-2_11

and used it to connect it to his understanding of the position of the analyst as he had theorized it in his Graph of Desire under the question "Che Voi?" (what do you want?).

In the chapter "Transference in the Present," which is the first chapter of the second part of the seminar, Lacan's ambition is to connect his previous reading of the final scene of the *Symposium* to the problem of transference, and thus to the way in which love is supposed to be manipulated by the analyst during a psychoanalytic session. To do so, Lacan proceeds in three steps. First, he proposes a short summary of his Graph, while emphasizing in it the function that love plays in relation to desire. Second, he connects his reflections on love and desire to the question of transference, offering a critique of the way in which the notion of transference was understood by the psychoanalytic institution, and substitutes for it a definition of transference as a paradoxical, but nonetheless necessary source of fiction. Third, Lacan returns to the final scene of the *Symposium* and shows how his definition of love and desire, as well as his definition of transference permits us to understand anew the meaning of Alcibiades' confession, and by the same token the meaning and the function that love and desire play in psychoanalysis.

The Terrible Commandment of the God of Love

To introduce his reflection on love and desire, Lacan starts by giving a brief account of his Graph of Desire.[4] The Graph, as Lacan summarizes it in this lesson, represents "the splitting, or fundamental doubling of two signifying chains by which the subject is constituted" (169). To make this splitting understandable, as well as to underline why this splitting underpins the very notion of the subject in Lacan's Graph, it is essential to emphasize from the start that the Graph puts in contact two very different levels of analysis. On the one hand, the Graph represents, through its horizontal lines, the subject of speech,[5] which is constituted by a chain of signifiers through which the subject expresses its demands in relation to an Other.[6] On the other hand, the Graph represents, through its vertical line, the subject of the drives, which is in relation to a primordial object (the maternal breast) that the very presence of the subject of speech posits as being forever lost.[7] And finally, the Graph, in its totality, has to be conceived as the representation of the divided subject of the unconscious, which is the reunion of the subject of speech and the subject of the drives. In turn, this divided subject, as the heir of the subject of speech, is grounded on a Symbolic lack (which stands for the missing signifier that could express perfectly the demand of the subject), and as the heir of the subject of the drives, on a fundamental fantasy (which covers, at an Imaginary level, the Symbolic lack). Desire, in regard to the lack, has to be conceived as a metonymical process that puts at the place of the lack "the possibility of the infinite sliding of signifiers owing to the continuity of the signifying chain" (169). Love, on the contrary, represents the possibility of encountering an object that stands as the perfect metaphor of one's lack, which is to say as what can concretely incarnate one's own fundamental fantasy.[8]

But if desire stands on the side of an infinite sliding, and love represents what puts an end to this sliding, "the whole problem," as Lacan has it, "is to perceive the relationship that links the Other to which the demand for love is addressed, to the appearance of desire" (170). While the experience of love always implies the presence of an Other to whom we address our demand for love, the structure of desire implies, on the contrary, the reduction of this Other to the status of an object that Lacan calls *a*, and that is not connected to the Other of speech but, rather, to the fundamental fantasy of the subject.[9] As such, love and desire, far from being equivalent, can, in fact, be opposed to one another. As Freud had already pointed out in "On the Universal Tendency to Debasement in the Sphere of Love," it is often because a subject loves that it cannot desire and, reciprocally, because it desires that it cannot love.[10] Likewise, for Lacan, if one wants to reconcile love and desire, one needs to resolve "what one might call the terrible commandment of the god of love. The commandment is to make of the object it designates something that, first of all, is an object, and, second, an object before which we falter, vacillate, and disappear as subjects" (170). It is, to put it differently, because we love that we are not only the ever-changing subjects of a metonymical desire. But it is also because we are in love that we are constantly threatened to disappear as subject in front of the Other to whom we address our most fundamental demand.

Transference as an Ambiguous Source of Fiction

Just like the experience of love, the experience of transference can either be described as something "positive" and necessary to the analytic treatment, or as something "negative" like an obstacle.[11] Herman Nunberg, for example, in "Transference and Reality"[12] distinguishes, within the phenomenon of transference, a negative aspect that he relates to the repetition compulsion, as well as to the drives and their demands for a static equilibrium; and a positive aspect, which he connects to what can potentially change in the fixity of the drives, through the relation to the analyst.[13] However, for Lacan, such a distinction does not grasp what actually happens when transference becomes a positive phenomenon. If transference, as a spontaneous process, involves, as Nunberg suggests, the most essential presence of the past, it is also, stresses Lacan, a phenomenon that is permeable "to the action of speech" (173). This is why transference, just like the terrible commandment of the god of love, raises an apparent paradox. "Transference is interpreted on the basis of and using the instrument of transference itself. It is thus impossible for the analyst not to analyze, interpret, and intervene in the transference from the position bestowed upon him by transference" (173). Transference is, at the same time, what needs to be modified and the tool through which it can be modified.[14] Just like the experience of love, transference can either trigger a "passivation of the subject" (174), through the return of an emotion or a trauma, or what can potentially be, through the development of an analysand's speech, a source of liberation.

To locate more precisely the origin of this creative dimension of transference, Lacan underlines its fictional character, before raising the question of who is being addressed when one fabricates under transference a fiction. Lacan asks, "What is the nature of this fiction? And second, what is its object(ive)? And if fiction is involved, what is being feigned? And since it is a matter of feigning, feigning for whom?" (175). Of course, in an analysis, the analysand is not addressing the person of the analyst as such, nor the person that the analysand potentially projects onto the person of the analyst. This is why, to go beyond the uncertainty that floats around the person for whom a fiction is fabricated during an analysis, Lacan suggests that this "person" is actually reducible to the one of the Other, which is to say to the coordinates of the signifying chain that structure the speech of a given analysand.[15] Each time an analysand constructs a fiction, he does so in the name of the Other. But this Other—and this is the crux of the matter—can either be an Other that dominates and subjugates the subject, or an Other who can help the subject to construct a fiction through which the first Other can progressively be known and manipulated. To illustrate this idea about the double nature of the Other, and its link to the fictional aspect of transference, Lacan uses Alcibiades confession at the end of Plato's *Symposium* to wonder to whom, and for whom Alcibiades is constructing his fiction.

Unveiling the Most Shocking Secret of Desire

Alcibiades's confession, very much like the speech of an analysand, is improvised. It is thus a speech that obeys, one could say, the principle of free association. However, contrary to the speech of an analysand, Alcibiades' confession is also a speech that is not neutral since it is a speech that is obviously addressed to Socrates. Finally, it is a speech that is also addressed, as Plato carefully notes, to those who will have to "deliver the verdict on Socrates' arrogant behavior" (Plato, 219c). It is thus a confession that is, at the same time, addressed to Alcibiades former philosophical master, but also a confession addressed to the Other of the Greek aristocratic society, which is to say the Other that has shaped Alcibiades fundamental fantasy. As such, Lacan suggests that Alcibiades' speech has a didactic value because it "gives the greatest possible weight to what might be called the Other as a tribunal" (176). When Alcibiades, for example, tells the story of how he tried to make of Socrates his lover, he does not emphasize Socrates's beauty of soul but, on the contrary, how Socrates humiliated his physical beauty when he said, "What you are trying to acquire is true beauty in return for apparent beauty, in fact you intend to 'get gold in exchange for bronze'" (219a). In other words, if Alcibiades makes a public confession, it is first because he is vexed.[16] And if he is vexed, it is not because Socrates, as his philosophical master, rejected him, but because "He [Alcibiades] wanted to see Socrates' desire manifest itself in a sign, in order to know that the other—the object, *agalma*—was at his mercy" (176).[17] When Socrates rejected Alcibiades as his love object, he did not reject Alcibiades as a lover, but as his philosophical disciple.[18] However, Alcibiades did not take it that way but accused Socrates, on the contrary, of having betrayed the code that was governing the Other of the Greek aristocratic society—and thus the desire that Socrates hoped to change in Alcibiades, but that was still, in fact, governing Alcibiades fundamental fantasy.

Thus what becomes apparent in Alcibiades speech is not so much Socrates' arrogant behavior than, as Lacan has it, the most shocking mainspring of desire, when desire is not correctly articulated to love. "The most shocking secret is unveiled before everyone; the ultimate mainspring of desire, which in love relations must always be more or less dissimulated, is revealed — its aim is the fall of the Other, A, into the other, a" (176). And it is precisely this fall that Socrates refuses, and that his interpretation of Alcibiades' speech highlights as what secretly keeps orienting his speech—namely the desire to inspire in Socrates' new lover, the young and handsome Agathon, a feeling of jealousy.[19] But if Socrates' interpretation is correct, it raises an ultimate paradox about Socrates' desire. If Socrates is capable, indeed, of designating to Alcibiades where his desire lies, he seems also eager to play, as Agathon's lover, the same desire's game. This is at least what Socrates seems to imply when he declares to Alcibiades, "Be nice, dear friend, and don't grudge my praising the young man [Agathon]. I have a strong desire to deliver a eulogy of him" (Plato, 223a). And it is also what Alcibiades confirms when he notes, "When Socrates is around it is impossible for anyone else to get a look in at attractive young men. And what abundant eloquence he found to make this one here take the place beside him" (Plato, 223a). Of course, Socrates never eulogized Agathon, and we as readers will never know what Socrates would have said about Agathon, and thus what he would have revealed, through his eulogy, about his own desire. As Lacan puts it, "we will never know what Socrates knew about what he was doing" (178). Even Plato, who "knew a bit more about what Socrates knew" (178), did not know it, since a Platonic interpretation of Socrates' desire is not, as Lacan underlines it, where the text of the *Symposium* necessarily leads its reader, especially when the reader is also a psychoanalyst.

Socrates as an Analyst

Socrates' desires, if one reads the *Symposium* as an analyst, are "to lead his interlocutor to Γνῶθι σεαυτόν (*gnothi seauton*) [know thyself], which is translated in an extreme manner, in another register, by "concern yourself with your soul" (178).[20] Of course, the extreme manner to which Lacan is referring here is the translation that Christianity, via Plato's reinterpretation of Socrates's maxim, gave to Socrates theory about love.[21] Isolating in Socrates' discourses what announces in it the figure of Christ—i.e., Socrates' denunciation of public fame, of desire for honor, of more importantly Socrates' idea according to which eros for the soul is more valuable than eros for the body (184a1)—this extreme translation made of Socrates "one of those to whom we owe to have a soul," (178) which is to say one of those to whom we owe to know what it means to be self-conscious about one's body needs, not to say to be self-critical about one's own sins. Deviating from such extreme interpretation, Lacan suggests, for his part, that it is possible to see in Socrates someone who knows how to locate desire and to become its accomplice, but also someone who does not know what desire is as such. And if one accepts seeing Socrates like this, then one can start to see Socrates as being, in relation to Alcibiades desire, in the position of the analyst.

If Socrates is capable of setting Alcibiades' desire ablaze, it is because, through his interpretations of Alcibiades speech, he is capable of redirecting Alcibiades to his true desire. For if the essence of desire is the desire of the Other, then the desire of the lover is nothing but the desire of the beloved, and the desire of the beloved is nothing but the desire of the lover, and desire on both sides is nothing but the mainspring that keeps engendering love. Commenting on this fragile dialectic in an almost poetical manner, Lacan says, "if love is what occurs in the object towards which we extend our hand owing to our own desire, and which, when our desire makes it burst into flames, allows a response to appear for a moment: the other hand that reaches towards us as its desire" (179). In the particular case of the relationship between Socrates and Alcibiades, Alcibiades failed to love Socrates inasmuch as he failed, once enflamed by the desire of Socrates, to respond to Socrates' desire with his own true desire. As Socrates puts it, Alcibiades remains a terrifying person because he is trapped in his "mad obsession with being loved," and thus trapped in his refusal to love in return the one who desires him.[22] This is why Socrates's merit, if one sees him as a Lacanian analyst, is to "designate [Alcibiades' love] as transference love, and to redirect him to his true desire" (179), which is neither the desire for the Good, nor the desire of the Other, but the desire to know better toward which desire his own true desire is directed.

Notes

1. See, for philosophical interpretations of the *Symposium*, Peckham (2015), Nussbaum (1969), and Sheffield (2006). And for Lacan's interpretation of the *Symposium* as an enigma, "Concerning the theme of love as it is presented to us in *The Symposium*, to which I have limited my attention here, it is difficult for us as analysts not to recognize the bridge that is standing there and the hand that is extended towards us in the articulation of the last scene in *The Symposium*— namely the scene that unfolds between Alcibiades and Socrates" (168).
2. Lacan writes, "(…) the final articulation of the *Symposium*—this apologue or scenario verging on myth—allows us to structure the situation of the analysand in the presence of the analyst around the position of two desires" (179).
3. For a detailed analysis of the notion of *agalma*, see Jacques Lacan, "Agalma," in *Seminar VIII, Transference*, Text established by Jacques-Alain Miller, Trans. Bruce Fink (Polity, Malden, 2015), pp. 135–148. Lacan writes, "*agalma*, from agallo," "to adorn, to ornament," signifies in effect—at first sight – "ornament, adornment." First of all the notion of ornament, of adornment is not that simple; it can be seen immediately that this may take us very far. (…) You should not see in it any taste for rarity but rather the fact that in a text which we supposed to be extremely rigorous, that of the *Symposium*, something leads us to this crucial point which is formally indicated at the moment at which I told you the stage revolves completely and, after these games of praising regulated as they had been up to then by this subject of love, there enters this actor, Alcibiades, who is going to change everything."
4. On the Graph of Desire, see, Jacques Lacan, *The Seminar Book V, Formation of the Unconscious*, J.-A. Miller (9th ed.), trans. R. Grigg (Malden:

Polity Press, 2017). See, also, Jacques Lacan, "The Subversion of the Subject and the Dialectic of Desire in the Freudian Unconscious," in *Écrits*, 2007. Finally, for a very good reading of the whole Graph of Desire, see Philippe Van Haute, *Against Adaptation: Lacan's Subversion of the Subject* (The Lacanian Clinical Field, The Other Press, 2001).

5. For a full analysis of the notion, see, Jacques Lacan, "The Function and Field of Speech and Language in Psychoanalysis," in *Écrits*, 2007; see also, Jacques Lacan, "The Instance of the Letter in the Unconscious, or Reason since Freud," in *Écrits*, 2007.
6. The Other with a capital O designates for Lacan "the locus that is always evoked as soon as there is speech." As such, the Other is not reducible to the (Imaginary) others to whom we address our speech (like the mother for the infant), neither to an absolute Other that would stand in an external position in regard to the subject that speaks (like God). On the contrary, the Other stands in a tertiary position in between the subject that speaks and the other with whom it is speaking with, and is thus constantly questioned as to what can validates it. This is why Lacan famously said that "there is no Other of the Other," which is another way to say that the Other is a perpetually vanishing Other, and that this vanishing Other is also what puts desire as the desire of the Other in a perpetually vanishing position too. Lacan says, "this Other, as I teach you to articulate it here, that is both necessitated and necessary as a locus, but at the same time constantly questioned as to what guarantees it, is a perpetually vanishing Other which, due to this very fact, places us in a perpetually vanishing position" (170).
7. See Jacques Lacan, *Le Séminaire Livre IV, La Relation d'objet*, J.-A. Miller (ed.) (Paris: Edition du Seuil, 1998).
8. Lacan says, "An object can thus assume, in relation to the subject, the essential value that constitutes the fundamental fantasy. The subject himself realizes that he is arrested therein, or, to remind you of a more familiar notion, fixated. We call the object that serves this privileged function, a" (170).
9. This object of desire that Lacan calls *a* will become, in his *Seminar X on Anxiety*, what Lacan will call *object a*—which is to say the object that causes desire, and not the object of desire (which is precisely the object agalma, and not the *object a.*). See Jacques Lacan, *The Seminar Book X, Anxiety*, J.-A. Miller (ed.), trans. R. Grigg (Malden: Polity, 2017). For an excellent

reading of this Seminar, see, Jacques-Alain Miller, 'Introduction to Reading Jacques Lacan's Seminar on Anxiety.' Trans. B. P. Fulks, *Lacanian Ink 26* (Fall 2005), pp. 6–67.

10. Sigmund Freud. *Sexuality and the Psychology of Love.* Trans. Philip Rieff (New York: Simon & Schuster, 1997).
11. See Sigmund Freud. 'Dora: An Analysis of a Case of Hysteria' (1905). The Standard Edition of the Complete Psychological Works of Sigmund Freud, Vol. VII, trans. J. Strachey, 24 vols. (London: Hogarth Press, 1953), pp. 3–124. In this text, Freud defines transference as the obstacle owing to which he failed to cure Dora from her hysteria. Lacan, taking up Freud's definition of transference in his paper 'Presentation on Transference,' suggested that such negative transference could become the point of departure of a series of dialectical reversals, if only the analyst was capable of providing to the analysand the correct interpretation. See Jacques Lacan, 'Presentation on Transference,' in *Écrits*, 2007, pp. 176–188.
12. Harman Nunberg, "Transference and Reality." *International Journal of Psycho-Analysis*, 32 (1), 1951.
13. Nunberg writes, "Repetition compulsion tries to fixate, to 'freeze', the old psychic reality, hence it becomes a regressive force; transference attempts to re-animate these 'frozen' psychic formations, to discharge their energy and to satisfy them in a new and present reality, and thus becomes a progressive force" (5).
14. This vicious circle is not Lacan's discovery. Ernst Jones, in "The Action of Suggestion in Psychotherapy," had already pointed to the difficulty. See Ernest Jones, "The Action of Suggestion in Psychotherapy," *The Journal of Abnormal Psychology*, 5(5), 217–254.
15. Lacan says, "Everything that we know of the unconscious right from the outset, on the basis of dreams, leads us to the conclusion that there are psychical phenomena which occur, develop, and are constructed in order to be heard [*entendus*, which also means "understood"] — which occur, develop, and are constructed for the Other who is there even if one does not know it" (175). This notion of the Other will be at the origin of the famous notion of the *subject supposed to know*, as well as the algorithm of transference developed by Lacan in 'Proposition du 9 octobre 1967 sur la psychanalyse de l'Ecole' (1967) in *Autres Écrits* (Paris: Edition du Seuil, 2001), pp. 243–260.
16. See Plato, 216b, "What I have felt in the presence of this one man is what no one would think I had it in me to feel in front of anyone, and this is shame."

17. See Plato 219c "Again, Socrates, you cannot deny that I am telling the truth. Yet, despite all that, he completely defeated me, and despised and mocked and insulted my beauty – and in *that* respect I really thought I was something, gentlemen of the jury (I call you that because it is you who will deliver the verdict on Socrates' arrogant behavior)."
18. Commenting on this idea in "defending Socrates as Educator," Sheffield (2006) writes, "In a dialogue concerned with the correct form eros should take, the inclusion of Alcibiades must be of particular significance. These associations are recalled when Alcibiades enters as the embodiment of drunken and lewd behavior: he threatens violence (213d2), rejects Eryxemachus' plea for justice (214c), and shows an overbearing attachment to Socrates (213d1–5). Alcibiades was also famed for his overbearing desire for honor. This character trait is recalled in the dialogue when Alcibiades explains that it is his desire for for honor from the crowd which draws him away from the path of philosophy (216b5)" (201–202).
19. "Though you were pretending otherwise, the reason for your entire speech was to make Agathon and me quarrel, because you think I ought to love you and only you, and Agathon ought to be loved by you and by no one else" (Plato, 222d).
20. See Plato (216a) "My soul wasn't in turmoil, and I wasn't disturbed by the thought that I was a slave to my way of living. But after listening to this Marsyas here I was often reduced to thinking that being as I was, my kind of life was not worth living. (…) For he [Socrates] compels me to admit that even with all my deficiencies I nevertheless take no care for myself, but instead I involve myself in the concerns of the Athenians."
21. For a very interesting interpretation of this movement from *eros* to *agape*, see Anders Nygrens, *Agape and Eros: The History of the Christian Idea of Love.* Trans. P. S. Watson (Harper Torchbook, 1969).
22. Commenting on the dialectic of love that Alcibiades fails to acknowledge, Anderson writes, in *The Masks of Dionysos*, "What Alcibiades has failed to recognize is the love as fundamentally dialectical. Thus Alcibiades fails – not because Socrates is (as claimed by Aristoxenos) a dedicated (and avid!) heterosexual; nor (as Rosen would have it) because he is 'abstinent or defective erotically,' nor more broadly (as argued by Nussbaum) because he has no interest in, or even contemns sex. Socrates is not stone, and Alcibiades does not fail because of its particularity. Alcibiades fails because of his own duplicity, his own unworthiness. He fails because he is offering philosophy as an inducement for sex, he is offering that which is the essence of humanity for that which humans share with other animals."

(124). See Stanley Rosen, *Plato's Symposium* (New Haven: Yale University Press, 1968), and see also Martha Nussbaum, *The Fragility of Goodness* (Cambridge: Cambridge University Press, 1969).

References

Anderson, Daniel E. 1993. *The Masks of Dionysos: A Commentary on Plato's Symposium*. Albany: State University of New York Press.

Cobb, S. 1993. William. *Plato's Erotic Dialogues*. Albany: State University of New York Press.

Freud, Sigmund. 1953. 'Dora: An Analysis of a Case of Hysteria' (1905). In *The Standard Edition of the Complete Psychological Works of Sigmund Freud, Vol. VII*, trans. J. Strachey. London: Hogarth Press, 3–124.

———. 1997. *Sexuality and the Psychology of Love*. Trans. Philip Rieff. New York: Simon & Schuster Press.

Lacan, Jacques. 2001. 'Proposition du 9 octobre 1967 sur la psychanalyse de l'Ecole.' *Autres Écrits*. Paris: Edition du Seuil, 243–260.

———. 2006. *Écrits: The First Complete Edition in English*. Translated by Bruce Fink. New York: Norton.

———. 2013. *Le Séminaire livre VI, Le désir et son interprétation (1958–1959)*. Edited by Jacques-Alain Miller. Paris: Edition du Seuil.

———. 2014. *The Seminar of Jacques Lacan Book X, Anxiety (1962–1963)*. Edited by Jacques-Alain Miller and Translated by A. Price. Malden: Polity Press.

———. 2015. *Transference: The Seminar of Jacques Lacan, Book VIII*. Edited by Jacques-Alain Miller and Translated by Bruce Fink. Cambridge: Polity.

Miller, Jacques-Alain. 2005. 'Introduction to Reading Jacques Lacan's Seminar on Anxiety.' Trans. B. P. Fulks, *Lacanian Ink 26* (Fall 2005), 6–67.

———. 2017. 'The Real Unconscious.' Trans. Frederic Baitinger and Azeen Khan. *Lacanian Ink 50* (Fall 2017), 22–41.

———. *L'Orientation Lacanienne, Le Banquet des analystes* (1989–1990). Unpublished. Unedited. http://jonathanleroy.be/2016/02/orientation-lacanienne-jacques-alain-miller/. Acceded December 15, 2018.

Nunberg, Harman. 1951. 'Transference and Reality.' *International Journal of Psycho-Analysis 32* (1), 1–9.

Nussbaum, Martha. 1969. *The Fragility of Goodness.* Cambridge: Cambridge University Press.
Nygrens, Anders. 1969. *Agape and Eros: The History of the Christian Idea of Love.* Trans. P. S. Watson. Harper Torchbooks Press.
Peckham, John C. 2015. *The Concept of Divine Love in the Context of the God-World Relationship.* New York: Peter Lang Publishing Inc.
Plato. 2008. *The Symposium.* Ed. M. C. Howatson and F. C. C. Sheffield and Trans. M. C. Howatson. New York: Cambridge University Press.
Rosen, Stanley. 1968. *Plato's Symposium.* New Haven: Yale University Press.
Sheffield, Frisbee C. C. 2006. *Plato's Symposium: The Ethics of Desire.* New York: Oxford Classical Monographs Press.
Van Haute, Phillipe. 2001. *Against Adaptation: Lacan's Subversion of the Subject.* The Lacanian Clinical Field, The Other Press.

12

"A Critique of Countertransference": Commentary on Session XIII

Miguel Rivera

Banging One's Head on the Walls

Jacques Lacan initiates his interrogation of the structure of countertransference using one of his greatest dictums, "one has no need for the blueprints of an apartment to bang one's head on the walls."[1] This dictum's timelessness is evinced by Joan Copjec's use of the turn-of-phrase at the outset of her chapter "The Unvermogender Other: Hysteria and Democracy in America" in *Read My Desire*[2] (1994). But in this case, Lacan insists what is most dangerous is not simply the ease with which one might bang his head on a home's wall without a blueprint, but rather the inability to formulate a blueprint moving through the home in the darkness. Still, one might believe he has created an adequate blueprint even though all he has done is bang his head against a wall. Lacan writes, "it is not enough to bang one's head on the walls to reconstruct the blueprints of an apartment, especially if one has this experience in the dark."[3] Thus, Lacan sets out

M. Rivera (✉)
Tufts University, Medford, MA, USA
e-mail: Miguel.Rivera@tufts.edu

G. Basu Thakur and J. Dickstein (eds.), *Reading Lacan's Seminar VIII*,
The Palgrave Lacan Series, https://doi.org/10.1007/978-3-030-32742-2_12

to find a blueprint for countertransference and the "communication of unconsciouses"[4] with the benefit of the light, or at least disabuse other analysts of their belief in a blueprint generated from bumbling forward in darkness. Lacan concludes that the lack of a schema to account for these psychic processes does not foreclose successful analytic work. He does concede, however, "This is perhaps a bit forced as a metaphor, though perhaps not as forced as it may still seem to you. It is what we are going to see put to the test, the test of what occurs in our times when analysts speak of transference."[5]

The danger is not in doing analysis without a "blueprint," but rather to proceed *believing* one has such a schema despite the lack of precisely that. An awareness of what is taken for granted in the phrase countertransference is firmly established by Lacan. He uses the word "faith," to describe this taken-for-grantedness. He writes of training analysts, "were one to neglect some corner of the analyst's unconscious, veritable blind spots would result therefrom … Yet one cannot but relate this view to another, which is that one must, in the end, have faith in the communication of unconsciouses to best provide the analyst with decisive insights."[6] This "communication of unconsciouses" is essential, in Lacan's view, for analytic work. Such an encounter is not foreclosed by the foreboding term of countertransference. In fact, it may be the case that countertransference is rendered inconsequential to analysis in the face of an essential facet of analytic work: the analyst's desire.

The Analyst's Desire: *Agalma*'s Orientation

Lacan has advocated the necessity of the analyst's desire throughout the body of his work. Bruce Fink gives a clear account of the analyst's desire in *A Clinical Introduction to Lacanian Psychoanalysis: Theory and Technique* (1997):

> In working with neurotics, the therapist must *always* express a desire for patients to continue, even if he or she feels that these patients have completed their work … Lacan's expression "the analyst's desire" refers not to the analyst's countertransferential feelings but rather to a kind of "purified

> desire" that is specific to the analyst ... It is an enigmatic desire that does not tell the patient what the analyst wants him or her to say or do.[7]

Lacan establishes this principle when accounting for a "purified desire" that should be "stronger than the other desires that may be involved — for example, the desire to get down to it with his patient: to take him in his arms or throw him out the window."[8] These "other desires" are the product of countertransferential feelings. But Lacan disputes the necessity of eliminating those "other desires" and problematizes the "Stoic ideal"[9] of the analyst. Lacan writes, "If the analyst deviates from the path of Stoic apathy, does this in and of itself mean that it is owing to some inadequacy in his training as an analyst? Absolutely not."[10]

Lacan, instead, returns to his notion of the *agalma* borrowed from Plato's *Symposium* and discusses the connection between *Philebus* and Freud's death drive. The *agalma* is synonymous with *objet petit a*, the object-cause of desire.[11] According to Lacan:

> In Plato's *Philebus*, Socrates says that the strongest of all desires must be the desire for death ... This argument is worth whatever it is worth, but it takes on an illustrative value here in relation to what I have already indicated to you concerning the direction in which the reorganization or restructuring of the analyst's desire can be conceptualized.[11]

If the death drive is restructured by "good personal analysis,"[13] the analyst's desire must be restructured according to that same logic. Lacan ventriloquizes Freud's claim that repetition compulsion can be redirected through analysis. Lacan writes, "[Freud] posits that it is conceivable that the fundamental repetition of the development of life may be nothing other than the long detour of a compact, abyssal drive."[14] Thus, it is not the issue of the *agalma* itself or of desire, but rather the location of the *agalma* and toward what desire is directed. Understanding the position of the *agalma* and the trajectory of desire, likely through the analyst undergoing analysis, makes the analyst's desire possible.

Just like in the case of a countertransferential relationship, the location of the *agalma* is problematic for Plato as well.[15] Lacan explores this idea throughout Chapters 11 and 12, leading up to Chapter 13. He writes,

"Alcibiades think[s] that inside Socrates lies a treasure, an indefinable, precious object which will fix his resolve after having unleashed his desire."[16] Lacan goes on, "A structure is revealed here, in which we can find anew what we are able to articulate as fundamental in what I will call the position of desire."[17] The notion of the *agalma* dramatizes the love relation between Alcibiades and Socrates. Alcibiades finds himself frustrated at Socrates's ostensible disinterest, indexed by his unwillingness to engage sexually with Alcibiades. Alcibiades says, "having slept with Socrates, it was nothing more than if I'd slept with a father or an elder brother."[18] But Alcibiades fundamentally misunderstands the nature of love and how one might return it. R. E. Allen writes, "Alcibiades portrays himself as a lover scorned by Socrates. But Socrates is in fact the true lover, who loves what is really beautiful and good, the proper object of love, instead of what only seems so."[19] Allen goes on, "[Alcibiades] has identified the object of love with someone who lacks that object, identified wisdom with the philosopher who loves wisdom and does not possess it."[20] Allen unintentionally evokes Lacan's dictum, "Love is giving what you do not have to someone who does not want it." What Alcibiades locates in Socrates, but what Socrates ultimately lacks, is the *agalma*, translated as "images" by Allen and "statues" by Christopher Gill and Alexander Nehamas.[21] Lacan writes, "Even if [*agalma*] seems to have to do with statues of the gods, look closely and you will see that it always has to do with something else … this term always emphasizes the fetishistic function of the object."[22] Alcibiades says in his final praise of Socrates:

> [Socrates] talks about packasses and smiths and cobblers and tanners, and forever appears to be saying the same things in the same ways, so that an inexperienced and unreasonable man might ridicule his arguments. But if the arguments are opened, and one sees them from the inside, he will find first that they are the only arguments with any sense in them, and next, that they contain within themselves utterly divine and multitudinous images of virtue.[23]

While Alcibiades might praise Socrates's virtue, it is something *more* that makes Alcibiades feel "enslaved" by Socrates. It is that something that must be seen from the inside, that thing revealed by opening up, the *agalma*.

Socrates comes to demonstrate a prototypical version of the analyst's desire as he lets Alcibiades continue speaking, his lack of interruption a tacit encouragement. What distinguishes Socrates and Alcibiades, and what makes Socrates the "true lover" in Allen's view, is the differing weight of the desires the two are subject to. Socrates embodies the analyst operating according to the proper desire whereas Alcibiades represents the analyst trapped in a countertransferential relation. Lacan corroborates this point, suggesting that Socrates is an exemplar of the analyst as subject supposed to know,[24] "It is neither beauty, nor ascesis, nor identification with God that Alcibiades desires, but rather this unique object, this special something he saw in Socrates and which Socrates turns him away from, because Socrates knows that he does not have it."[25]

The Reserve Unconscious

The question of countertransference, in the context of the clinic, is one of analytic training and of analysis itself. Lacan and most psychoanalytic thinkers suggest that analysts should be undergoing analysis themselves. Analytic training for the analyst helps develop the analyst's desire and resolves the issues that emerge when the analyst assumes herself to actually possess what the analysand imagines her to: knowledge. For the analysand, the analyst is cast in the role of subject supposed to know and possessor of the *objet a.* Lacan writes, "no one ever undergoes an exhaustive elucidation of the unconscious, regardless of how far his analysis is taken."[26] For the analyst who has taken her analysis quite far, then, Lacan theorizes a "reserve unconscious" that facilitates the "communication between unconsciouses." This reserve unconscious is one of a particular kind, "It is certainly not a raw unconscious we find in him, but rather a supple unconscious, an unconscious plus experience of that unconscious."[27] Lacan takes this position in opposition to both the prevailing opinion of psychoanalysts in support of the "Stoic ideal" and the view more permissive of countertransferential feelings derived from Melanie Klein and her adherents.

Lacan explicitly identifies Paula Heimann's "On Counter-transference" (1950) and Roger Money-Kyrle's "Normal Counter-transference and

Some Deviations" (1956) as examples of misunderstanding the orientation of *agalma* and its function in relation to countertransference. Unlike the analysts who advocate the stoic ideal that Lacan opposes earlier in the chapter, the Kleinian circle and Heimann in particular argue for the use of countertransferential feelings as an analytic tool. Heimann writes in "On Counter-transference," "My thesis is that the analyst's emotional response to his patient within the analytic situation represents one of the most important tools for his work. The analyst's counter-transference is an instrument of research into the patient's unconscious."[28] Lacan does not entirely disagree, but argues that the analyst's desire needs to outweigh the countertransferential urges. Money-Kyrle's misunderstanding is founded in his investment in understanding the projection of the "bad object." Lacan writes, paraphrasing Money-Kyrle, "It is only when the analyst does not understand the patient that he is affected and that a deviation from normal countertransference occurs."[29] For Money-Kyrle, as long as the analyst *understands* that the analysand is projecting the "bad object" onto the analyst, the analyst will not suffer the effects of irregular or excessive countertransference. Lacan ultimately disputes this point, however. He writes, "I am of the opinion that it is not possible to understand [Money-Kyrle's approach] outside of the register of what I have pointed to as the place of *a*, the partial object, *agalma*, in desire."[30] Lacan goes on to dispute the category of countertransference as a whole. He writes:

> [W]hat is presented to us here as countertransference, whether normal or not, in fact has no reason to be specially qualified as such. What is at work is but an irreducible effect of the transference situation itself.
>
> By the sole fact of transference, the analyst is situated in the position of he who contains *agalma*.[31]

Thus, it is not countertransferential (or transferential) feelings but this "supple unconscious" fostered through analysis that provides analytic insights. Rather than follow the whims of countertransferential feelings as Heimann claims, it is the analyst's desire that must outweigh countertransferential feelings. Heimann does suggest something similar in "On Counter-transference." She writes, "Our basic assumption is that the analyst's unconscious understand that of his patient. This rapport on the deep level comes to the surface in the form of feelings which the analyst notices in response to his patient, in his 'counter-transference'."[32] It is this second qualification of Heimann's that Lacan rejects, however. The "communication between unconsciouses" comes not from countertransferential feelings, but rather by way of the analyst's desire. The analyst's desire is what emerges through the analyst's developing her unconscious through her own analysis.

(Counter)Transference in Social and Political Life

It is not countertransference in and of itself that is dangerous, but rather a belief that what transferential feelings suggest about the analyst and the analysand is actually true. The analyst assumes the position of the subject supposed to know,[33] but should be aware that she does not, in fact, have anything to tell the analysand about himself. Lacan anticipates his formulation of the subject supposed to know, writing:

> His occupying the correct position is not contingent on the criterion that he understand or not understand [the mechanism of countertransference] … his lack of comprehension can be preferable to an overly great confidence in his understanding. In other words, he must always call into question what he understands and remind himself that what he is trying to attain is precisely what in theory he does not understand.[34]

This danger is mirrored in the manifestation of transference and countertransference in social life. Molly Anne Rothenberg gives an account of how transference functions in political groupings:

> In psychoanalytic theory, groups are composed of individuals who identify with the group's aim in their own ways and for their own reasons. Similarly, any group as a whole might identify with another group's political agenda in its own way and for its own reasons. In theoretical terms, we are speaking of the modes of transference: any given individual identifies by way of an internalized unary trait idiosyncratic to *itself*.[35]

For Rothenberg, transference governs the logic of group identification as a whole. While Lacan, in this chapter, is discussing countertransference as a clinical phenomenon rather than transference as a social phenomenon, the rearticulation of countertransference against the preexisting conception articulated by Heimann and Money-Kyrle suggests that Rothenberg's notion of transference is spot-on. There must be a desire that exceeds the transferential identification in order to function both in analysis and politics. Political agency may well have the prerequisite of a sort of "analyst's desire," polished through analysis and intervened on by the "supple unconscious" fostered through analysis.

Avoiding the Issue

In Lacan's 1964 seminar, *The Four Fundamental Concepts of Psychoanalysis*, Lacan continues to repudiate the notion of countertransference altogether. He writes:

> The transference is a phenomenon in which subject and psycho-analyst are both included. To divide it in terms of transference and countertransference—however bold, however confident what is said on this theme may be—is never more than a way of avoiding the essence of the matter.[36]

One might read Lacan's suggestion of avoidance as a clinical observation. For analysts to avoid their own implication in transference is precisely the blind spot Lacan suggests as he makes an account of "the stoic ideal" and the analyst's desire. For it is not countertransference, or transference, that is the issue for the analyst but rather the absence of a desire that outweighs transferential desire. However, Lacan points to the way in which analysts imagine that desire can be completely tamed through repeated analysis or that countertransferential feelings should be the primary source of analytic insights. While, as Lacan says at the outset, banging one's head against the wall with no blueprint is certainly not a desirable situation—an incorrect blueprint is a dire issue indeed.

Notes

1. Jacques Lacan, *Transference Seminar Book VIII* (1960–1961), trans. Bruce Fink (Cambridge, UK: Polity Press, 2015), p. 180.
2. Copjec writes in *Read My Desire*, 'You don't have to know the plan of a building in order to bang your head against its walls; as a matter of fact, it is precisely through your ignorance that you *guarantee* such accidents' (London, UK: Verso), p. 141.
3. Lacan (2015, p. 180).
4. Ibid., p. 181.
5. Ibid., p. 180–181.
6. Ibid., p. 181.
7. Bruce Fink, *A Clinical Introduction to Lacanian Psychoanalysis: Theory and Technique* (Cambridge: Harvard University Press, 1997), pp. 5–6.
8. Lacan (2015, p. 185).
9. Lacan writes, 'The path of Stoic apathy demands that we remain unmoved by the attempts at seduction — as well as by the punishments that may be meted out — by this other with a lowercase *o* found outside of us' (2015, pp. 183–184).
10. Ibid., p. 184.
11. Lacan writes, 'This object, *agalma*, little *a*, the object of desire' (2015, p. 147).
12. Ibid., p. 186.
13. Ibid.
14. Ibid.
15. C. D. C. Reeve writes, 'In Plato, an *agalma* (from the verb *agallein*, meaning to glorify or honor something) is a figurative statue in honor of a god or, more often, a figurative statue of any sort—the puppets which cast their shadow on the walls of the cave in *Republic* VII are *agalmata.*' 'A Study in Violets: Alcibiades in the *Symposium*' in *Plato's Symposium: Issues in Interpretation and Reception*, ed. James Lesher, Debra Nails, and Frisbee Sheffield (Cambridge: Harvard University Press, 2006), p. 125.
16. Lacan (2015, p. 152).
17. Ibid., p. 169.
18. Plato, *The Symposium*, trans. R.E. Allen (New Haven: Yale University Press, 1991), p. 165.
19. Ibid., p. 104.
20. Ibid., p. 107.

21. Lacan writes, 'It is clear that *agalma* cannot be translated in any way, shape, or form by 'ornament' or 'jewelry' here, or even, as we often see in published texts, by "statue"' (2015, p. 140). Lacan also addresses issues with translation on page 151.
22. Ibid., p. 140.
23. Plato (1991, p. 168).
24. Lacan writes in *The Four Fundamental Concepts of Psychoanalysis. Seminar Book XI* (1973), 'As soon as the subject who is supposed to know exists somewhere ... there is transference.' Trans. Alan Sheridan (New York: Norton, 1998), p. 232.
25. Lacan (2015, p. 159).
26. Ibid., p. 182.
27. Ibid.
28. Paula Heimann 'On Counter-transference.' *The International Journal of Psycho-Analysis* 31 (1950), p. 81; pp. 81–84.
29. Lacan (2015, p. 191).
30. Ibid., p. 192.
31. Ibid., p. 193.
32. Heimann (1950, p. 82).
33. Lacan comes to the idea of the subject supposed to know in 1964, in *Seminar XI: The Four Fundamental Concepts of Psychoanalysis*, three years after the conclusion of *Seminar VIII: Transference.*
34. Lacan (2015, p. 193).
35. Molly Anne Rothenberg, *The Excessive Subject: A New Theory of Social Change* (Cambridge, UK: Polity Press, 2010), p. 141.
36. Lacan (1998, p. 231). See also Dylan Evans, *An Introductory Dictionary of Lacanian Psychoanalysis* (London: Routledge, 1996), p. 30.

References

Copjec, Joan. 1994. *Read My Desire.* London, UK: Verso.

Evans, Dylan. 1996. *An Introductory Dictionary of Lacanian Psychoanalysis.* London, UK: Routledge.

Fink, Bruce. 1997. *A Clinical Introduction to Lacanian Psychoanalysis: Theory and Technique.* Cambridge: Harvard University Press.

Heimann, Paula. 1950. On Counter-Transference. *The International Journal of Psycho-Analysis* 31: 81–84.

Lacan, Jacques. 1998. *The Seminar of Jacques Lacan, Book XI: The Four Fundamental Concepts of Psychoanalysis* (1964). Translated by A. Sheridan. New York: W. W. Norton.

———. 2015. *Transference: The Seminar of Jacques Lacan, Book VIII.* Edited by Jacques-Alain Miller and Translated by Bruce Fink. Cambridge: Polity.

Plato. 1991. *The Symposium: The Dialogues of Plato Volume 2.* Trans. R. E. Allen. New Haven: Yale University Press.

Reeve, C.D.C. 2006. A Study in Violets: Alcibiades in the *Symposium.* In *Plato's Symposium: Issues in Interpretation and Reception*, ed. J. Lesher, D. Nails, and F. Sheffield. Cambridge: Harvard University Press.

Rothenberg, Molly Anne. 2010. *The Excessive Subject: A New Theory of Social Change.* Cambridge, UK: Polity Press.

13

In the Name of Desire: A Reading of Lacan's "Demand and Desire in the Oral and Anal Stage"—Commentary on Session XIV

Frederic C. Baitinger

A Critique of Ego-Psychology

Lacan's implicit goal in Chapter 14 "Demand and Desire in the Oral and Anal Stages" is to critique the Anglo-Saxon community of psychoanalysts for having reduced Freud's definition of psychoanalysis to the goal of re-adapting the "deviant" subject to the rules and norms of the society.[1] More specifically, Lacan's critique is aiming at deconstructing the conception of transference developed after the Second World War by ego-psychologists such as Heinz Hartmann, Anna Freud, and Ernest Kriss, who argued that psychoanalysis' primary task was not, as Freud thought, to reveal repressed primitive impulses, but to repair the ego structure already there. Hartmann posited within the sphere of the ego, which is normally the place where the sexual demands of the Id and those of the superego meet and battle, a "conflict-free" ego zone with which the analyst, just like a good parent, could form an alliance. Likewise, Anna Freud, in

F. C. Baitinger (✉)
Department of Romance Languages at Hunter College, The City University of New York, New York, NY, USA

G. Basu Thakur and J. Dickstein (eds.), *Reading Lacan's Seminar VIII*,
The Palgrave Lacan Series, https://doi.org/10.1007/978-3-030-32742-2_13

The Ego and the Mechanisms of Defense (1936), made of the ego the cornerstone of the child's psychic ability to adjust itself to reality. She argued that the ego was the only psychic faculty that had the ability to use and channel the unconscious conflicts constitutive of the human psyche—i.e., the conflicts between sexual drives (Id), aggressive drives (super-ego), and moral ideals (ego). She proposed to isolate, within the ego defenses, the ones that were socially valuable, and those that only represented an impediment for the person, or a direct threat for society. By doing so, she emphasized the reality-based ego (the part of the ego working in agreement with the reality principle) and downplayed the ego's involvement in the constitution of the fantasy (the part of the ego working in agreement with the pleasure principle).

Opposing this normative vision of psychoanalysis, Lacan suggests in Chapter 14 that as long as an analyst knows what the structure of desire is (in relation to love and satisfaction), he does not need necessarily to understand the demand of his analysand. On the contrary, an analyst should never understand too quickly his analysand and respond like a "good parent" to his demand. For if he was to do so he would become incapable of turning his analysand, who is at first like Alcibiades in the position of an *eromenos*, which is to say in the position of an object of desire demanding parental love from Socrates, into an *erastes*, which means into an analysand in possession of its own desire. It is around this reversal that Lacan situates the question of the desire of the analyst and more broadly the question of his responsibility in regard to his analysand. And it is this responsibility that Lacan starts to locate in regard to his broader conception of desire in "Demand and Desire in the Oral and Anal Stage."

Desire as the Beyond and the Shy of Demand

What Lacan questions first is the definition and the function that ego-psychologists give to the notion of understanding. "It is," writes Lacan, "around the term 'understanding' [compréhension] that what I intend to show you today revolves, in order to hone in on what one might call, in our terms, the relation between the subject's demand and his desire" (239). Of course, Lacan agrees with ego-psychologists when they argue that to understand correctly an analysand's demand, an analyst needs to know how to respond adequately to it. However, to believe that an analysand's demand, and especially the one of a neurotic, coincides with what he truly needs would be also quite foolish. It would amount, in fact, to not taking into account that when a neurotic expresses in speech its needs, there is always a part of them that is "situated both in a beyond [au-delà] and a shy [en-deçà] of demand" (198). To understand this remark, one needs to remember that Lacan in his Seminar V, *Formations of the Unconscious,* showed how in any form of demand, i.e., in what "in need gets conveyed by means of signifiers addressed to the Other" (77), there is always a beyond that takes the form of a demand for love, which is to say a demand for recognition and approval addressed not only to an imaginary other, but to the symbolic Other (i.e., the locus of the code where the demand gets registered).[2] Reciprocally, what Lacan calls in this chapter the "shy of demand" needs to be understood in relation to what he defines, in his Seminar VI, *Desire and Its Interpretation*, as being the place of desire, i.e. the unavowable parts of the needs that cannot be expressed inasmuch as to express them would put in jeopardy one's self-image, and by implication one's relation to the Other. This is why, for Lacan, if an analyst does not want to reinforce what is repressing his analysand's desire but, on the contrary, help him to reconnect with his unconscious desire, such analyst should not adopt a parental position toward him. If he was to do so, his analysand would necessarily fall "into the very same position in relation to the analyst as the one he occupied during his whole upbringing in relation to people around whom were constructed the fundamental situation that constitute for him the signifying chain and repetition automatism" (198).

Freud, underscores Lacan, was actually of that opinion too when he pointed, in the third chapter of *Beyond the Pleasure Principle*, that the ultimate goal of the analytic treatment was not the reinforcement of the analysand's ego defense mechanisms, as ego-psychologists claim, but the opposite, which is to say remembering the repressed. Of course, to achieve such goal, Freud was also well aware that an analysand had to be able to "re-experience a certain portion of his past life" (SE XVIII 18–19), while remaining at a critical distance from such experience in order to be able to become conscious of it. Freud, it is well known, used the term *Überlegenheit* (which means superiority or dominance) in *Beyond the Pleasure Principle* to name the ability to gain such critical distance and argued that the only quality that was needed on the side of the analysand, as well as on the side of the analyst, was a capacity to be "cognizant at every turn that what appears to be reality is in truth the refracted image of a forgotten past" (SE XVIII 18–19). Unfortunately, the term *Überlegenheit*, as well as the way in which Freud used it, was somehow mistranslated in French and English, and thus largely misinterpreted by ego-psychologists. While the French translation situated the kind of superiority (in regard to the past) implied by the notion of *Überlegenheit* on the side of the analyst, the English translation situated it on the side of the analysand, in the so-called healthy part of the ego, as Heinz Hartmann had it. As a consequence, none of them, according to Lacan, remained faithful to Freud's true intention. Worst, even, they betrayed him, and with him, the potentially subversive goal of psychoanalysis. This is why Lacan, for his part, initiated his "Return to Freud," and claimed that to understand properly what the term *Überlegenheit* means in Freud's work, one needs to understand first how this notion is connected to the different kind of demands that a subject expresses in relation to the different stages of development of its libido.[3] For it is only with this condition that one will be able to understand how a subject can remain superior to the demand that the Other has made on him during his childhood, and thus capable of becoming a subject of desire, and not only the object of the desire of the Other.

Oral Demand and the Killing of Desire

The most primitive demand that a subject learns to express in relation to the Other is the one that Freud associates with the oral demand.[4] The oral demand is a demand to be fed. This demand, inasmuch as it is articulated in speech and addressed to an Other, is also a demand that calls for "an inverted response from the Other" (200). In other words, to the demand to be fed corresponds the demand to let oneself be fed. As such, underscores Lacan, what is added to the primitive oral demand is the desire to be fed in a certain way by the Other. This is why, concludes Lacan, as soon as the need to be fed is articulated in speech and addressed to the Other, one can no longer conceive the feeding relationship between a child and its mother as the meeting up of two natural tendencies, but one has to acknowledge, also, that this meeting up relies on a fragile encounter between two desires that are sometimes not well adjusted to one another. It is not rare in the clinic, for example, to see conflicts breaking out in the nursing relationship between a child and its mother, to the point of giving birth to cases of mental anorexia. Commenting on the structure of this conflict between demand and desire, Lacan suggests that it can be broken down in four parts, "[1] a desire goes beyond [déborde] this demand; [2] the demand cannot be satisfied without the desire being extinguished; [3] it is so that the desire which goes beyond demand not be extinguished that the subject who is hungry does not let himself be fed (…) and refuse in some sense to disappear qua desire by being satisfied qua demand; [4] the extinction or crushing of demand through satisfaction cannot happen without killing desire" (201).

Desire needs to be killed in order for the demand to be satisfied. Such is the vexing contradiction that lies at the core of every nursing conflict between a mother and a child, and more broadly between the subject and the Other. To explain this vexing contradiction, Freud argued in *Contribution to the Theory of Sex* that it is because the other also stands as the partial object of the oral drive that a conflict between the demand to be fed and a sexual desire for the breast can emerge in the subject.[5] Put differently, it is inasmuch as the other to whom the baby addresses its demand is also what the baby desires as such [*tu es le désir*] that the Other is not only conceived as the one who can satisfy the demand of the subject but also as the one who can potentially kill the desire it represents [*tué le désir*]. This is why, concludes Lacan, the libido should not be conceived in the manner of "surplus energy manifested in a living being once its needs related to self-preservation have been satisfied" (202),[6] as Franz Alexander does, but as a "surplus that renders vain any satisfaction of need wherever libido is situated" (202). In the case of anorexia, for example, the subject can even go as far as refusing the satisfaction of need to preserve the function of desire. This is why, for Lacan, the proper analytic attitude in front of such conflict is not, as most ego-psychologists would argue, to turn a "compensated frustration into the end-all of analytic intervention" (202) but, on the contrary, to help the patient assert his desire against the omnipotent power of the Other's desire.

The Myth of Oblativity and the Gaping Maw of Life

The stakes of such reversal become all the more visible if one takes the example of what happens to the demand of the subject during the anal stage.[7] Within the anal stage, indeed, what comes at the forefront is no longer "the simple relationship of a need to its demanded form, linked to surplus sexuality [excédent sexuel]" (203) but it is "a matter of disciplining need, and sexualization is produced only in a movement of return to need" (203). During the anal stage, the child's need, so to speak, becomes a gift addressed to the mother, and the mother's desire the law of the child's need. In turn, it is because the child's need becomes submitted to the law of the mother's desire that its needs are sexualized, are at least, as Lacan has it, introduced in a kind of sexual relationship in which the child becomes the phallus of the mother at the expense of its own desire. This is why, for Lacan, the sexualization of the need that happens during the anal stage should not be taken, as Freud and ego-psychologists do, as the prefiguration of any form of genital love but, on the contrary, as the foundation of obsessive neurosis, which itself supports the very "myth of oblativity" in which the polymorphous perversity of sexuality is supposed to find its normal resolution. Lacan writes, "the true field of oblativity is the field of the anal dialectic" (203). But if the anal dialectic is the true field of oblativity, then one is also entitled to conclude, as Lacan aptly does, that "the room that remains for the subject—in other words desire—is symbolized in the situation by what is flushed away in the process. Desire literally goes down the tubes" (204).

Moreover, the anal stage is not only what gives rise to "the myth of oblativity" (203), but it is also the stage to which is associated, in an inverted way, the notion of anal-sadism.[8] Indeed, it is only in the anal stage, underscores Lacan, that the Other becomes truly dominant, and that the subject becomes truly submitted to the Other's desire. In this regard, the sadism at stake in the anal stage is not the same as the one at play in the oral stage. While, in the oral-sadistic stage, the sadistic element rises from life itself in the form of a cannibalistic fantasy of a gaping maw ready to devour its object, in the anal stage, sadism comes from the oblative subject itself who imagines that the other is being the victim of the gaping maw of life itself.[9] Commenting on this sado-masochist structure, Lacan says, "Suspending the imaginary other over chasm [gouffre] of suffering forms the apex and axis of sadomasochism eroticization" (205). In other words, it is because the other is imagined as being the victim of the Other itself that this imaginary other [here the mother] becomes a sexual partner for the subject, and that the desire of this other can take over the desire of the subject itself. In Chapter 24 of his *Seminar VI* entitled "The Dialectic of Desire in the neurotics," Lacan said, "The relation of the desire of the subject to the desire of the Other is dramatic inasmuch as the desire of the subject has to situate itself in front of the desire of the Other, while this Other literally sucks him in, and leaves him without recourse" (my translation 502). Consequently, if one does not want to see the analysand's desire being flushed down the tubes by the analytic institution, one needs to recognize that the notion of oblativity is nothing but a *myth* in which the gap between the desire of the subject and the Other's demand is falsely bridged by giving to the Other's demand the upper hand.[10] "As long as you have not located at this point the basic, fundamental relationship of the subject as desire with the most disagreeable object, I assure you that you will not have made great strides in the analysis of the condition of desire" (204).

In Praise of Desire

This is why, concludes Lacan, if an analyst does not want to leave its analysand without recourse in front of the Other's desire, this analyst should not understand too quickly his analysand demand. Otherwise, this analyst will not restore in his analysand the place of desire but, by responding to its demand in the form of a counter demand, he would simply reinforce his analysand's identification to the little excremental *a*, and thus reinforce the very obliteration of his desire. Put differently, if the analyst was to respond to the frustrated demand of his analysand with a "nourishing signifier," he would do nothing else than to give consistency to the very symptom that he was supposed to cure. As such, Lacan even argues that such analyst, far from helping his analysand moving beyond the demand of the Other, would, in fact, perform a "therapeutical abuse" that would be of the same kind as "the locus in which everything the outside world can add by way of a supplement to the construction of the super-ego" (207). This is why, in order to avoid such normative outcome, Lacan suggests that what is more important than understanding the analysand's demand is to understand what is going beyond this demand, which is to say the counter demand that has shaped its super-ego in the first place. Taking thus the exact opposite position defended by ego-psychologist, Lacan affirms that "the space occupied by not understanding is the space occupied by desire" (208).

Notes

1. After the death of Freud, in 1939, a controversy arose among Freud's followers that ended with a division of the *British Psychoanalytic Society* in three different groups: the "A" group, supporters of Melanie Klein, which gave birth, in England and the United States, to a branch of psychoanalysis called "Object Relation Analysis" (Fairbairn and Winnicott); the "B" group, supporters of Anna Freud, which lead to the creation of "Ego Psychology Analysis" (Heinz Hartmann, Ernst Kris, and Rudolph Loewenstein), a group that eventually took control of the I.P.A and imposed on the rest of the analytic community—especially the American one—its own vision of psychoanalysis; and the "C" group, composed of all the people who did not want to pick a side, which will give birth to either "Interpersonal Psychoanalysis" (Horney, Fromm, Thompson, and Sullivan), or to the "Psychologies of Identity and Self" (Erikson, Kohut). This divide between three psychoanalytic groups is of crucial importance to understand the many complex alliances that will be formed after the Second World War between feminism and psychoanalysis, and more importantly, to understand the reason why Jacques Lacan, in France, claimed, as early as the 1940s, that Freud's discovery was in danger of being lost, or that it was, at the least, being severely betrayed by Anna Freud and her group of followers.
2. Commenting on this mechanism in Chapter Five "A Bit-of-sense and the Step-of-sense" of his *Seminar V Formations of the Unconscious*, Lacan writes: "For, in actual fact, there you have it all—demand is in itself so relative to the Other that the Other is immediately in the position of accusing and rejecting the subject, whereas by invoking need he authenticates, assumes

and ratifies it, he assumes it and is already beginning to recognize it, which in itself is an essential form of satisfaction" (78).

3. The word drive, in Freud's theory, designates any form of biological or psychological need that has the power of driving the behavior of an individual. Freud isolated four different kind of drives: the oral, the anal, the phallic, and the genital drives. More importantly, Freud argued that each of these *drives* needed to be separated in four elements: the *source* of excitation, the *pressure* that it imposes on the organism, the *object* to which the excitation gets attached, and the *aim*, i.e., the way in which the satisfaction is obtained. In the case of the oral drive, for example, the drive arises from the cavity of the mouth (the source), creates the need for sucking activities (the aim), and gets attached to particular external objects, such as the mother's breast (the object). For a full explanation of the notion, see Sigmund Freud, *Standard Edition, XIV, Papers on Metapsychology*, trans. James Strachey, Standard Ed. London: Hogarth Press, 1957.
4. The oral stage is the first stage of the libidinal development. This stage is linked to the activity of nutrition, as well as to the excitation of the oral cavity that accompanies feeding. This is why Freud has argued, in *Three Essays on the Theory of Sexuality*, that the love relationship to the mother is marked during this stage by a polarity between *eating* and *being eaten*. Likewise, Karl Abraham proposed to subdivide this stage in two opposite types of activities, one that is related to the process of eating and to which is attached the activity of sucking (early oral stage), and one that is related to the fear of being eaten and to which is attached the activity of biting (oral-sadistic stage). For more details, see Sigmund Freud, *Standard Edition, VII*, trans. James Strachey. London: Hogarth Press, 2001, 179 and 198. See also Karl Abraham, "A Short Study of the Development of the Libido, Viewed in the Light of Mental Disorders," in *Selected Papers*. London: Hogarth Press, 1927, 442–453.
5. Lacan said, "Oral demand has another meaning beyond that of the satisfaction of hunger. It is a sexual demand. It is cannibalism at its root, as Freud tells us right from the *Three Essays on the Theory of Sexuality*, and cannibalism has a sexual meaning" (201).
6. Franz Gabriel Alexander was born in Budapest in 1891. His father, Bernhard Alexander, was a philosopher and literary critic, and his nephew, Alfréd Rényi, was a Hungarian mathematician who made contributions in combinatorics, graph theory, number theory but mostly in probability theory. Alexander studied in Berlin where he was part of an influential group of German analysts mentored by Karl Abraham, and which

included Karen Horney and Helene Deutsch, and gathered around the Berlin Psychoanalytic Institute.

7. The anal stage designates Freud's second stage of libidinal development. It is supposed to occur between the ages of two and four. In his *Three Essays…*, Freud describes this stage as the first one in the pregenital organizations in which there is a polarity between activity and passivity. Activity coincides with sadism, and passivity with anal eroticism. For more details on this stages, see, Sigmund Freud, *Three Essays on the Theory of Sexuality*, trans, Strachey. New York: Verso, 2017.
8. The notion of anal-sadism is linked to the active part of the anal stage, which is to say to the sadistic instinct of expulsion, which itself is related to the destruction of the object.
9. Lacan, commenting on this movement through the example of the little Hans's relationship to his mother's desire writes, in his *Seminar VI*, "At this moment, she [the mother] appears to him as the person that could respond to all its demands, but she appears to him with a supplementary mystery to be herself opened to a lack about which the meaning appears to Hans to be in a certain relationship to the phallus—the phallus that he is not. It is at the level of the lack-in-being of the mother that opens up for Hans the drama that he can only resolve by conjuring it up through a phobic signifier about which I showed you the polyvalent function" (my translation, 503).
10. Lacan had already introduced this idea in his Seminar VII, when he said: "The most archaic aspirations of the child are… a nucleus that is never completely resolved under some primacy of genitality." See, Jacques Lacan, *The Seminar Book VII, The Ethics of Psychoanalysis, 1959–60,* Trans. Dennis Porter. London: Routledge, 93.

References

Abraham, Karl. 1927. "A Short Study of the Development of the Libido, Viewed in the Light of Mental Disorders." In *Selected Papers*. London: Hogarth Press, 442–453.

Freud, Anna. 1936. *The Ego and the Mechanisms of Defense*. Standard Ed., Vol. 1. London: Hogarth.

———. 1971. "Problem of Termination in Child Analysis." *Problem of Psychoanalytic Technique and Therapy*, Vol. 7. London: Hogarth.

Freud, Sigmund. 1955. "A Child Is Being Beaten." Standard Ed., Vol. 17 (1917–1919). Trans. by James Strachey. London, Hogarth Press, 175–204.

———. 1957. *Standard Edition, XIV, Papers on Metapsychology*. Standard Ed. Trans. James Strachey. London: Hogarth Press.

———. 1961. *Beyond the Pleasure Principle*. Trans. James Strachey. New York: Norton.

———. 2017. *Three Essays on the Theory of Sexuality*. The 1905 Ed. Trans. Herman Westerink and Haute P. Van. Brooklyn: Verso.

Hartmann, Heinz. 1939. *Ego Psychology and the Problem of Adaptation*. New York: International University Press.

Lacan, Jacques. 2013. *Le Séminaire de Jacques Lacan Livre VI, Le désir et son interpretation*. Edited by Jacques-Alain Miller. Paris: La martinière Edition.

———. 2015. *Transference: The Seminar of Jacques Lacan, Book VIII*. Edited by Jacques-Alain Miller and Translated by Bruce Fink. Cambridge: Polity.

———. 2017. *The Seminar of Jacques Lacan Book V, Formations of the Unconscious*. Edited by Jacques-Alain Miller and Translated by Russell Grigg. Malden: Polity Press.

14

"Oral, Anal, and Genital": Commentary on Session XV

Jonathan Dickstein

One would be remiss to suggest that the core theme of psychoanalysis, at least as Sigmund Freud founded it, is anything but sexuality. There are nonetheless ways of orienting oneself toward this theme to generate different understandings of its features. One such feature is the theory of the so-called developmental phases of psychosexual organization (titled "Entwicklungsphasen der sexuellen Organisation"). Jacques Lacan's lecture XV from his eighth series of seminars *Transference* focuses on this feature of Freudian doctrine in order to raise questions about one orientation toward it. Lacan calls this orientation the "naturalist view" (SVIII, p. 209). He makes it clear that in raising questions about this orientation that his aim is not to reject this orientation outright, but to ask readers to consider its functions more carefully. Following Lacan, my goal is to review what these functions entail in an attempt to present an account of their modern, technical implications.

J. Dickstein (✉)
Fort Lauderdale, FL, USA

G. Basu Thakur and J. Dickstein (eds.), *Reading Lacan's Seminar VIII*,
The Palgrave Lacan Series, https://doi.org/10.1007/978-3-030-32742-2_14

Freud's theory of the developmental phases of psychosexual organization is one of his most well-known teachings in and beyond psychoanalytic communities. Nonetheless, value is to be found in a recapitulation of this theory's common interpretation. This interpretation, typical in most introductory psychology courses, consists of a chronological presentation of its five main components: the oral, anal, phallic, latent, and genital. Each component is characterized by some operation that has a standard and non-standard trajectory. For example, according to Freud, the oral phase is related to the psychic notion of identification, the anal to the activity and passivity of personality types. Frustrations during these operations, he also suggests, could lead to fixations which once under the sway of the "normal sexual life of the adult" might come to be designated as "perverse" (Freud, *Three Essays*, p. 29).

There are three primary factors Lacan claims bear on the way one understands these component phases and the possible frustrations of them. These factors are conceptually denoted by need, demand, and desire. The naturalist is essentially the one who emphasizes the primacy of need over and against demand and desire. The need to eat, for example, might be said to be what lends value to oral erotogeneity insofar as the object of this need (typically, in psychoanalytic literature, the "nipple") is withheld and in being withheld is negotiated by the deployment of sexual energy or libido. This tale regarding the transformation of need into libido sets up what Lacan calls the "fantasy of natural perversion" (211/355) or the belief that what in later life is assumed to be an over-deployment of sexual energy in conjunction with one or more of the phases indicates some physical limitation in the subject. The term most often used to describe this limitation is animalism.

Lacan, however, is careful to insist from his earliest seminars that everything must be taken from the vantage point of the symbolic, that is, from the social architecture that governs how we think and act (language). As he puts it in his first seminar, *Freud's Papers on Technique*, "I insist on the notion of the symbolic by telling you that it is always advisable to start with that notion in order to understand what we are doing when we intervene in analysis, and especially when we intervene in a positive fashion, namely through interpretation" (Lacan, *Seminar I*, p. 107). This insistence echoes Freud, who in his *Three Essays On Sexuality* already emphasized that "[t]he assumption of the pregenital organizations of the sexual life is based on the analysis of the neuroses and hardly deserves any consideration without a knowledge of the same" (Freud, *Three Essays*, p. 56). In other words, the theory of the developmental phases of the sexual organization is not to be understood as a pure scientific account of a world in which neuroses might come to emerge but rather as the speculative supposition that unfolds as a result of observations regarding these neuroses. Psychoanalysis, especially the form championed by Lacan, takes the symptom as given, not as some effect under which lies the cause.

The shift here results in a reconsideration of the phases in terms not of the way need gives rise to libido but instead of the way demand links up to desire. In Seminar VIII, Lacan invokes one of his famous metaphors of a female praying mantis to illustrate this point. The impact of this metaphor stems from the fact that oral erotogeneity seems to be involved given that the female praying mantis consumes the head of the male praying mantis after intercourse. The phrase I have used—seems to be involved—is crucial. It amounts to our tendency to subjectivize the animal world. What this process of subjectivizing entails, for Lacan, is the attribution to this world the experience of "sexual jouissance" or enjoyment (Lacan, *SVIII*, p. 211).

Whether or not this enjoyment is actually experienced by the praying mantis though is beside the point. More significant is how this attribution of the possibility of enjoyment functions. In the case of the praying mantis, Lacan explains: "If we speak of the jouissance of the praying mantis as an other, … it is because she either gets off where the male organ is, or she gets off elsewhere as well. But wherever she gets off … the fact that she may get off elsewhere only takes on meaning on the basis of the fact that she gets off (or does not get off …) there" (p. 212). In other words, enjoyment is grasped through the framework of choice or decision. As Lacan concludes, "[t]he Other is thus not merely hunger, but articulated hunger—hunger that demands. And the subject is thereby open to becoming an object, but the object of a hunger that he chooses" (p. 215).

To generalize, in the oral stage, the movement is not from a simple need to eat (i.e., hunger) to a pleasure in being fed (satiation). Rather the movement is from a demand to be fed or, as Lacan puts it, the "cry of hunger" to a desire to be fed by something in particular, the nipple (p. 209).

Demand is already caught up in a symbolic (a relation between the subject and its other), which through the process of the given developmental phase (in this case, the oral phase) is refined by an object to function as desire. Lacan states: "there is a place for desire in the margins of demand" (SVIII, p. 209). This is to say that there is a logical relationship between demand and desire that must be presupposed insofar as we take ourselves as being beings who have wants that can be represented through speech. To be more precise, we are already beings who speak. Desire thus can only be thought in terms of this speech. In psychoanalytic terms, it can only be understood "Nachtraglich," "retroactively," or "after the fact" (210).

This final consideration has significant technical consequences, particularly on the field known today as natural language processing. Around the same time Lacan gave his eighth series of seminars, a major development in this field was already underway. This development was the program known as Eliza. Created in 1966 by Joseph Weizenbaum at MIT's then newly established Computer Science and Artificial Intelligence Laboratory, Eliza was a project interestingly named after George Bernard Shaw's famous speech-inept protagonist from *Pygmalion*. The project at the highest level, as Weizenbaum put it, was intended to make "conversation between man [also, we should add, woman] and computer possible" (Weizenbaum, "Eliza," p. 36).

Perhaps the most well-known script (i.e., program script) from within the project consists of a series of language-based directives that were intended to approximate the methods of reflective listening, which had been made popular around the same time by the psychoanalytically inspired psychologist Carl Rogers. The influence of this script on modern technology cannot be overestimated. It represents a paradigmatic case of a program that challenges the assumptions of the famous "imitation game" Alan Turing proposed in his 1950 paper "Computing Machinery and Intelligence" to answer the question: "[c]an machines think?" (Turing, p. 433). Furthermore, as one of the first chatbots, this script prefigures many of the name-brand digital communication interfaces, like Apple's Siri, Amazon's Alexa, Microsoft's Cortana, and Google's generically named assistant. The popular computer science writer Douglas Hofstadter even coined the phrase "Eliza Effect" to refer to the way similar software can fool humans into believing it is not entirely mechanical (Hofstadter, *Fluid Concepts*).

The most striking feature of Eliza though is not the weight of its heritage but the simplicity of its operations. For the psychotherapeutic script in particular, the program operates by way of two basic functions—one that discerns patterns in input text, the other that determines responses based on the discerned patterns. While Weizenbaum's original program was written for the now obsolete MAD-SLIP, modern variations of the program written in more contemporary languages, like the browser-based JavaScript or the data scientific Python, illustrate this simplicity. To be somewhat precise, such variations reveal that, once the user interface is determined, whether this interface is a basic dialogue window with an input field or a more elaborate design replicating popular chat services, such as iMessage or WhatsApp, the steps behind the scenes are as straightforward as, firstly, matching words or phrases to a dictionary containing these same words/phrases and, secondly, generating appropriate responses, with the minimally complex intermediary step of pronoun reflection (cf. versions by Michael Wallace, George Dunlop, Keith Weaver).

Contemporary approaches to natural language processing tend to focus on refinements of one or both of these steps, whether through an elaborate encoding to tease out subtle input patterns or a complex network to generate unique output. However, anyone who has interacted with a chatbot knows that the relevance and novelty of the response alone does not lead one to mistake the program for a human interlocutor. As crucial as the quality of the response's content is the timing of the response's production.

Weizenbaum himself had reflected on this topic in his original implementation of the program insofar as hardware limitations could, but did not, produce "truly intolerable delays" of response (Weizenbaum, "Eliza," p. 36). Certain modern versions of Eliza have addressed the same topic by including a simple function that implements random number generators to introduce an unexpected delay prior to the response.

The assumption of these modern solutions is that peoples' delivery time follows a regime that cannot be reduced to a periodic formula. I maintain that this assumption maps onto the assumption that humanity begins with the movement from need (natural randomness) to pleasure (unnatural randomness) as opposed to the relation between demand (articulated need) and desire (individual choice). Lacan's emphasis on the latter thus raises questions not only about the proper mode of treatment but also about the possibility of what today is called artificial intelligence.

Currently, researchers approach this possibility as if humans are at base a progression of interrelated statistical filters through which a singular worldly input flows, whether this input is light-based, sound-based, or abstract (read: language). The issue is that humans, at least observationally in the present, appear to desire, and desire cannot be neatly folded into the statistical progression. Rather, desire operates, to repeat Lacan's phrase, "in the margins of demand," implying that its object draws its value "retroactively" or "after the fact" (pp. 209–210). Philosophically put, this supposed cause of desire has chronological priority but logical posteriority. In other words, a function of desire must intervene in the function determining the appropriate response time all while desire is grasped by way of this function.

Of additional significance is that desire is not the final note of Freud's theory of the developmental phases of sexual organization. While this theory is commonly explained as involving five components, it in reality has two: the pregenital (oral and anal) and the genital (phallic, latent, genital). The reason for this more basic division is that Freud introduced his theory to provide reason for the way human sexuality tends to be localized in a single bodily region in the service of reproduction.

Lacan's conclusion to Chapter 15 offers a kind of riddle to address this topic. He states the following: "little *a* is the Other minus *phi*" (219). For Lacan, the shift at the heart of the developmental phases concerns not only the introduction of desire but also the distinction between this so-called little *a* or the object of desire and the phi or phallus. The latter, as Lacan emphasizes, is "not the simple specification, homologue, or homonym of the little imaginary *a*" (p. 218). He continues: "*phi* [instead] comes to symbolize what the Other is missing because it is the noetic A, the full-fledge A, the Other insofar as one can have faith in its response to demand" (p. 219).

To summarize, for Lacan, the transition to the genital phase amounts to the following flow: since one cannot have pure faith in the Other's response to demand given the ever-developing hole of the Other's desire (i.e., what does this Other want? what is this Other's preferred source of pleasure?), one is faced with the instance of the fact that what the Other is missing is missing because it was taken away. As Lacan puts it: "The function taken on by the phallus ... is not that of being identical to the Other as designated by the lack of a signifier, it is that of being the root of this lack" (p. 219). To mirror Lacan's own recourse to confusion, I wish to end this review with a question to match this quotation up with my digression into the practicality of a program like Eliza: If we pursue the course of artificial intelligence in these terms, do we stop at the point where the machine desires, or ought we proceed to the point at which we encounter its castration?

References

Freud, Sigmund. 1953. *Three Essays on Sexuality* (1903). In *The Complete Psychological Works of Sigmund Freud.* Ed. James Strachey. Vol. VII, pp. 125–243. London: Hogarth Press.

Hoftstader, Douglas. 1995. *Fluid Concepts and Creative Analogies: Computer Models of the Fundamental Mechanisms of Thought.* New York: Basic Books.

Lacan, Jacques. 1991. *The Seminar of Jacques Lacan, Book I: Freud's Papers on Technique (1953–1954).* Translated by John Forrester. New York: W. W. Norton.

———. 2015. *Transference: The Seminar of Jacques Lacan, Book VIII.* Edited by Jacques-Alain Miller and Translated by Bruce Fink. Cambridge: Polity.

Turing, Alan. 1950. "Computing Machinery and Intelligence." *Mind.* Vol. 59, No. 236. Oxford: Oxford University Press.

Wallace, Michael, and George Dunlop. 2016. *ELIZA: A Very Basic Rogerian Psychotherapist Chatbot.* Retrieved July 10, 2019, from https://web.njit.edu/~ronkowit/eliza.html.

Weaver, Keith. 2017. *Keithweaver/eliza.* Retrieved July 10, 2019, from https://github.com/keithweaver/eliza.

Weizenbaum, Joseph. 1966. "Eliza—A Computer Program For the Study of Natural Language Communication Between Man and Machine." *Communications of the ACM.* Vol. 9, No. 1, 36–45.

15

Killing the Soul with Zucchi's Painting: Commentary on Session XVI

Joseph R. Shafer

There are moments in Lacan where the subject deviates from its overdetermined chain of signifiers. Such short circuits occur, for instance, when Poe's Dupin perceived and physically held the enveloped purloined letter, suspending its function as a signifier, however momentarily. In Chapter 16 of *Transference*, Dupin's grasp of the hidden letter is briefly compared to Lacan's own encounter with a particular painting, where Lacan beholds in the canvas what it symbolically negates—the phallus. The painting, from 1589, is *Psiche sorprende Amore* [Psyche surprises Cupid], "about which I have never heard anyone speak," by a Florentine Mannerist, Jacopo Zucchi, who is "not a very well known artist."[1] Lacan's experience is illuminating, as he devotes a series of lectures to analyzing the precise angle from which the spectator perceives what Psyche's lamp truly unveils when looking upon her naked nocturnal lover. For while the painting will suggest

J. R. Shafer (✉)
School of English, University College Cork, Cork, Ireland
e-mail: jrs0166@auburn.edu

G. Basu Thakur and J. Dickstein (eds.), *Reading Lacan's Seminar VIII*,
The Palgrave Lacan Series, https://doi.org/10.1007/978-3-030-32742-2_15

that Cupid's phallus is actually missing from Psyche's perspective, providing the lack which gives birth to Psyche's desire, the painting obstructs the spectator's view of this absence with a vase bouquet, redirecting our attention toward the illumination of Psyche's light itself. In other words, the missing object represented as giving birth to Psyche's desire is simultaneously presented to the viewer as a shining presence.

Rather than offering an ekphrasis or interpretation of Psyche (soul/mind) and Cupid (love), as if the painting were representational, Lacan aims at confronting "the relations between soul and desire" as Dupin had done previously.[2] After all, the soul for Lacan is that specific instrument of discourse which enables thought to think the body. Thus, the birth of the soul commences as Psyche enters the signifying chain of discourse with a desire for what is seen as lacking. Existing criticism concerning this lecture has indeed focused on its given theme by Jacques-Alain Miller, "Psyche and the castration complex," what Lacan emphasizes here as "the point in which the soul is born."[3] But Lacan's over-emphasis regarding this point is far more striking. Preceding lectures subtly yet consistently suggested that Plato played his audience with the delusion of the soul's immortality, especially since Socrates' "assertion of immortality" was "a desire for infinite discourses"; that is, an eternally uninterrupted discourse detached from the body.[4] Lacan plays his audience similarly. For a tacit counterpoint looms, targeting the philosophical discourse Lacan addresses: that if the soul is born, it dies. It seems that enmeshed within the very image of the soul's birth, when Psyche enters the castration complex, the spectator-analyst is able to sensibly perceive what is lacking: "the real presence of the Other's desire." This sublime shock, in suddenly and sensibly perceiving the Other's desire in an object of art, disrupts the signifying chain at the soul's expense. Therefore, by questioning Lacan's own vantage point as spectator-analyst, two central yet somewhat implicit and overlooked theses are exhibited. First, *Psyche surprises Cupid* illustrates at least one angle of what could be called Lacan's aesthetics. Second, this aesthetics involves killing the soul.

The aesthetics found in *Psyche surprises Cupid* can be contextualized by adjacent seminars, where the desire deferred by the symbolic order begins to crop up within negative space. In Seminar VI, *Desire and Its*

Interpretation, a methodology is introduced which moves from philosophical discourse toward poetry. Initially surveying how philosophical discourse represents and defines desire, Lacan turns to Freud, who relied not on discourse but an analysis of translated images of excitation (*Vorstellungsrepräsentanz*). Yet it is within poetry's dramatic manipulation of the signifying battery—"poetic discourse" and "the effects of poetry," even the "tragic poetry" of *Oedipus* and *Hamlet*—where desire is situated in the gaps of the signifying chain.

In Seminar VII, *The Ethics of Psychoanalysis*, Lacan critiques the field of aesthetics proper. The poetry of courtly love, composed by the troubadours, the trouvères, the Minnesänger, created a poetic relationality with the unattainable feminine object, the Lady, the Thing the Law prohibits, the beyond-of-the-signified. Poetic presentations of *the Thing* [*das Ding*] evolved, Lacan observes, in later movements like Mannerist painting, in the late fifteenth and early sixteenth centuries, where new geometrical laws of perspective, such as anamorphosism, resituate *the Thing* not only within the signifying gaps but also in the perceptible structures of space. Two forms of empty space now become framed: The gaps unconsciously structured by the signifying chain, and the unconscious bodily space comprising the perceptual field, which is also split by the former. Mannerist techniques can nevertheless symbolically situate *the Thing* within the empty space of the viewer's scopic field. When *the Thing* is perceived in relation to an object, two forms of "transgression" may arise which Kant's aesthetics did not account for: "excessive object sublimation" and "perversion."[5] According to Kant, the sublime could not be experienced as an object of art. The pyramids, for Kant, prove that the imagination is incapable of grasping the monument in totality. It is precisely because the Kantian sublime locates a disagreement between the subject's sensory experience and its imagination that reason was given autonomous freedom over the supersensible.[6] In Lacan's aesthetics of the sublime, however, the subject is not freed, nor driven by discourse, but shocked in facing the alteriority of the Other's desire as *the Thing* within a sensible object of art. Contrary to discourse, all art bares traces of filling empty space with desire rather than with signs: "All art is characterized by a certain mode of organization around this emptiness,"[7] Lacan concludes, "a work of art always involves encircling *the Thing*."[8]

Unlike Merleau-Ponty, who often described artworks by imagining the artist's own spatial perception of an object (Cézanne with his apples, Van Gogh, his fields),[9] Lacan, on the other hand, does exemplify Cézanne in similar fashion when invoking Merleau-Ponty in *Ethics* but was more inclined to view the artwork itself as an object in space. This is one reason why Mannerism is so privileged by Lacan. Particularly after Rafael's death in 1520, Mannerists began stylizing the perfected naturalism and classicism of their High Renaissance predecessors by distorting object proportions, through fantasy, artificiality, and technical innovation, in order to set up the spectator's spatial relationship to the work itself. In contrast to twentieth-century avant-garde movements like Suprematism or Abstract Expressionism, where the dissolution of the symbol or sign is ostensibly sought, Mannerism utilized symbolic relations in bringing the Other's desire into the viewer's perceptual field (a trait resonant with Lacan's other cherished movement, Surrealism).

Mannerism spread from Rome, Florence, then Mantua, like the plague of 1522,[10] running contemporaneously with the German Renaissance of Hans Holbein and Albrecht Dürer, each featured in Lacan's famous lectures on the gaze in Seminar XI. There Lacan reinterprets the "aesthetic world" and "the flesh of the world" in the late Merleau-Ponty, before employing Dürer's *lucinda* (or screen) as a model for how and where the subject is being painted. As Lacan sees it, the unconscious Other (the artist) gazes upon its object (the woman being painted) through the *lucinda* (veil of desire). The squares of the screen organize the feminine body into proportional, partitioned parts, which, when transposed onto the corresponding squares of the canvas, can display the object from the exact vantage point of the viewer. And where is the subject in this schematic process? The subject is that which is being painted within the canvas' empty spaces. Even when one is looking at an object of art, the subject is being mimetically sketched by the Other's desire. Lacan therefore becomes enthralled when those geometrical and optical relations which Mannerist art projects from the vantage of the spectator come into alignment with those already constituting subject formation. Here is where short circuits occur.

The viewer stumbles upon this alignment when leaving the room of Holbein's *The Ambassadors*, as Lacan found it in Baltrušaitis' *Anamorphoses*

(1955). Glancing back from a specific angle, the painting's hidden object of desire reveals itself in the canvas—the skull (*objet petit a*), capturing the subject in its "trap."[11] This trap results not from vision but from coming into the "line of light" within the structures of space, where the subject sensibly perceives the remainder of the Other's desire within the symbolic that bars it. And what is the reward for embodying the image of the Other's desire in this previously split space? Annihilation: "All this shows that at the very heart of the period in which the subject emerged and geometrical optics was an object of research, Holbein makes visible for us here something that is simply the subject as annihilated—annihilated in the form that is, strictly speaking, the imaged embodiment of the *minus-phi* [$(-\varphi)$] of castration, which for us, centres the whole organization of the desires through the framework of the fundamental drives."[12] Three years earlier, *Psyche surprises Cupid* not only illustrated how the object of desire appears as the imaged embodiment of the *minus-phi* of castration, in relation to the Other's desire, but how the phallus itself, the lack as the Other's desire, enters the frame as real presence within the sensible. Zucchi's painting accomplishes such through what Lacan experiences as its "Mannerist mainspring," "Mannerist flavor," and "Mannerist procedure."[13]

Lacan's lecture begins by disseminating copies of the painting (with a related abbozzo by his brother-in-law, André Mason) and by recalling how he gravitated toward its hanging space when entering Rome's Borghese Gallery: "Experience has taught me to always look at what is near an elevator, as it is often significant and people never look there," and, "at the moment I left the elevator," "I saw something people never really pause to look at."[14] When entering the gallery with an over-the-shoulder paranoia similar to Baltrušaitis' when exiting the room of *The Ambassadors*, *Psyche surprises Cupid* appears in a blind spot, giving pause before its Mannerist traits take effect. Unlike other renditions, Psyche stands armed, with a blade in one hand and a lamp held over "Cupid's phallus," which both Cupid and Psyche look down upon. Yet the phallus is hidden from the viewer, behind a vase bouquet at "the visual, intellectual center of the painting." The vase, moreover, sits rather like "a black mass" in the painting's foreground while the background beams, as Psyche "shines an intense light" over Cupid's thighs. It is this precise angle of obstruction that implicates the viewer. Lacan does not mention the small puppy glaring at the viewer when cowering from Psyche's light in the shadows, but the vase does deflect Lacan's line of light back toward Psyche's well-lit torso as an object of desire. The spectator is drawn into the scene of the soul's shining form.

The difference in Psyche's relation to the phallus, compared to Lacan's, is pivotal. And it is not one based upon sex. Lacan reiterated, "Psyche is not a woman, but rather the soul" "[t]he tale is not about relations between men and women,"[15] since "[t]he castration complex is at work in men and in women."[16] Psyche's relation to the phallus is one of lack. For the phallus is not just an ordinary signifier, lacking a signified, but it signifies the lack in the entire chain, the locus of the Other, "the signifier of the Other's desire."[17] This symbolic phallus is never seen. If its mere presence is entered, it disappears. Yet it is this presence or absence that renders the phallus "the signifier of this very *Aufhebung*, which it inaugurates (initiates) by its disappearance. That is why the demon of Αἰδώς (*Scham*) springs forth at the very moment the phallus is unveiled in the ancient mysteries (see the famous painting in the Villa of the Mysteries in Pompeii)."[18] In Pompeii's mural of Αἰδώς, shame stretches her immortal wings in looking away from the cornucopia being unveiled, but Lacan stipulates that despite Psyche and Cupid being traditionally winged, Psyche is alarmingly unwinged when looking upon what ought to be Cupid's phallus in the painting. Why is Psyche unwinged?

Her position is comparable to Aidos, since Psyche does not see the phallus, for Cupid's organ is found missing. Lacan was keen to note that the flower petals obstructing our view of the phallus are so tiny that it's clear there is nothing to be seen from Psyche's end: "What Psyche is about to cut off has already disappeared."[19] Psyche's siege upon the absent phallus is unshameful, perhaps mortalizing, yet Lacan calls it the birth of the soul:

> Thanks to this painting, you must see that the castration complex is, in its structure and instinctual dynamic, centered in such a way that it coincides exactly with what we might call the point at which the soul is born.
>
> If this myth has any meaning, it is indeed that Psyche only truly becomes Psyche – in other words [...] the subject of a pathos which is, strictly speaking, that of the soul – at the moment at which the desire that fulfilled her slips away and takes flight. Psyche's adventures begin at that very moment.[20]

The soul is born into desire with the vanishing phallus. And with the Other symbolically lacking, Psyche's subsequent adventures in love consist of a sexual relationship that does not exist. Instead, she is born into the signifying chain that had already prompted the act, via her sisters' "chattering."[21] But if Psyche's birth into a fear of losing the phallus (castration complex) inaugurates the unending chain of discourse, should this not carry the soul eternally? Lacan remarks that unlike Venus, who is born daily, or Cupid, conceived daily, the birth of the soul occurs once, implying a life span. This sense, that the very point of the soul's birth could be the point of its demise, is the "paradox" facing Lacan.[22]

The point is one of divergence, for when encountering the Other's desire, the subject either enters a debt in trying to give the Other what it cannot, out of fear of losing the symbol of desire (the phallus), or the subject grasps desire itself, which is hardly ever the case: "What analytic practice reveals to us is that it is more precious to hold onto desire's symbol – the phallus – than to hold onto desire itself. This is the problem with which we are presented."[23] Lacan follows the soul's birth into desire, while grasping at its substance. "But the birth of the soul," Lacan writes, "is, in both universal and the particular, for all of us and for each of us, an historic moment. It is from this moment on that the dramatic story with which we are faced unfolds in all its consequences."[24] The "both universal and the particular" birth of the soul speaks to the Aristotelian soul analyzed at length in Seminar XX, *On Feminine Sexuality, the Limits of Love and Knowledge*, where discourse of the soul registers the sniveling effects of a threatening body it cannot know.

In Seminar XX, Plato and Aristotle are nevertheless found making discursive strides when speaking of what cannot be spoken, "the sexual relationship," because, while elevating the soul as that which gives form to matter and animates it, they tease out the object of desire despite being unable to think it: "something, albeit something ambiguous, nevertheless got through, namely, that this animation is nothing other than the *a* with which the agent animates what? [Aristotle] animates nothing – he takes the other as his soul."[25] Aristotle assumes that the remainder of the Other's desire in the symbolic is part of the soul's agency, and thus fails to make the presumed link between thought and what grounds being: the body. The fallacy, Lacan continues, is "that man thinks with – instrument – his soul, that is, as I just told you, the presumed mechanisms on which the body is based."[26] In other words, the incomprehensibility of the body reinforces the instrumental function of thinking the soul in Aristotle. "Isn't it plain to see that the soul is nothing other than the supposed identicalness [*identite*] of this body to everything people think in order to explain it? In short, the soul is what one thinks regarding the body – on the winning side."[27]

From the outset of *Transference*, Lacan is fascinated by the love of discourse in *The Symposium* and surprised when Socrates refuses it, in light of Alcibiades' desire for Socrates to speak, offering Diotima in his stead. Scientific discourse was Plato's world: "In a sense, there will never be any universe other than a universe of discourse," which was, "in the end, their only instrument of experimentation."[28] Already by Chapter 7, Lacan was mocking Socrates' notion of immortality as discourse, these "verbal exercises for all eternity," which, in the *Phaedo*, is an endless deliberation "about even and odd, the just and unjust, the mortal and immortal, hot and cold."[29] Carrying on this way "for all eternity is a very odd conception of happiness."[30] Lacan's rebuff rather condones Plato's seriouslessness, and their joined project, to slight the soul, is alluded to as early as Chapter 4:

> At this point, when everything I am telling you about Plato has perhaps led you to open up the *Phaedo*, for example, it is important that you realize that the goal of the *Phaedo* is perhaps not entirely to demonstrate, appearances notwithstanding, the immortality of the soul. I would even say that its goal is obviously the contrary. But let us set that aside.[31]

Plato's skepticism concerning the immortality of philosophical discourse seems evident in the opening passages of the *Phaedo*, where Socrates is found discrediting "the art of philosophy" for a new "kind of art," which Socrates recently discovered in translating his dreams into poetry, "in obedience to the dream" "I realized that a poet, if he is to be a poet, must compose fables, not arguments."[32] Signs of the Other's desire enter discourse here, although Lacan does not mention this example of Socrates' surrealist poetry, nor any other example. He merely insinuates that Plato's sense of the eternal Idea in the *Phaedo* could not honestly disavow corporeality: "The idea that anything whatsoever that exists could participate in the Platonic idea as incorporeal essence proves to be fictional in nature, an illusion. Things go so far in the *Phaedo* that it is impossible not to remark that there is no reason to believe Plato was any less aware of this illusion than we are."[33] In respect to the soul, Lacan's objective, however muffled, nevertheless appears more forthcoming than Plato's:

> Let us put things in perspective. One man thus experienced the question of the immortality of the soul. I would go even further: [...] the soul we deal with in the Christian tradition has as its internal brace, frame, or truss the by-product of Socrates' delusion of immortality. We are still living off it.[34]

To substantiate the "delusion of immortality," Lacan turns to the moment the soul is born, and Zucchi's painting holds the key to its ruination. Through its "Mannerist application" in particular, the desire in Psyche's symbolic relation becomes approachable, as the painting's artifice does not reveal nor represent the lacking phallus but the visual illusion necessary for viewing what cannot be seen. "It is clearly in this register that we see, in the composition of this canvas, the way in which the question of what is at stake in what must concern us here – namely, Psyche's act – is sustained."[35] To hold desire rather than chase its symbol is to sensibly interrogate sign exchange, "to put a stop to the deferral":

> The point is to find the guarantor of the chain that, transferring meaning from sign to sign, must stop somewhere – to find what gives us the sign that we have a right to operate with signs. [...] Of all possible signs, isn't it the one that brings together in itself the sign and means of action along with the very presence of desire as such? If we allow the phallus to come to light in its real presence, isn't that apt to put a stop to the deferral that takes place in the chain of signs and, furthermore, to push the signs back into some kind of shadow of nothingness?[36]

The question arises: Can "we allow the phallus to come to light in its real presence"? This play of words, "come to light [*au jour*]," though often found in Freud [*an den Tag zu bringen*], is a double entendre connoting a surfacing into consciousness and/into perception. Lacan calls attention not toward a sign or object, painted or imaginary, nor the lack from Psyche's perspective, but a once invisible "light" rendered sensible as the "real presence" of desire. Illuminating the light of desire in the moment the soul is born may just push signs of the soul "back into some kind of shadow of nothingness."

Lacan's "light," in the context of *Psyche surprises Cupid*, invokes Hegel's shining [*Erscheinung*], the actual or essential manifestation of a thing, and Merleau-Ponty's concurrent phenomenology, where sensible perception consists of the anteriority of light, the field as contrived by the body, and that which is illuminated (e.g., colors).[37] Zucchi's "Mannerist flavor" orients the spectator toward the light shining rather than its object. With the visual illusion of the vase bouquet, Psyche's view of symbolic lack is obstructed and perception is redirected in beholding the materializing light itself, as Lacan's eye is initially drawn to a literal line of light—a "shaft"—pointing from Psyche's lamp to Cupid's bust: "there is something like a shaft of light which runs from the lamp and goes straight toward Cupid's shoulder. Nevertheless, the angle of this shaft does not allow us to believe that it is a drop of oil, but rather a ray of light."[38] In Apuleius' description of this scene in *The Golden Ass*, which Lacan compares to France's recent erotic and sadomasochistic novels, a drop of oil had burned Cupid, but the burning substance here is a shaft of light. It is this substance that reflects not the object at center but the soul's radiating torso: "In the painting, Psyche is the one who is illuminated."[39] With light materializing into the sensible form of Psyche, the perceptual space of the viewer's soul and desire becomes implicated in relation to the Other (artist).

The painting's focused projection of Psyche's body highlights, on the one hand, how she internalizes the other body. "Because of this," Lacan continues, "we realize that it is neither the woman nor the man who, in the final analysis, is the medium of the castrating action; it is the [phallic] image itself insofar as it is reflected – reflected onto the narcissistic form of the body."[40] The narcissistic form of the body, in Psyche's case, identifies and internalizes the other as specular image (of lack) with the empty form of the body. On the other hand, Zucchi's redoubled imagery of this scene magnifies the illumination of her embodiment: "In this image, the artist has grasped what last time I called the moment of the appearance or birth of Psyche – the sort of exchange of powers whose effect is that she becomes embodied."[41] What the artist "grasps" here is critical. Lacan repeatedly acknowledges the hand of the Mannerist artist within the viewer's unfolding trap. For the illumination of Psyche's embodiment of light is the procedure by which the artist sustains the act of desire. That which the vase bouquet truly hides, the artist reveals in light—the Other's desire: "something is hidden behind that [bouquet] and, if we are to believe what is revealed to us here by the painter's intuition, it is no other than the decisive moment that he painted."[42] The "decisive moment" Zucchi painted reveals an "intuition" buried in the "historical moment" of Psyche's birth, and the spectator gets caught in sensibly (not visually) perceiving the Other's desire within the canvas.

Grasping the real presence of the Other's desire halts the signifying chain and finds the soul on the losing side. The lecture's closing passages make two swift gestures toward this end. The first succinctly notes how Socrates refuses discourse, and the second is embedded in Lacan's final phrase—"the demise of the soul," quoted from Rabelais. Lacan first concludes, "If the Other's desire is essentially separated from us by the mark of a signifier," then we should surely understand why Alcibiades sought Socrates' desire discursively, for Alcibiades knew the Other's desire existed, and he wanted "to see it in the form of a sign" "This is also why Socrates refuses. For this is but a short circuit."[43] Socrates, in this moment, manages to hold desire, not in a sign but in perceiving its real presence, ceasing the signifying chain. *Psyche surprises Cupid* offers this potential position for the spectator-analyst, though not by representing it (as Psyche and the castration complex), for "[r]epresenting something to someone is precisely what must be disrupted," Lacan continues. Rather, this disruptive position is "being presented with this painting, in what non-negative, but positive, sense Rabelais says that it is 'the demise of the soul.'"[44] Rabelais' original line, "*ruine de l'âme,*"[45] from *The Life of Gargantua and of Pantagruel* (1532–1564), comes as a warning, from Gargantua to his son, to seek wisdom with a righteous mind, knowledge with conscience, to serve, love and fear God. In this way, Rabelais, like Plato and Lacan, validates the soul's purpose in a mischievous manner. At the height of Mannerism, Rabelais the satirist, as Bakhtin himself underlined in *Rabelais and His World* (1965), was reacting to High Renaissance divination from within the Paduan school of Pomponazzi, believing that the soul cannot be separated from bodily material, from either its most base excrements (urine and feces) or images mixed with such.[46] Bakhtin concludes: "The parody of the medieval topography is obvious; the soul's beatitude is deeply immersed in the body's lowest stratum."[47]

Notes

1. Jacques Lacan, *Transference*, trans. Bruce Fink (Cambridge: Polity Press, 2017), p. 200.
2. Ibid., p. 225.
3. Ibid., p. 226.
4. Ibid., p. 102.
5. Jacques Lacan, *The Ethics of Psychoanalysis*, trans. Denis Porter (New York and London: W. W. Norton, 1991), p. 109.
6. Jacques Rancière, *Aesthetics and Its Discontents*, trans. Steven Corcoran (Cambridge: Polity Press, 2009), p. 93.
7. Lacan (1991, p. 141).
8. Ibid., p. 130.
9. Maurice Merleau-Ponty, *Signes* (Paris: Gaillimard, 1960), pp. 64–66.
10. John Shearman, *Mannerism* (Middlesex: Penguin, 1967), p. 24.
11. Jacques Lacan, *The Four Fundamental Concepts of Psycho-Analysis*, trans. Alan Sheridan (New York: Penguin, 1979), p. 89.
12. Ibid., pp. 88–89.
13. Lacan (2015, p. 236).
14. Ibid., p. 220.
15. Ibid., pp. 224–225.
16. Ibid., p. 227.
17. Jacques Lacan, 'The Signification of the Phallus,' in *Écrits: The First Complete Edition in English*, trans. Bruce Fink (New York and London: W. W. Norton, 2006), p. 583.
18. Lacan (2015, p. 581).
19. Ibid., p. 229.
20. Ibid., p. 226.
21. Ibid., p. 243.
22. Ibid., p. 227.
23. Ibid., p. 229.
24. Ibid., p. 227.

25. Jacques Lacan, *On Feminine Sexuality*, trans. Bruce Fink (New York and London: W. W. Norton, 1999), p. 83.
26. Ibid., p. 111.
27. Ibid., p. 112.
28. Lacan (2015, p. 78).
29. Ibid., p. 102.
30. Ibid.
31. Ibid., p. 61.
32. Plato, *Phaedo*, in *Complete Works*, trans. G.M.A. Grube (Indianapolis: Hackett Publishing Company, 1997), pp. 52–53, 60d–61c.
33. Lacan (2015, pp. 73–74).
34. Ibid., p. 102.
35. Ibid., p. 237.
36. Ibid., p. 243.
37. Maurice Merleau-Ponty, *The Phenomenology of Perception*, trans. Colin Smith (London and New York: Routledge, 2005), p. 363.
38. Lacan (2015, p. 222).
39. Ibid., p. 244.
40. Ibid.
41. Ibid., p. 237.
42. Ibid., p. 235.
43. Ibid., p. 232.
44. Ibid., p. 233.
45. François Rabelais, *Les Cinq Livres de Rabelais, Tome II* (Paris: Magnard, 1965), p. 107.
46. Mikhail Bakhtin, *Rabelais and His World*, trans. Helene Iswolsky (Bloomington: Indiana University Press, 1984), p. 371.
47. Ibid., p. 402.

References

Bakhtin, Mikhail. 1984. *Rabelais and His World.* Trans. Helene Iswolsky. Bloomington: Indiana University Press.

Lacan, Jacques. 1999. *The Seminar of Jacques Lacan, Book XX: Encore, On Feminine Sexuality (1972–73)*. Translated by Bruce Fink. New York and London: W. W. Norton.

———. 1991. *The Seminar of Jacques Lacan, Book VII: The Ethics of Psychoanalysis (1959–1960)*. Translated by Denis Porter. New York and London: W. W. Norton.

———. 2015. *Transference: The Seminar of Jacques Lacan, Book VIII*. Edited by Jacques-Alain Miller and Translated by Bruce Fink. Cambridge: Polity.

———. 1979. *The Seminar of Jacques Lacan, Book XI: The Four Fundamental Concepts of Psycho-Analysis (1964)*. Translated by Alan Sheridan. New York: Penguin.

———. 2006. 'The Signification of the Phallus,' in *Écrits: The First Complete Edition in English*, Translated by Bruce Fink. New York and London: W. W. Norton.

Merleau-Ponty, Maurice. 1960. *Signes*. Paris: Gallimard.

———. 2005. *The Phenomenology of Perception*. Translated by Colin Smith. London and New York: Routledge.

Plato. 1997. *Complete Works*. Trans. G.M.A. Grube. Indianapolis: Hackett Publishing Company.

Rabelais, François. 1965. *Les Cinq Livres de Rabelais, Tome II*. Paris: Magnard.

Rancière, Jacques. 2009. *Aesthetics and Its Discontents*. Trans. Steven Corcoran. Cambridge: Polity Press.

Shearman, John. 1967. *Mannerism*. Middlesex: Penguin.

16

The Art of Questioning "Real Presence"

Joseph R. Shafer

In the previous chapter, Zucchi's Mannerist painting, *Psyche surprises Cupid* (1589), represented one thing for Lacan and presented another. The painting represents Psyche, shining her lamp upon what seems to be Cupid's missing organ. The phallus, as the missing signifier, is the lack which begets Psyche's desire. On one level, therefore, Zucchi offers Lacan a figurative interpretation of Psyche and the castration complex. On the other hand, what Lacan beholds cannot be represented. As spectator, Lacan cannot visually see from Psyche's angle, nor the apparent lack, since a vase bouquet, at the center of the canvas, obstructs our view of the object between Cupid's thighs. Unlike Psyche, who imagines this lost object, Lacan does not succumb to the imaginary, for part of the Mannerist contrivance lies in the finely placed thinness of the flower's stem, which more than suggests that behind its masking there is absence. As a result, Lacan neither sees absence visually nor imagines it completely, but has his perception drawn by the vase toward that which is actually being illuminated: Psyche's own

J. R. Shafer (✉)
School of English, University College Cork, Cork, Ireland
e-mail: jrs0166@auburn.edu

G. Basu Thakur and J. Dickstein (eds.), *Reading Lacan's Seminar VIII*,
The Palgrave Lacan Series, https://doi.org/10.1007/978-3-030-32742-2_16

reflected body in her materializing light. With the embodied light implicating our viewing space, Lacan not only encounters "soul and desire," in witnessing Psyche momentarily basking in the presence of her own desire, but comes to sensibly perceive "the real presence" of the Other's desire in relation to the canvas.

In his following lectures, however, Lacan questions the necessary conditions for experiencing this relation to the lost object, whereby "real presence" may arise, and he does so by illustrating its altogether unlikeliness, and the delusion required in sustaining it. If so-called real presence of the phallus is manufacturable, as Lacan purports by way of certain Mannerist techniques, then it is inevitable that the object is exchanged and incorporated into the psychical economy of imaginary objects. The task is then to question the objects that continually mask, or reveal, real presence. Yet even if Lacan's particular manner of questioning were to miraculously make the "real presence" of the phallus known, the risk of serving that illusion behooves the analyst to then "break [real presence] or mash it up in the mechanisms of desire."[1]

Despite all precautions, Lacan nevertheless reaffirms that the phallus under question can surface within what might be considered certain art forms. Midway through Chapter 17, he reiterates:

> This signifier [the symbolic phallus or uppercase *Phi*] is always hidden and veiled – to the extent, good gracious, that one is astonished, that one takes it to be a peculiar and almost exorbitant enterprise, to see its form in some obscure representation or artwork. It is more than rare, though of course it happens, to see it brought into a hieroglyphic chain or into a prehistoric rupestrian painting. We cannot say that it plays no role in human imagination, even prior to analytic exploration, and yet it is, of all our fabricated, signifying representations, the one most often elided or eluded. What does this imply? [...]
>
> An either/or relationship becomes established between this signifier of desire and the entire signifying chain.[2]

Before the end of this three-part series concerning "real presence" in *Psyche surprises Cupid*, a quite stark either/or relationship is established on account of what seems impossible and what is not. Nonetheless, Lacan cites two prime examples: hieroglyphs and cave paintings.[3] It is not digressive here to note that these are extremely rare occurrences, unlikely to be seen by non-specialists. Looking closer, they are a kind of symbolic art with a most primordial function; using a language of images to surround that missing thing which cannot be written despite a most proleptical need to symbolize it. Lacan calls this thing "the unnameable symbol."[4] The distinctness of this absent symbol warrants a hard either/or as a result of our desire to artificially preserve and reconstruct it.

The middle ground of this either/or is at issue, and problems arrive in how the unnameable symbol becomes so naturally confused with real or imaginary objects. Chapter 17 begins by returning to "a fundamental ambiguity between Φ and φ, between uppercase *Phi* as a symbol, and lowercase *phi*."[5] The difference between Φ and φ is between the symbolic and the imaginary, but the ambiguity occurs as symbol Φ is rendered ubiquitous through the displacements, substitutions, and slippages of imaginary objects. "Lowercase *phi* designates the imaginary phallus insofar as it is concretely involved in the psychical economy at the level of the castration complex where we first truly encountered it, where the neurotic experiences it in a way that represents his particular mode of operating and maneuvering, with the radical difficulty that I am trying to articulate for you through the use I make of the symbolic capital *Phi*."[6] The ambiguities between the object of the symbolic phallus and that of the imaginary are not exactly elucidated by Lacan in Chapter 17, nor in *Transference*, but in Seminar IV, *La relation d'objet et les structures freudiennes*. There, the structure of fantasy transforms the missing object into the imaginary.

In *The Object Relation*, the object in question can no longer be conceived within the subject–object relation of philosophy since Plato, nor within the mother–child relation of psychoanalysis, for Lacan divides and triangulates that dyad with the third term of the phallus. Lacan thus turns to contemporary debates in object relations theory, particularly those centered around Winnicott and Klein, which revolve around an intermediary object between mother–child. Yet Lacan repeatedly locates a third object still missing from each formation: the symbolic object that is lack itself. The object of lack is not a real object, like a mother's real breast, which certainly exists in having once imposed itself upon the child. Neither is it one of the mutatious imaginary objects. It is not a "transitional object," like a teddy bear, real yet fictional, nor one of the other imaginary objects of "frustration," such as a child's imaginary image of the mother's breast, which provides a constant image promising a pleasure that can now never be completely satisfied. Nor is it the imaginary object of castration: What the child imagines as the lost object, albeit his own body—the object of the mother's desire. Nor is it a fetishized object, the mother's shoe, for example, which objectifies what is imagined to be missing under her dress. It is neither the objects of *frustration* nor *castration* (nor perversion) that trouble Lacan in *The Object Relation*, but the object of *privation.* Lacan asks: Is there not some thing always already found missing in the real itself? Is there not this real hole, this hole in the real, energizing the economy of imaginary objects? Must not this very lack be symbolized? Moreover, isn't it all too easy to let this missing object or signifier slip into another signifier? In this way, *The Object Relation* deciphers the act of giving what one doesn't have, which is the act of love so central to *Transference*. In Chapters 16–18 of *Transference*, Lacan does not again parcel out this missing object but instead questions how the analyst may or may not come to know its real presence.

Chapter 17 returns to *Psyche surprises Cupid* to recommence "my difficult discourse," "which is ever more difficult owing to its aim"; an aim that asks: When looking at any assemblage, persons or paintings, how does the spectator-analyst perceive the real presence of this symbol without identifying with any object or image, real or imaginary? The painted vase bouquet in *Psyche surprises Cupid*, which obstructed the spectator's vision of Cupid's missing organ, for example, is a centered "black mass" that offers itself as a signifier for the clearly absent object behind it, yet taking either the vase or Psyche's own reflected body as the phallic object is an imaginary ploy. Lacan's forewarning, of this fundamental ambiguity between Φ and φ, is followed by juxtaposing *Psyche surprises Cupid* with a contemporary of Zucchi's, the Mannerist Giuseppe Arcimboldo, whose portraits are comprised entirely of objects. Lacan's commentary on Arcimboldo coincides with a general rediscovery of the artist, and the timeliness of Lacan's invocation is no doubt due to a personal fascination with Mannerism and his proud friendship with Salvador Dali, who, with Max Ernst, seemed to mimic Arcimboldo,[7] though Lacan makes that connection explicit: "[Arcimboldo] is known for a singular technique which sent out its most recent shoot in the work of my old friend Salvador Dali in what he called paranoiac drawing."[8] What Arcimboldo captures is a vision of how objects reconstitute "persona," as the persona "is always in the foreground in the economy of human presence."[9] Persona's duplicity and dissimulation are apparent from its etymological roots, as the Greek πρόσωπον already attributes the hypostasis of one's "person" to a theatrical mask, but here Lacan pries into the economy of objects which both delimits and confounds that composite.

This economy is foregrounded in Arcimboldo's more famous paintings, when serving as court portraitist for Rudolf II, King of Bohemia, as seen in the portrait of "Rudolf II's librarian," and others with "the symbolic theme of a season."[10] The former refers to a 1566 portrait, later entitled *The Librarian* by Olof Granberg in 1911,[11] and the latter to a 1572 series known as *Spring*, *Summer*, *Autumn* and *Winter*. In each, Arcimboldo employs what Lacan calls "the Mannerist application." And "the word 'application' must be used both literally and figuratively," since "the image of a face," or "the disguise of a human face," continues Lacan, consists of nothing but objects associated with the subject being painted. *The Librarian*, for instance, is a portrait composed of a stack of books resembling a bust, a typical librarian's duster for what is a beard, a book's open pages to act as a hat, and the library's curtain thrown over the pile's shoulder to suggest a cape. The fact that scholars in Arcimboldo's day had attempted to identify what authors were being represented in *The Librarian* simply extended the underlying critique, that identity is superficially constructed by its associated objects. Lacan, uncharacteristically, does not dabble in such contexts but states: "this Mannerist procedure consists in creating the essence of a human image through the coalescence, combination, or accumulation of a pile of objects, the sum total of which is given the task of representing what is thus manifested both as substance and illusion."[12]

The persona, which "results from a complex grouping [of objects]," is instructive for Lacan, since ultimately a more objective mask is painted that can be removed to unveil the object behind, where "all form slips away and vanishes."[13] Facing the complex yet concrete assemblage of objects that is the persona, in other words, offers a tangible sense of the facade that must be stripped for the symbol to emerge. "Here indeed lies the illusion [*leurre*] and the fragility of [the persona's] subsistence. Behind it, we know nothing of what can be sustained, for it is a twofold appearance that is suggested to us, a redoubling of appearance that leaves unanswered the question of what there is there in the end."[14] Lacan, however, does not intend to leave unanswered the question of what's behind imaginary objects, as the answer is sought in that signifier which cannot be signed and is always missing: the phallus as symbol Φ.

Questioning the presence of the phallus is not only required in light of its ubiquitous illusions, but as a means of breaking through the mask. Reemploying signs for interrogation purposes is to create the very obstacles meant to be overcome. An initial obstacle lies in the fact that there can be nothing left unsaid in a language. Citing Jakobson, Lacan confirms, "There is no language, however primitive it may be, in which everything cannot in the end be expressed, with the exception that [...] what cannot be expressed in that language is, quite simply, neither felt nor subjectified."[15] Yet it is precisely because what ex-ists outside a language cannot be felt or subjectified that the chain must be questioned quite militantly: "At what moment can a lack of a signifier possibly begin to appear? In the dimension that is subjective and that is called questioning."[16]

Lacan exemplifies the notoriously endless questioning of the child—"What is running?" "What does 'stamping your foot' mean?" "What is an imbecile?"[17], but he admonishes the philosophical and psychoanalytic idealization and normalization of the "child." Returning the subject to the ideal child position is not merely a cyclical practice but an inherently rhetorical one. For underlining this developmental line of questioning is the question of "What am I?", the essential question which all too comfortably finds the subject relating to (or as) "the child." Put another way, the very sign this question provokes immediately re-identifies infantile objects. Lacan briefly illustrates this in his Graph of Desire.[18] An utterance of "What am I?" simultaneously, though not synchronically, reestablishes the object it meant to upset. Invoking the Hegelian dialectics of propositions, where the predicate identifies the reflected subject (e.g., God is Love),[19] and referring to *Nachträglich* in Freud, the object summoned in "What am I?" retroactively incarnates and crystalizes the ideal ego. From here the chain of questioning unfolds, for in questioning the ideal ego, the ego-ideal takes shape. The ethical dimension of the super-ego's self-criticism is well underway. It is this wheelwork that begs a different question, Lacan argues, which does not address "What am I?" but rather the Other, or the Other's desire, in "What do you want?" "This is how the question must be understood. It is here that the lack of a signifier at stake in the phallus as Φ intervenes."[20]

Lacan relates this mode of questioning to Freud's "reality testing," except Lacan concludes Chapter 17 by recalling how Freud deceived himself through his interrogative approach, specifically in the case of Dora the hysteric. According to Lacan, the main difference between his approach and Freud's, in the case of Dora, is in the object questioned. Freud had directed his questions as a master of knowledge, and thus fell prey to the imaginary objects substantiated by the "What am I?" dialectic with Dora. With hysteria, moreover, such questioning becomes far more imposturous, as the path of "What am I?" not only produces the normal metonymy of signs for the hysteric to identify with, perpetuating the standard "ethical and philosophical blunders" described above, but the hysteric also takes those signs with "full and absolute meaning,"[21] which further beguiles Freud. Lacan, on the other hand, questions knowledge as such, and thus the analyst's position, by targeting the Other's desire.

This contrast stems from a different understanding of the Oedipus complex. For Freud, Oedipus sleeps with Jocasta as a result of murdering the father: The son replaces the father as master. The master has what the son desires. Lacan sees Freud representing this cycle, of subverting the father, in Freud's attempt to subvert all religion. But as Lacan elaborates in Seminar XVII, *The Other Side of Psychoanalysis*, Freud, like this primordial definition of the father, does not appear on the scene in possession, but as already castrated.[22] The father is not the master of symbolic truth, he is found lacking. For Lacan, Oedipus assumes the tragic position of master by solving the sphinx's riddle. Oedipus is the master of solving riddles, of obtaining knowledge, and this is Freud's own tragic mistake, because the master is caught in the dialectics of desire, seeking the lost object of truth in the imaginary forms of the signifying chain. In other words, Freud is seen chasing imaginary forms (φ) of the phallus in Dora, which are linked to Dora's objects of desire, her little other (*a*), but he does not question the real presence of the phallus (Φ), the desire of the Other (A).[23]

Indeed, it is dizzying to follow Freud's pursuit of what Dora is, what woman is, in relation to her object of desire, and the case famously exemplifies Freud's own impotence as master, as the elusive Dora is exchanged in relation to one object after another. She had visited Freud with symptoms developing after an incident where she was propositioned by her father's close-friend, Herr K. Although Dora slapped Herr K. and reported the event to her father, Dora eventually admits to fancying Herr K., knowing that he could not please his wife. It is this impotence that associates Herr K. with her father, whose own impotence flagrantly neglected Dora's mother, as he spent all his spare time with Herr K. and his wife. Although Dora's mother was in the picture, her father's abandonment, and Dora's enmity toward her, aided Freud in determining Dora's sexual desire for the father. But when the father is seen as Dora's object of desire, Dora's true desire appears to be for her father's not-so-secret mistress, Frau K., who was always so affectionate with Dora, and, in Dora's words, had an "adorable white body."[24] Dora's homosexual attraction speaks not only to what Freud considers a universal bisexuality but Dora's self-identification with the phallus in relation to Frau K: Dora takes the position of the father in desiring woman. And yet, as soon as this paradigm is validated, Freud realizes that Dora is not infatuated with, nor simply jealous of, Frau K, but self-identifies with her, in order to reimagine herself as the woman-object of her father's desire. The non-competitive nature of this love triangle is telling, for it becomes clear that Dora is not pursuing Frau K., nor her father, but has positioned herself as their enabler, their mediating object, since the mutual caring for Dora by her father and Frau K. is the performance that enables them to carry out the affair. From here, Freud's chase continues. Dora, growing weary of Freud's inability to rise to the occasion, terminates the analysis prematurely. Freud is left concluding, in hindsight, that Frau K. was most likely the real object of Dora's desire, while her Oedipal fantasies placed Freud in the paternal position, though her hostility toward Freud resulted from being associated with Herr K. In Chapter 17 of *Transference*, Lacan continues by observing: "Freud himself stumbles and loses his way here. You know that he is mistaken concerning the object of her desire, precisely because he seeks to situate Dora as an hysteric, first and foremost, with regard to her choice of object, an object that is no doubt little *a*."[25] Lacan's point is that Freud is deceived by positioning himself as a master-analyst who knows the object of Dora's desire, but only because Freud overlooks the object of the Other's desire, lack. We might see this failure poignantly represented in Freud's ironic admission: "I did not succeed in mastering the transference in good time."[26]

Lacan argues that the hysteric's evasiveness maintains a paradoxical relationship with the father/master. The hysteric stays in relation to a master, a master who represents authoritative knowledge (e.g., the father, rabbi, analyst), yet this master must be also found and kept lacking, impotent, and without knowledge. The paradox is compounded, as the relation can hold only if the master is one without desire, as the true master for the hysteric must be above (sexual) desire (e.g., the father, rabbi, analyst), yet the hysteric's elusivity still manages to solicit and excite the master's desire by granting him certain bits of knowledge while manufacturing a semblance of lack.[27] As Lacan concludes: "This is why [Dora] resorts to all kinds of substitutes, the closest forms, let it be noted, she can find for this sign, Φ. If you follow Dora's operations, or those of any hysteric, you will see that what is always involved is an intricate game by which she can, so to speak, complicate the situation by slipping φ, the lowercase *phi* designating the imaginary phallus, where it is needed."[28]

Lacan had himself reevaluated Dora's relation to lack [*manque d'objet*] at great length in *The Object Relation*, where everything revolves around impotence, or rather what the father cannot give. After all, the object of lack is the greatest gift one can give, the gift of love. And although the question of love is integral for *Transference*, it is not the issue in this lecture. If we wish to outline Dora's mediating symbolic position, among objects of frustration, castration, and privation, Lacan explicitly encourages us to return to *The Object Relation*. For to detail those functions in this chapter is to veer from Lacan's more limited thesis, which comes in the form of a warning. The hysteric reveals to the spectator-analyst the illusion of real presence—how easily that presumed relation with the symbol slips into other signifying forms within the psychical economy. "There is one thing that [Dora] prefers to her own desire," Lacan concludes, "she prefers to let her own desire go unsatisfied and have the Other hold the key to her mystery."[29] Lacan's use of the word "key" [*clé*] is key here. The "key" to Dora's locked "jewelry-box," as described in her first dream, was for

Freud a common allusion to the father's penis and the girl's genitals. Thus, Freud is left deciphering the real and imaginary object Dora has slipped into the Other's hands. For Lacan, there is no key. The real presence of the Other's desire is experienced in beholding the object of lack. Yet the hysteric shows the Other holding an illusion. The only more distrustful and dangerous appearance of "real presence" is found in the case of the obsessive, discussed in the following chapter, Chapter 18.

Notes

1. Jacques Lacan, *Transference*, trans. Bruce Fink (Cambridge: Polity Press, 2015), p. 258.
2. Ibid., p. 243.
3. The cave paintings invoked are most likely those of Lascaux, discovered in 1940 near Montignac among other prehistoric paintings of the Vézère Valley.
4. Ibid., p. 234.
5. Ibid., p. 235.
6. Ibid.
7. Werner Kriegeskorte, *Arcimboldo* (Cologne: Taschen, 2004), p. 30.
8. Lacan (2015, p. 236).
9. Ibid., p. 237.
10. Ibid., p. 236.
11. Derek Sayer, *Prague, Capital of the Twentieth Century: A Surrealist History* (Princeton: Princeton University Press, 2013), p. 51.
12. Lacan (2015, pp. 236–237).
13. Ibid., p. 237.
14. Ibid.
15. Ibid., p. 238.
16. Ibid.
17. Ibid.
18. Ibid., p. 240.
19. "Only in the end of the proposition does the empty beginning become actual knowledge." G.W.F. Hegel, *Phenomenology of Spirit*, trans. A.V. Miller (Oxford: Oxford University Press, 1977), pp. 12–13.
20. Lacan (2015, p. 241).
21. Ibid., p. 245.

22. Jacques Lacan, *The Other Side of Psychoanalysis*, trans. Russell Grigg (New York and London: W. W. Norton, 2007), p. 101.
23. Lacan (2015, p. 244).
24. Sigmund Freud, *Dora: An Analysis of a Case of Hysteria* (New York: Simon & Schuster, 1997), p. 54.
25. Lacan (2015, p. 244).
26. Freud (1997, p. 108).
27. Philippe Van Haute and Tomas Geyskens, '"Freud's Dream"?: Lacan and Oedipus,' in *Jacques Lacan: Between Psychoanalysis and Politics*, ed. Samo Tomšič and Andreja Zevnik (New York: Routledge, 2016), p. 56.
28. Lacan (1997, p. 245).
29. Ibid.

References

Freud, Sigmund. 1997. *Dora: An Analysis of a Case of Hysteria*. New York: Simon & Schuster.

Geyskens, Tomas, and Philippe Van Haute. 2016. 'Freud's Dream'?: Lacan and Oedipus. In *Jacques Lacan: Between Psychoanalysis and Politics*, ed. Samo Tomšič and Andreja Zevnik, 56. New York: Routledge.

Hegel, G.W.F. 1977. *Phenomenology of Spirit*. Trans. A.V. Miller. Oxford: Oxford University Press.

Kriegeskorte, Werner. 2004. *Arcimboldo*. Cologne: Taschen.

Lacan, Jacques. 1994. *La relation d'objet et les structures freudiennes, Livre IV (1956–1957)*. Edited by Jacques-Alain Miller. Paris: Seuil.

———. 2007. *The Seminar of Jacques Lacan, Book XVII: The Other Side of Psychoanalysis (1969–1970)*. Translated by Russel Grigg. New York and London: W. W. Norton.

———. 2015. *Transference: The Seminar of Jacques Lacan, Book VIII*. Edited by Jacques-Alain Miller and Translated by Bruce Fink. Cambridge: Polity.

Sayer, Derek. 2013. *Prague, Capital of the Twentieth Century: A Surrealist History*. Princeton: Princeton University Press.

17

"Real Presence": Commentary on Session XVIII

Stephanie Swales

"Real Presence," the eighteenth chapter of the seminar, focuses on the function of Φ and on its role in obsessional neurosis. In the previous chapter, Lacan reminded us that the Φ is what "arises in the place of the missing signifier"[1] in the symbolic order. He also spoke for the first time about Φ as the "real presence" of desire and, as such, an unbearable "shadow of nothingness."[2]

In the opening section of the eighteenth chapter, Lacan tells us that the question of the symbolic function of the phallus "is so ubiquitous in [Jonathan Swift's] work that one could say that, if we take his work as a whole, it is articulated in it."[3] Lacan then quotes extensively from the section in Jonathan Swift's *Gulliver's Travels* about the kingdom of Tribnia, or Langden, as it was called by its inhabitants. Lacan does not, for all this, explain the connection between these passages and the symbolic function of the phallus.

S. Swales (✉)
University of Dallas, Irving, TX, USA

G. Basu Thakur and J. Dickstein (eds.), *Reading Lacan's Seminar VIII*,
The Palgrave Lacan Series, https://doi.org/10.1007/978-3-030-32742-2_17

What can be gleaned from the text? We are told that the majority of the citizens of Langden were involved in the government or the law. The Informers, specifically, with regard to their enemies would take "effectual Care…to secure all their [enemies'] Letters and other Papers, and put the Owners in Chains. These Papers are delivered to a Set of Artists, very dexterous in finding out the mysterious Meanings of Words, Syllables and Letters."[4] These Informers thereby found ways to interpret the written word in a fashion which suited their purposes of criminally implicating their enemies. The Informers functioned via methodology such as deciphering anagrams,

> Thus, N, shall signify a Plot; B, a Regiment of Horse…So for Example, if I should say in a Letter to a Friend, Our Brother Tom has just got the Piles; a Man of Skill in this Art would discover how the same Letters which compose that Sentence, may be analysed into the following words: Resist, ----- a Plot is brought home ----- The Tour.[5]

The Langden society, in which any word can be made to mean anything, provides a striking example of the function of the symbolic phallus insofar as the hole in the system of language is made apparent. We can see there that all communication, as Lacan has said elsewhere, is miscommunication. The author of a letter in Langden might mean to communicate something entirely different from the message the Informers discover. In their deciphering, the Informers make clear the absence of an indelible link between signifier and signified. This absence is a consequence of the lack at the heart of the symbolic where Φ arises. What is more, the Φ as the signifier of the real presence of desire is evident since it is the desire of the Informers that runs the show.

In the fifth chapter of Part III of *Gulliver's Travels*, the narrator visits the grand academy of Lagado, where Swift has much occasion to poke fun at academia and its production of knowledge. The Lagado professors in the school of languages, reasoning that the effort of speech diminishes one's lung capacity and thus shortens one's life, proposed as an alternative a system of communication which cannot be called a language, since people would—instead of speaking—carry the objects to which they needed to refer to conduct their business. As Mary Klages has commented about this proposition of the Lagado professors, given the presence of the objects and the absence of lack, language could not function.[6] Even as "real presence," the symbolic phallus is the cornerstone of language as absence. It is because something is absent, or because a signifier can never fully call forth a referent, that we need language. The Φ as the real presence of desire can only arise from a place of absence.

At the conclusion of this chapter, Lacan mentions that perversion bears some relevance to the symbolic phallus because it can signify the lack in the signifying system. As the signifier that is excluded from the signifying system, it can only enter the signifying system in the guise of the imaginary phallus, but yet, paradoxically, we can talk about the symbolic phallus as a signifier; we are able to do so because of what Lacan calls "the perverse mechanism."[7] What could be meant by this perverse mechanism? The symbolic phallus is a sign and a signifier of desire that "does not simply serve to make a sign to someone but, at the same moment of the signifying mainspring or instance, to make a sign of someone."[8] In other words, the perverse moment is when this someone becomes the phallus—not the imaginary phallus, as in perversion, but the symbolic phallus.

The signifying function of the phallus has to do with the fact that it is both a signifier of desire and that it designates something beyond signification—real presence. The real presence of desire, as Lacan mentioned at the end of the seventeenth chapter, is unbearable in its unveiled form. Lacan devotes the middle section of the eighteenth chapter to discussing how the obsessional neurotic defends against real presence or enacts "an insult to real presence."[9]

Fantasy in Obsessional Neurosis

Lacan presents the formula for the obsessive's fantasy: the lacking Other in its desire for $\varphi(a, a', a'', a''', \ldots)$. This formula represents the way in which the obsessive tries to overcome his castration and reach out toward his objects of desire; as such, it is a defense against lack which is his particular brand of insult to real presence. So how does his insult manifest? The obsessive's relation to the object is situated as a function of φ, meaning that his objects of desire have a certain erotic equivalence for him. For instance, the breast, a drug, a ham sandwich, a woman who wears high heels, and so on, all are rendered roughly equivalent in the economy of the obsessive's desire.

Lacan cites the paradigmatic example of Freud's Rat Man, or Ernst Langer. As we are told by Freud, the rat is an object of desire which causes the Rat Man's jouissance: When speaking of the Turkish rat torture, Ernst Langer's "face took on a very strange, composite expression. [Freud] could only interpret it as one *of horror at pleasure of his own of which he himself was unaware*."[10] Lacan asks why Freud calls him "*Rattenmann*, the Rat Man or 'man with the rats,' 'rats' being plural"[11] when in his fantasy there is only the one rat, the one that is part of the Turkish torture. As an aside, this seems technically incorrect, since the Rat Man spoke of a pot of rats—in the plural—being turned over onto the buttocks of an individual who then bored their way into the person's anus.[12] Nevertheless, Lacan's observation rings true: that Ernst Langer is the man with the rats because the rat is the embodiment of but one of the objects *a* in the series for the obsessional. The rat plays its role "in the whole economy of the peculiar exchanges, substitutions, and permanent metonymy of which the obsessive's symptomatology is the living example."[13] The rats and the florins are among the myriad of objects symptomatically taken up by the Rat Man.

When working with an obsessive in analysis, it is often easy to feel lost amid the plethora of objects and symptoms. It is in that vein that Lacan's observation about the obsessional fantasy is helpful. First, to stick with the example of the Rat Man, Lacan tells us that the rat symbolizes φ insofar as it can be considered a degraded form of Φ.[14] Lacan emphasizes that "φ is precisely what underlies the equivalence instituted between objects at the erotic level"[15] for the obsessive. This is because the obsessive, wanting to deny his own castration and being averse to owing anything to the Other's desire, depreciates the signs of the Other's desire. The obsessive strikes the phallus in the Other "at the imaginary level in order to heal symbolic castration."[16] Lacan asks his audience to perceive the status of the symbolic phallus in the unconscious as manifested by the obsessive's symptomatology, where the symbolic function emerges in a degraded form. In other words, the rats represent the function of the imaginary phallus with which the obsessional tries to plug up the lack in the Other. In Ernst Langer's case, we might say that the rat functions to plug up both a literal and a figurative hole in the Other.

Lacan says that it is in this context that we can turn our attention to the function of *Verneinung* or negation, since the obsessive's object appears to be out in the open. The function of the imaginary phallus in the obsessional is both blatant and repressed thanks to the fact that he is a subject and is not reducible to the psychologistic or Sartrean observing ego. The subject's relationship to the object *a* is not something straightforward which the subject can recognize through conscious knowledge. As a subject, however much he may consciously be aware of his objects or of his symptoms, it still shares in repression and "is not avowed by the subject without the analyst's help."[17] Since being a subject means "to have one's place in the Other [A], in the locus of speech,"[18] and as, for instance, the obsessive's myriad thought disturbances all speak to his inability to tolerate the origins of his thought coming from anyone other than himself, he defensively fails to recognize himself at the moment when he manifests "himself as the *phi* function in relation to the object."[19]

Aphanisis and the Wall of Desire

In the second section of the chapter "Real Presence," Lacan reminds us of what he called "the wall of language"[20] in his Rome discourse. According to Lacan, both the analyst and the analysand are on the same side of the wall of language, and the analyst must "try to respond to the echo of his speech."[21] This comment in the Rome discourse comes just after Lacan spoke of the importance of manifesting disdain for the product of the obsessive's egoic "working through," as the analyst can often be seduced by the detailed introspections of the obsessive—or even by erudite or political commentary. In this chapter in the eighth seminar, Lacan alludes to the wall of language when he comments that "[n]othing is more difficult than to back the obsessive neurotic up against the wall of his desire."[22] Just as it is necessary in analysis for the obsessive to be brought to aim at something beyond the wall of language, so too is it both difficult and necessary to help the obsessive have a different relationship to desire.

To clarify what is at stake in backing the obsessive up against the wall of his desire, Lacan brings up the term *aphanisis*, or the disappearance of desire. Lacan tells us that when obsessives engage in self-analysis—as they sometimes are wont to do—and attempt to make manifest what they want, what happens instead is *aphanisis*. In order to explain this further, Lacan speaks of the analogous situation of the limited duration of a subject's erection. Lacan points out that the subject is dealing with an obstacle "that is fundamental in his relation to his fantasy. What is at stake for him is the end of the line: erection and then the fall of desire."[23] Descartes perhaps being the paradigmatic obsessive provides us with the mantra of the obsessive in "I am thinking, therefore I am."[24] The obsessive equates thinking with existence, and fears that *aphanisis* will occur should he stop thinking. At the end of the line, as Lacan put it, at the moment of orgasm, there is often a brief pause in thinking, and it is this *aphanisis* that the obsessive fears.

In obsessional neurosis, desire is impossible because the closer he gets to his object, the more keenly he feels the presence of the Other which threatens the obsessive with *aphanisis*. *Aphanisis* is at one and the same time the disappearance of his desire and his disappearance as a subject. In response to the threat of *aphanisis*, the obsessive typically keeps his distance from the object of his desire. He invents ways to render the realization of his object impossible, such as falling for a person who is married or otherwise inaccessible. It is in this vein that Lacan comments "that the obsessive has no greater fear, in the end, than of what he imagines he aspires to: to act freely and to live in the state of nature."[25] Acting freely results in approaching the object of his desire and with *aphanisis*.

The obsessive in fantasy props himself up via the imaginary phallus, imagining, for example, that he will be so irresistible to a woman that she will orgasm as soon as he touches her. As Lacan puts it in the twenty-fifth chapter in the seminar, in fantasy, the obsessional subject imagines himself as his semblable, as *i(a)*, with "the illusion of having one's object in hand."[26] Since what occurs is produced at the lower level of the Graph of Desire, the subject's fantasy is at odds with being capable of grasping himself as desiring.

Along those lines, we see a disparity between the fantasy of the obsessive and any actual sexual relations with a woman, which always involve, literally and figuratively, the fall of the erection and of desire. Underlying the obsessive's experience is a fear of *aphanisis* and a related fear of "deflating related to phallic inflation."[27] The obsessive attempts to deny his symbolic castration, to deny the Φ function of the phallus through exchanging it for the φ function, which invariably involves falsely elevating his phallic status. Lacan provides the analogy of La Fontaine's "fable of the frog that wanted to become as big as an ox. 'The puny ninny,' as you know, 'swelled so much that it burst'."[28]

A Hat That Does More Than Cover a Head

In the third section of the eighteenth chapter, Lacan returns to highlighting the phallic function in terms of "real presence." He calls our attention to its homonymical relation in its usage in the Apostolic and Roman Catholic dogma of the Eucharist. Lacan then quotes from Maurice Bouvet's case vignette of an obsessive: "She imagined to herself that there were male genitalia in the place of the communion wafer."[29] This, Lacan says, is an excellent example of real presence. The communion wafer, as the real presence of the body of Christ, is replaced and degraded by the male genitalia which take on a signifying form. The obsessive thus eliminates this real presence, enabling her own desire to function.

Lacan then gives us a rare glimpse into one of his cases. He says that the example he gives is paradigmatic of the obsessive, and not unusual. He tells us that his obsessive analysand found a partner who was willing to join him in degrading the Other into an other. The obsessive felt guilty about his way of enjoying himself, but his desire outweighed this guilt. The obsessive's fantasy was that he would place a communion wafer in the woman's vagina, so that "the host would wind up serving as a hat atop the subject's penis at the moment of penetration."[30] As with Bouvet's example, the communion wafer functions as the real presence of the Other's desire. Lacan criticizes Bouvet and those who take up such fantasies in the imaginary register, who are concerned with the objectivity of the outside world. Instead, this real presence, Lacan insists, must be situated in the lack in the Other, in the lack in the symbolic. In the fantasy of Lacan's analysand, his desire is able to manifest through debasing the Other by turning the body of Christ into a wafer hat for his penis. What is more, we may recall here that the desire of a subject is shaped in accordance with the law—either for or against. The analysand is turned on by acting against the moral and religious dictates to protect the sanctity of the body of Christ (as materialized in the communion wafer).

Lacan then comments that the symbolic phallus is a real presence which "can only appear in the intervals between what the signifier covers (over)."[31] The obsessive cannot tolerate this lack in the Other very well, and so he symptomatically fills in "everything that can present itself as a gap in the signifying system."[32] Lacan provides the example of the Rat Man's compulsion to count up to forty or fifty between each lightning flash and its accompanying thunderclap. Lacan asks about the reason for this need to fill in the signifying gap and explains that the signifying interval poses a threat to the obsessive that his fantasmatic relation to the Other would be revealed for what it is. This common type of compulsion—not counting, per say, but the experienced need to fill in the signifying gap—is comparable to the function of the phobic object. Both operate to fill in the lack in the Other, "the gap…where real presence threatens."[33]

Reducing the Other to an other is an exhausting process for the obsessive, as the compulsions such as the Rat Man's counting ritual have to be repeated over and over again. The obsessive tries to strike at the symbolic phallus in the Other at the imaginary level in order to attempt to heal his symbolic castration, but this degrades the Other to be a "function of the phallus' imaginary elision."[34] What is more, degrading the Other harms the subject's own desire, since man's desire is the Other's desire. Although Lacan does not speak of transference love in this chapter, we might say that the obsessional who engages in psychoanalysis has a way to climb the wall of his desire through transference love. If to love is to give what one lacks, loving involves admitting that one is lacking. In analysis, this leads to a greater acceptance of the Other's lack.

Notes

1. Jacques Lacan, *Transference: The Seminar of Jacques Lacan, Book VIII* (1960), trans. B. Fink (Malden, MA: Polity Press, 2015), p. 237.
2. Ibid., p. 243.
3. Ibid., p. 248.
4. Ibid., p. 249. In eighteenth century English writing (as well as German and Danish writing, for example), it was common to capitalize all proper nouns.
5. Jacques Lacan, *Transference: The Seminar of Jacques Lacan, Book VIII* (1960), trans. B. (Malden, MA: Polity Press, 2015), pp. 249–250.
6. Mary Klages, http://www.Colorado.EDU/English/ENGL2012Klages/1997lacan.html.
7. Jacques Lacan, *Transference: The Seminar of Jacques Lacan, Book VIII* (1960), trans. B. Fink (Malden, MA: Polity Press, 2015), p. 260.
8. Ibid., p. 261.
9. Ibid., p. 246.
10. Sigmund Freud, Notes Upon a Case of Obsessional Neurosis, In *The Standard Edition of the Complete Psychological Works of Sigmund Freud, vol. X* (1909), trans. J. Strachey (London: Hogarth Press, 1955), p. 166.
11. Jacques Lacan, *Transference: The Seminar of Jacques Lacan, Book VIII* (1960), trans. B. Fink (Malden, MA: Polity Press, 2015), p. 252.
12. Sigmund Freud, Notes Upon a Case of Obsessional Neurosis, In *The Standard Edition of the Complete Psychological Works of Sigmund Freud, vol. X* (1909), trans. J. Strachey (London: Hogarth Press, 1955), p. 165.
13. Jacques Lacan, *Transference: The Seminar of Jacques Lacan, Book VIII* (1960), trans. B. Fink (Malden, MA: Polity Press, 2015), pp. 252–253.
14. Ibid., p. 253.
15. Ibid., p. 252.
16. Ibid., p. 247.
17. Ibid., p. 254.
18. Ibid.
19. Ibid.
20. Jacques Lacan, 'The Function and Field of Speech and Language in Psychoanalysis' (1955), In *Écrits: The First Complete Edition in English* (2006), trans. B. Fink (New York and London: W. W. Norton, 2006), p. 260.
21. Ibid.

22. Jacques Lacan, *Transference: The Seminar of Jacques Lacan, Book VIII* (1960), trans. B. Fink (Malden, MA: Polity Press, 2015), p. 254.
23. Ibid., p. 255.
24. Ibid., p. 361.
25. Ibid., p. 256.
26. Ibid., p. 362.
27. Ibid., p. 256.
28. Ibid.
29. Ibid., p. 258.
30. Ibid.
31. Ibid., p. 259.
32. Ibid.
33. Ibid.
34. Ibid., p. 247.

References

Freud, Sigmund. 1955. Notes Upon a Case of Obsessional Neurosis (1909). In *The Standard Edition of the Complete Psychological Works of Sigmund Freud, vol. X*, translated by J. Strachey, 24 vols. London: Hogarth Press.

Lacan, J. 1955. The Function and Field of Speech and Language in Psychoanalysis. In *Écrits: The First Complete Edition in English* (2006), translated by Bruce Fink. New York and London: W. W. Norton.

———. 1960–1961. *Transference: The Seminar of Jacques Lacan, Book VIII.* Translated by Fink. Malden, MA: Polity Press.

18

The Claudel Sessions: Commentary on Sessions XIX–XXII

Ed Pluth

At the beginning of psychoanalytic thought was the father.[1]

In this group of sessions, Lacan discusses three plays by Paul Claudel (1868–1955) collectively known as the Coûfontaine trilogy, written between 1911 and 1920. It was not uncharacteristic of Lacan to discuss theater in his seminar—he had discussed *Hamlet* in Seminar VI and *Antigone* in Seminar VII. But there are two important differences in this case: here he is dealing with three contemporary works, and while Claudel may have been well known to Lacan's audience at the time, he is certainly less well known to us now, compared to Sophocles and Shakespeare. The relative obscurity of these plays and their author is an issue when trying to understand and assess Lacan's commentary on them: and it is even possible to wonder how well known the trilogy was to the seminar participants, given the amount of time Lacan spends on plot summaries.

E. Pluth (✉)
California State University, Chico, Chico, CA, USA
e-mail: EPluth@csuchico.edu

G. Basu Thakur and J. Dickstein (eds.), *Reading Lacan's Seminar VIII*,
The Palgrave Lacan Series, https://doi.org/10.1007/978-3-030-32742-2_18

While it may not be the case that Paul Claudel is an entirely forgotten figure in the Anglophone world, it is questionable how familiar his work ever was to it. He did appear on the cover of TIME magazine in March 1927, but this was on the occasion of being named France's ambassador to the United States.[2] And while the Anglosphere did have its share of conservative Catholic intellectuals in the early twentieth century, there was likely something too Gallic about Claudel's version of Catholicism for it to have had much appeal.[3] His older sister, the sculptor Camille Claudel, is perhaps currently better known than he is, thanks to the internationally successful 1988 film about her starring Isabel Adjani and Gerard Depardieu.

With some caveats, the plays in the trilogy can be considered tragedies. Generally speaking, Lacan discussed tragedies in his seminar in order to focus on some aspect of desire that was related to that year's seminar topic. In *Hamlet*, his focus was the role of the mother's desire as a formative as well as inhibitory factor in the development of the subject's desire. In *Antigone*, the main point was about the ethical appeal and beauty of a figure who persists with her desire, let the world be damned. The role of the Other's desire, and the notion of persisting with desire, are both present in Lacan's discussion of Claudel. What is added to the discussion of desire in these sessions that is relatively novel is a focus on the status of the father, and the use of a multigenerational story to outline a psychoanalytic theory of subject formation (a theory that in my opinion is rather incomplete here, and does not come together fully until Seminar XI).

But how does Lacan's discussion of Claudel relate to the overall topic of the seminar: transference? Lacan makes a distinction early in these sessions that gives us some clues. He tells us that there have been historically two main approaches to desire, one that he calls either philosophical or "scientific" (in the sense of the word that "has been proposed since Socrates' time," he tells us) and the other, tragic.[4] In other words, there is desire as it is portrayed in philosophical, scholarly, and moral treatises, and then there is desire as it is portrayed in tragedy. There is an echo of the old difference between the God of the philosophers and the God of Abraham, Isaac, and Jacob here. The two contrasts line up rather neatly and are relevant, Lacan thinks, to the then-current situation of psychoanalysis. He accuses many of his psychoanalytic colleagues of taking the wrong approach to desire, such that the split he is referring to in antiquity is being repeated in his own day: Analysts should not be taking the philosophical, scientific, and moral route when thinking of desire. They should instead learn from what is shown of desire in tragedy, and they can learn something from tragedy about the position they should be adopting in the clinic as well. For example, we know post-Freud that "desire does not show itself openly."[5] And in addition desire is not "where the secular experience of philosophy…has designated it in order to contain it and, in a certain sense, rule out its right to govern us."[6] It could of course be argued that tragic figures are governed by desire: Analysts are too, or they should be, especially insofar as they are put in this position by an analysand's demands. This is the connection to the topic of transference.

One of the main tracks of these four sessions on Claudel deals clearly and in some depth with the Coûfontaine trilogy itself, focusing on the plot and the themes peculiar to the plays—tragedy, fate, faith, myth, and what in Lacan's eyes is a contemporary yet parodic version of Oedipus, as we shall see. Another track hews closer to the main topic of the eighth seminar, which is transference. On this track, throughout these sessions, Lacan brings up now and again some of his typical critiques of other analysts on such topics as countertransference, desire, and fantasy. I will not have much to say about this track here, since his comments along these lines do not seem unique to his oeuvre, whereas his discussion of Claudel in these sessions is. The two tracks may seem quite far apart, but they do intersect, at least in principle. I say this because the final play of Claudel's trilogy is dominated by a character, Pensée de Coûfontaine, who Lacan reads as desire or desirousness incarnated. Lacan describes her as an "indisputably seductive figure" presented to the audience "as the object of desire, strictly speaking."[7] The phrase "object of desire" is ambiguous; the "strictly speaking" suggests we should understand it to mean not only that she is someone who is herself very desirable, but that she is *desire objectified* or better *personified.* This is a topic we find in Lacan's reading of Socrates earlier in the seminar, and it aligns with his view of what the analyst's position in transference needs to be. So in this respect, spending four sessions on Paul Claudel is not entirely off-topic in a seminar on transference, since the discussion fits into his effort to present transference, as he puts it in the first line of the seminar, "in its subjective disparity, its supposed situation, and its excursions into the realm of technique."[8] Evidently, Lacan thinks Pensée and Claudel's trilogy generally has something to say about all this.

The conditions of Claudel's characters are unique compared to other tragic figures, both ancient and modern. Lacan evokes Nietzsche when he tells us that he wants to think of their condition as one that is linked to the impasses of subjectivity after the death of God. As Lacan sees it, one of the important changes from antiquity to modernity entails a shift in the status of Fate, a shift that is itself due to Christianity, whose central doctrine is the word become incarnate.[9] The following passage provides a good set up for Lacan's commentary on the plays, even though it appears late in the third session:

> To us, the Word is not simply the law into which we insert ourselves in order that each of us bear responsibility for the debt that constitutes our fate. It opens up for us the possibility or temptation on the basis of which it is possible for us to curse ourselves, not only as a particular destiny or life, but as the very pathway by which the Word commits us, and as an encounter with the truth, as the moment of truth. We are no longer solely subject to feeling guilty owing to symbolic debt. We can, in the most proximate sense that the word indicates, be reproached for bearing responsibility for the debt. In short, it is the very debt that gave us our place that can be stolen from us; and it is in this context that we can feel totally alienated from ourselves. Antiquity's *Até* no doubt made us guilty of this debt, but to give it up – as we can now – makes us responsible for a still greater misfortune owing to the fact that fate is no longer anything [for us].[10]

This passage can be taken as Lacan's thesis statement on Claudel. Compared to the figures of ancient tragedy, the contemporary tragic hero or heroine has a different relationship to Fate, and in this passage at least it sounds as if Lacan is saying this is linked to a contingent historical event: Christianity. For Lacan's purposes what is important about Christianity is what is thematized and thought in the incarnation and crucifixion: The word become flesh, which suffers. As we shall see, this is exemplified well by the main character in the first play of the trilogy, Sygne de Coûfontaine.

The word being incarnated entails a change in our relationship to language, one that has everything to do with the word becoming mundane, descending into our changing, flawed, sublunary sphere (to put in in appropriately Platonic terms). It is as if the ability of language to bind, to act as an authority, is in fact undermined and called into question by the doctrine of incarnation, or, in other words, by the fact that language has in some sense descended from the "ultra-world" down into the muck of empirical existence. Interestingly, and not uniquely, Lacan seems to be equating incarnation with the death of God. "In short, what we learn every day from psychoanalytic practice is that the guilt we still have, the guilt that is palpable to us in our work with neurotics, is the exact price we have to pay for the fact that the God of fate is dead. The fact that this God is dead is at the heart of what Claudel presents us."[11]

Claudel himself was a very religious man who struggled much of his life with whether he should follow a clerical or secular vocation. It is safe to say that most of his works have faith as their theme: especially the difficulties of maintaining faith in the contemporary, materialistic, hedonistic world. To the atheist writing these lines, what makes Claudel's work somewhat interesting rather than annoying is its sort of jaded sentimentalism. He presents us with characters who are attached to a lost world, to lost authority, to lost traditions…and they know it quite well. Yet unlike run-of-the-mill conservatives and reactionaries, Claudel (and his characters) also seem to possess an awareness that even if the world they were attached to were to return—if their desires were to be realized—it could only be as a parody of what used to be. In the trilogy, we in fact see the French monarchy and the Papacy restored after the revolution, as the Franco-Prussian war looms (the period covered in the plays is from the 1810s to about 1870), but it is also clear that the world has moved on from such agencies, and their continued presence is nothing short of farcical.

This is the tragic situation Claudel's main characters are in. How to continue with, or live with, their desire under such hostile circumstances? How to persist with a desire in the keen awareness of its futility? Put this way, it is not difficult to see how their situation echoes the libidinal situation Freud presents us with in his discussions of the Oedipus complex and its resolution in the castration complex, in which every subsequent libidinal object is also always "not it."

This gives us another way to get at the relevance of some of Lacan's points in the long "thesis statement" passage cited above. There seem to be two main factors in what I'll call the Claudelian condition. While Claudel does not say anything about the death of God explicitly, he has much to say about the changed status of authority, tradition, and the father—the last play in the trilogy is even called *The Humiliation of the Father* and the first, *The Hostage*, could be referring to Pope Pius VI, who was in fact imprisoned by Napoleon (but in Claudel's play, in a bit of alternative history, is set free by George de Coûfontaine). There is a none too subtle scene at the end of the second play, *Crusts*, in which a giant bronze crucifix, a family heirloom featured prominently onstage, is in the process of being assessed and sold off for scrap by the new head of the family, the rather politically/historically ridiculously named Louis-Napoleon Turelure de Coûfontaine.

So this is one condition under which Claudel's characters function: Living in a materialistic, post-feudal world in which the nature of authority is in flux. The other is the one I mentioned above, concerning their relationship to their unsatisfiable, impossible desire. Each of the main characters in the three plays deals with this situation in slightly different ways, and this is perhaps why Lacan is inclined to read the trilogy as a series of structural variations on a basic theme, with the character Pensée in the last play presenting us with a resolution to the impasse.[12] In a crucial remark, Lacan tells us that what he sees in Claudel's plays is

> an exemplary structural decomposition of the function of what, in Freud's myth, takes the form of a type of hollow or vacuum toward which things are drawn, a vertiginous point of the libido that is represented by the mother.[13]

In the Freudian Oedipus, it is fair to say that attachment to the mother is the center of gravity. Everything rotates around it: reactions to the father, identifications with the father, reactions to castration, interpretations of sexual difference…truly, the whole Freudian psychoanalytic universe can be said to gravitate around this point. But what Lacan sees in Claudel's trilogy is what he refers to as a "structural decomposition" of this "vertiginous point of the libido" that is the mother-function in Oedipus. And this correlates to what he was seeing in the psychoanalytic clinic in his own day.

What is a structural decomposition? The French *décomposition* could be translated as "analysis," and "deconstruction" is even a suggested, viable translation according to one source. It might be a stretch to say that Lacan thinks Claudel was already deconstructing Oedipus…but perhaps we must say that something like that is going on! In the Freudian Oedipus, the father is the dead father, while the Claudelian/Lacanian father is a living father, and for this reason all the more problematic, as the father's presence calls into question the legitimacy of the law—with a host of consequences. This is a theme that I will return to in a moment.

The trilogy follows the Coûfontaine family through three generations. About twenty years separate each play, and each play, despite changing venues and characters, repeats a basic template. The main character is required to give up a libidinal object, and is given in return one that is either less desired, or somehow problematic, or actively detested: in any event the replacement object is a mere shadow, and even a parody, of the original, and this is keenly felt. I will get into a bit more detail about each play in a moment, but for now a brief synopsis. In the first play, Sygne de Coûfontaine gives up on the true object of her desire, her cousin George (but also in fact what her cousin represents—her family history, their estates, their traditional status…) and receives in return the enemy and destroyer of her family, Toussaint Turelure. They have a child, the aforementioned Louis-Napoleon Turelure-Coûfontaine: After his birth, she refuses to see him. The second play focuses on him and his relation to his father, Toussaint. Louis loses the object of his desire, the Polish revolutionary Lumîr, and after his father's death (by his hand, but it's complicated as we'll see, making him into a sort of parodic Oedipus) he receives not his mother, of course, but the object of his father's desire (his father Turelure's mistress Sichel). The third play centers on their child, Pensée. The object of her desire, Orian, refuses to marry her (he would rather serve the Pope as a soldier) and tries to get her to marry his brother Orso instead. But Pensée manages to have a child out of wedlock with Orian anyway, and after he dies she does end up marrying his brother Orso while, at the same time, there is a suggestion that the child she is carrying has just been ensouled by her dead lover (whose decapitated head has just been brought to her in a basket of flowers by Orso).[14]

The different subject positions, and actions, of each character with respect to the same basic situation is noteworthy; we will briefly track in what follows how each reacts, or is not able to, and why. This is a major part of what Lacan's reading of what the plays are trying to do. In fact, he wants to read these plays structurally, as a series of permutations of basic attitudes and positions within the same basic template.

Let's return to what I take to be Lacan's overall thesis on the plays: that they show us how "man becomes a hostage of the Word because he tells himself…that God is dead."[15] The first play is of course called *The Hostage*, and in it we see the direct impact of the signifier upon an individual illustrated in the form of a facial tic developed late in the play by the main character Sygne. She is compulsively shaking her head as if to say "no." (The word become flesh indeed!) This symptom is developed after she breaks her vows to her cousin George and prepares to marry her family's mortal enemy, the post-revolutionary, crass, and very materialistic Toussaint Turelure. This was not exactly a free choice. She was presented with an intolerable option: either marry her mortal enemy Turelure or see both her cousin and the recently liberated Pope turned over to the authorities. Of course, by choosing to marry Turelure she does not really save her cousin and the Pope either, as their return to power is a façade. So we should see in this a precursor to the "alienating vel" Lacan discusses a few years later in his eleventh seminar, which he makes into a central moment in the development of neurosis; a different way of thinking about what Freud called the choice for neurosis (*Neuronenwahl*). This is a forced choice, one in which there is really only one option, entailing the loss of something essential. In the scene in which she wrestles with her dilemma, Sygne concludes by repeating "not my will but Thine, not my will but Thine"—not a bad way to get across the fact that she does not want what she is choosing.[16]

Her subjective reaction to this forced choice is one that Lacan describes as a *Versagung*, which he wants to understand in terms of refusal rather than frustration. (Frustration is how the German term is translated in the English Standard Edition of Freud.) Lacan claims that "at the origin of every neurosis there is…something that is much closer to a refusal than to frustration" and that there is not "a sequential order from normal, to the possibility of *Versagung*, and then on to neurosis": Instead, there is "a

Versagung right at the origin, beyond which a path may lead to neurosis or to normality, neither being worth more than the other in relation to what is, at the outset, the possibility of *Versagung*."[17] So on Lacan's reading, Sygne's position presents us with a condition sine qua non of neurosis, and a precondition of any subject formation whatsoever. And yet, subjectively, Sygne is at an impasse.

What Sygne has already done, yet is refusing at the same time, involves the loss of her essential libidinal object. In a sense this is personified by her cousin George, as I pointed out above, but the deeper symbolic resonances of her engagement to him, made in the first scene of the play, should not be overlooked. George represents everything about her family name, tradition, and status that she had been working to restore for years, after their land had been parceled and sold off during the revolution, and their pre-revolutionary world essentially destroyed. Her future husband Turelure played a key role in that dismantling.

Her loss is clear. But what should not be overlooked is that by marrying Turelure she is assured that her family name will be restored, as well as her estates, and the authority of the Church and Crown in France... and indeed, after her wedding it is all returned, but is obviously not what it used to be. These are the circumstances of her *Versagung*: again, not necessarily her frustration (which would be understandable, of course) but her refusal. A refusal that, and this is important, is not fully articulated, but instead emerges as a symptom, a tic. A compulsive shaking of her head, 'no'. Lacan describes this as a "twitching on the part of life" that takes Sygne beyond the limit of beauty that he had discussed in his reading of *Antigone* in the previous year's seminar.[18]

Sygne is also described as going beyond the limit of what he had called in Seminar VII the second death. This is because Sygne—unlike Antigone—is being asked to "renounce her very being – the pact that has kept her forever faithful to her own family."[19] (This is of course what Antigone adhered to.) Agreeing to marry Turelure is the ultimate betrayal of everything her family stood for (even if it did save her family name and the Pope's life). The notion of a second death, which was developed from a reading of Sade, is typically taken to mean bringing the cycle of generation and destruction to an end. If the first death is one in which the cycle of life is perpetuated, or, if one can still persist symbolically even after one's "first" death insofar as one's names and deeds live on, the Sadean second death was about in some way leaving no lasting trace behind whatsoever, bringing an end to continuity in and of the symbolic itself. Antigone does not cross that line, hence she is described as "between two deaths." For Antigone's death is one in which her family, and her name, lives on. Sygne's choice, however, can be taken to entail the death of the entire symbolic universe in which the name Coûfontaine meant something. She goes past the limit of the second death in this respect.[20]

In his seventh seminar, Lacan explained that a figure who is suspended between the first and second death radiates with beauty. Given Sygne's different status, we see not beauty but an ugliness, a distortion of the flesh, what Lacan calls a "twitching" or grimace on the part of life itself.[21]

What does it mean to see in Sygne's *Versagung* a precondition to neurosis and subject formation? One can think of this as a moment at which one is marked by the symbolic, but is protesting and resisting that marking at the same time, remaining libidinally attached to what was supposed to have been renounced. Sygne presents us with the precondition for neurosis (but perhaps not the thing itself) by her refusal to accept signifiers as a replacement for what she has lost—a refusal that assumes that she has in fact already been indelibly marked by the symbolic. The signifiers she refuses have done their work on her, so to speak. It's too late.

But what Lacan refers to as Sygne's "radical stance" is not the end of the story. He tells us that the remaining plays in the trilogy are going to show us the following: "As it develops through the three stages of the tragedy, the drama is that of knowing how – based on this radical stance – a desire can be reborn and of knowing what desire is."[22] He's thinking of Sygne's granddaughter Pensée here while also suggesting that in some sense Sygne's desire is blocked.

But before getting there we have to consider Louis now, the subject of the second play, *Crusts*, who is something like a very Oedipal (but also not) vanishing mediator. To get at this, we must spend some more time on the role the decline of the father plays in Lacan's treatment of Claudel.

Louis's father is of course the vile Toussaint Turelure, and the relationship between father and son in *Crusts* is quite awful. Turelure has an open contempt for his son. (Louis's mother, Sygne, refused to see him after his birth. She died shortly thereafter, throwing herself before a bullet meant for Turelure, and shot by her beloved cousin George…) *Crusts* takes place about twenty years after the events of *The Hostage*. Louis is in love with Lumîr, a revolutionary Polish nationalist who is seeking money for her political cause. She targets Louis's father, who has recently been given 10,000 francs for the sale of the Coûfontaine estates (a paltry sum, given their true scale and worth). He won't give the money so Lumîr hatches a plot to take the money from him violently. She coaxes Louis into murdering his father. A bit reluctant to be a parricide, Lumîr tells Louis that she'll give him two guns, only one of which will be loaded. Given his father's excitability and ill health, she banks on the idea that the fright of the moment and the sound of the gunshot will probably be enough to cause his death. She's right: Turelure does die after Louis fires what he thinks is a blank. (Lumîr had actually loaded both guns though. The one Louis shot just happened to misfire.) Lumîr makes off with the money, and Louis ends up marrying Turelure's mistress Sichel. In this manner, Louis becomes a de facto parricide and is rewarded with the loss of the money from the sale of his family estate, and a partner he doesn't really want.

Lacan's discussion of *Crusts* is heavy on plot details and other marginalia. But his substantive remarks gravitate around the portrayal of the father in it, and how the status of the father has changed from Freud to his own day. I will focus on only a couple of pages from the session devoted to *Crusts* in which Lacan is reflecting on the role of the father, and even claims that "at the beginning of psychoanalytic thought was the father, and in a form whose scandalous traits comedy is well designed to help us bring out."[23] Lacan is probably thinking here of the father of the primal horde in Freud's *Totem and Taboo*, a figure he would later designate as *père jouissance*. In fact, like this figure, Toussaint Turelure blocks his son's possible satisfaction at every opportunity. The story of the primal horde is a "drama" that psychoanalysis "had to articulate…at the origin of the law" but when a figure like the father of the primal horde is presented on the contemporary stage we can see "not simply its criminal character but the possibility of its caricatural or even abject decomposition."[24] With this remark, Lacan is getting to his main point, to what it seems to me really interests him about what Claudel is showing us. The very shape of desire has changed, not just from antiquity to modernity, but from Freud to the present. And perhaps surprisingly, Lacan gets at this point by talking about the role mothers play in castration.

While it may be true that in the beginning was the father, Lacan observes that "we have begun to see the mother ever more at the root of this Other that we evoke in our patients"—the mother becoming more of a factor in psychoanalytic practice than the classical prohibitive and law-giving father of Oedipus or even the perverse hyper-enjoying father of the primal horde.[25] Lacan notes that "the mother is all the more castrating insofar as she is not busy castrating the father."[26] Presumably, when analysts of his day would focus on the figure of the castrating mother they were focusing on the mother/child relationship (and thus probably the pre-Oedipal), neglecting the position of the father altogether, or else making even the father prone to the mother's castrating agency. Lacan's view is that "mothers who are busy castrating the father exist, but we would not bother talking about the castrating mother if there was no father, whether we see him or not."[27] So in the beginning was the father, and even in the era of the castrating mother, there is still something of the father…

From the prohibitive father to the castrating mother, Lacan moves on to the effect this shift has had on the analyst's status. One consequence is that analysts can no longer intervene the way Freud did—Lacan says that Freud's behavior as an analyst was such that he had "adopted the position of the father." This is no longer viable, and instead given the shift to the mother analysts of Lacan's time were more inclined to say to their patients "'you take me to be a bad mother.'"[28] Yet Lacan says this "is not the position we must adopt either"—the position of a mother, whether good or bad.[29]

I take this to be a central issue for Lacan in these sessions. Perhaps the very selection of the topic of transference for this year is due to reflections along these lines. There was a crisis about the status of the analyst in psychoanalysis, and it had everything to do with the cultural shift Lacan is talking about here, a shift in the father's status—such that Freud's position in analysis becomes a position the analyst could no longer adopt—and what it all means for desire. All of this, Lacan alleges, is reflected in Claudel's trilogy. The shift in question entails that the "very instrument of desire: the phallus" no longer occupies the same "symbolic place" that it used to.[30] This is what Lacan is driving at with his remarks about the father and the death of God, then, and why he is interested in the scenarios the plays are presenting. How is it possible to stake out a place for desire in post-Oedipal circumstances?

Returning to my hypothesis that each play presents us with a similar template, with different subject positions being taken (Sygne's being one of refusal), in Lacan's reading it is not Louis but Lumîr, the Polish revolutionary who is the figure in *Crusts* who follows her desire. In her case, it was a desire for death. With her pursuit of her desire for a cause that will kill her, she "rehabilitates our excluded son, our unwanted child, our drifting partial object [Louis]. She reinstates him, recreating with him the father who has been defeated. The result of the operation is thus to give him the father's woman."[31] This is what Lacan calls a "structural decomposition" of the mother-function in the Oedipus complex. If Lacan thinks the plays are going in the direction of a character who is a reconstitution of desire, we are not there yet with Louis. Louis's status as a pure, disdained object is transitory phase.

It is in the third generation that we see that all the other plays are "artificial decompositions"—"they are the antecedents of the only one that is of concern" (296). According to Lacan, the main character of the last play, Pensée, illustrates how "between the mark of the signifier and [the] passion for the partial object…desire is composed."[32] Sygne being where we obviously see the mark of the signifier, and her son Louis's story being "the passion for the partial object" in that he is, as Lacan puts it just a little bit earlier, "an object that is totally rejected, an object that is not desired, an object inasmuch as it is undesired."[33] Between the mark of a signifier and a rejected object, how is desire composed? Pensée shows us, insofar as she is according to Lacan something like desire or desiring or desirousness incarnate… Not a desired object but desire or desiring *as* an object.

The Humiliation of the Father opens in Rome, with Pensée, blind, but able to walk around and navigate the world as if she isn't. She is the child of Louis and Sîchel, thus the granddaughter of Sygne and Turelure. She falls in love with Orian, a soldier for the pope. Orian does not want to get married and tries to convince Pensée to marry his brother Orso instead. He leaves for battle against the Prussians, but not before Pensée and Orian have a tryst. Pregnant, Orso returns posing as Orian, but Pensée figures it out after a while. He tells her of Orian's death in battle, and while he was unable to bury his brother he did manage to sever his head and bring it back with him.

Although, like her grandmother, Pensée capitulates to an intolerable situation, it is not without her persisting in her desire for Orian, and in some sense succeeding in realizing it—they do have a child together, and in a strange concluding scene the child becomes something like the very location where their souls merge.

Conclusion

It seems to me that Lacan was trying to accomplish two things in his reading of Claudel. One of his goals was in line with what he had been doing and saying about tragedy in the previous years—tragedy can be used to think about desire. These points are rather clear and relatively unproblematic. One can see where Lacan is going, why Pensée may be read as sort of a concluding, resolving figure relative to the impasses Sygne and Louis represent. The points about the death of God and the decline of the father are clearly important to Lacan's reading, but less fleshed out. It seems to me that the latter especially becomes an increasingly more important and developed point as Lacan's work continues.

Notes

1. Jacques Lacan, *Transference: The Seminar of Jacques Lacan, Book VIII*, ed. Jacques-Alain Miller, trans. Bruce Fink (Cambridge: Polity, 2015), p. 293.
2. Claudel had an active and successful diplomatic career, with posts in China, Japan, Brazil, and Belgium.
3. Claudel's French biographer even refers to G. K. Chesterton as the *English* Claudel!
4. Lacan (2015, p. 269).
5. Ibid., p. 266.
6. Ibid.
7. Ibid., p. 303.
8. Ibid., p. 3.

9. Ibid., pp. 301–302.
10. Ibid., p. 302.
11. Ibid.
12. In my opinion, there is a more relevant connection between Antigone and Pensée than between Antigone and Sygne, as we shall see. Although it is true that in some respect, all of Claudel's main characters meet the Antigonian ethical requirement to persist with their desires. But what we see in Lacan's discussion is not a focus on the beauty of such figures, but on the difficulty of attaining that status, as if to acknowledge that we cannot be Antigone anymore; the world that made her possible is gone.
13. Ibid., p. 324.
14. There is an error on this point in Lacan's seminar. Lacan says that Orian's *heart* was eviscerated, and that the flowers were planted in the soil in which his heart was buried: "With the flaps of her shawl, Pensée wraps herself, as it were, around the basket of flowers that the brother, Orso, had sent, flowers that grew in soil that – as we learn from the dialogue, constituting a macabre note – contains the eviscerated heart of her lover, Orian" (Lacan 2015, p. 310). But there is nothing of this in the play! And in fact, the situation is even more macabre than Lacan tells us. Orian was shot in the heart by the Prussians in battle. Claudel has Orso explain in troubling detail why he had to hastily decapitate his brother's corpse and bring his head back to Pensée, covered up by a bouquet of flowers (Paul Claudel, *Three Plays*, trans. John Heard [Boston: John W. Luce Company, 1945], p. 220).
15. Ibid., p. 303.
16. Paul Claudel, *Three Plays*, trans. John Heard (Boston: John W. Luce Company, 1945), p. 62.
17. Lacan (2015), p. 322
18. Ibid., p. 277.
19. Ibid., p. 275.
20. It is surely worth noting that the phrase "second death" actually appears in the play *The Hostage*! It is uttered by the family priest and confessor Badilon and refers to a death he says Christ endures every day since his crucifixion; a death he suffers due to the "mortal sin of those He loves" (Claudel 1945, p. 109).
21. Lacan (2015), p. 277.
22. Ibid., p. 303.
23. Ibid., p. 293.
24. Ibid.

25. Ibid., p. 294.
26. Ibid.
27. Ibid.
28. Ibid.
29. Ibid.
30. Ibid., p. 295.
31. Ibid., p. 324.
32. Ibid., p. 296.
33. Ibid.

References

Claudel, Paul. 1945. *Three Plays.* Trans. John Heard. Boston: John W. Luce Company.

Lacan, Jacques. 2015. *Transference: The Seminar of Jacques Lacan, Book VIII.* Edited by Jacques-Alain Miller and Translated by Bruce Fink. Cambridge: Polity.

19

Paradoxes of Transference and the Place of the Psychoanalyst: Commentary on Session XXIII

Rodrigo Gonsalves

An Introduction to Lacan's Seminars

Before reading any of Lacan's lessons from the Seminars, it seems relevant to take into consideration a few elements. First of all, to realize the fact that these are Seminars. And, although risking stating the obvious or being repetitive, to acknowledge the Seminars means also to understand that it consists of the transcriptions of the lessons taught by the French psychoanalyst over the course of around twenty-seven years (1953–1980). And it goes without saying that, the Seminars are different from the *Écrits* or the *Other Écrits* (1966), which were texts published by Lacan himself and established already in a written form. Lacan's Seminars are a particular moment where he was establishing his teachings, testing and developing his metapsychological pursuits and inventiveness concerning his return to Freud. In this sense, to accompany Lacan on a

R. Gonsalves (✉)
European Graduate School, Saas Fee, Switzerland
e-mail: rodrigo.gonsalves@egs.edu

Universidade de São Paulo, São Paulo, Brazil

G. Basu Thakur and J. Dickstein (eds.), *Reading Lacan's Seminar VIII*,
The Palgrave Lacan Series, https://doi.org/10.1007/978-3-030-32742-2_19

lesson from his Seminars means that, on the one hand, there will always be a certain excitement of following the provisional and constructive movement of a metapsychological pursuit occurring on these pages, but on the other hand, this very movement comes with some hermetic passages and a great amount of associations which are left open as threads to be further pursued. This does not presuppose a hierarchy regarding Lacan's developments, but it sure allows room for possible considerations on some "rough edges" present on a few of his lessons.

The psychoanalytic field, in its fairly recent history, has a significant amount of theoretical troubles, which could never be fully covered or even properly summarized in here. And concerning some of the points brought up earlier, it makes sense to consider the discussion about the locus of psychoanalysis and its relationships to some other fields of knowledge—especially, because these are major concerns and objects of the psychoanalytic development for Lacan. So, the way that Lacan approaches psychoanalytic texts along with other fields like Literature, Philosophy, Mathematics, as well as others, did inspire further discussions and consequences to the field. But to be fair, it is crucial to remember that this is not an odd theoretical attempt or a new inventive step—this is simply a Freudian heritage which follows the field since its very beginning. The difference is that Lacan gives dignity to it by debating it, instead of simply indulging previous definitions in a dogmatic fashion. So, perhaps, a good approach to Lacan lies parallelly to the way he approached Freud—debating it. After this brief and yet, necessary detour, it becomes clear that some lessons of the Seminars are a way of putting under the microscope, some specific theoretical constructs of the field, but also, a way to put further to the test some metapsychological investigations of Lacan's praxis. Such movement, with all its twists and turns, composes the way in which the French psychoanalyst aims at constructing and establishing his own theoretical developments to the field.

After this advertently rushed introduction concerning the Seminars, it becomes evident that a multiplicity of readings and understandings will always derive from it. So, this one is an investigative appreciation of Jacques Lacan's psychoanalytic developments, out of the many other possible ones, and highlights some of the main points considered by the thinker in his eighth Seminar, at the lesson dated May 31, 1961. To succeed at the strategy of covering the most prominent topics pursued by Lacan in this lesson, this text is tactically separated into three different subsets, entitled: (1) *The psychoanalysts and their crowd*; (2) *Paradoxes of transference*; and (3) *The place of the psychoanalyst*. Well, this is not a theoretical separation done by Lacan himself, but an attempt to circumvent subsets from within his main discussion about transference. Or, to put in other words, let's consider transference as a theoretical set and the subsets proposed here allow the consideration of the relationship between some of its elements. So, these subsets will contain some theoretical elements which belong to one another and some others which do not.

The Psychoanalysts and Their Crowd

Lacan's theoretical investigations were certainly clinically driven, but his developments led him straight to a ghostly structural feature of the field, a haunting element which spooks by its absence. A ghostly presence which is always already there, a heritage of the field which was established through Freud's formalizations and his practices: the political, as previously pointed out by Mladen Dolar (2008). Lacan's investigation on the political took many directions, but he did not soften his criticism because he was dealing with Freud, quite the opposite he denounces Freud's lack of political oomph and clarifies the institutional consequences which derive for the field, even until our days, because of it.

In the previous year before this Seminar, Lacan addressed the *Ethics of Psychoanalysis* (1960) which was popularized for being a more "social" interaction of psychoanalysis or a psychoanalytic approach beyond the walls of the private practices of the analysts. This could be considered as his attempt on addressing the crowd (*masse*), the social and organizational elements of society through ethics. But Lacan in this Seminar addresses another crowd, a more specific one, he focuses further on the internal politics of the field and the crown of psychoanalysts. So, Lacan examines this ghostly element of psychoanalysis within the formation of psychoanalysts, an unaddressed organization element which is silently rooted to the field.

Lacan turns his attention to the internal political articulation within the field throughout its history. This is why he insists in this lesson, that a probable reason why Freud was problematizing divergences concerning technical developments in his article *Ich-Analyse und Massen-psychologie* (1921) must have something to do with the fact that the psychoanalytic community was now established. Lacan presents criticism over the institutional agency of psychoanalysis, questioning its occurrence as an effects of the *komintern* like establishment of Freud's inner circle. Ambiguously positing how this heritage was embedded at the organizational level of psychoanalysis or, perhaps, could have even had become a kind of symptomatic institutional repetition for the field. And since Lacan considered this analogy, it is fair to elaborate that he did not call it a *nomenklatura*, but a *komintern* and this makes a difference. While the *nomenklatura* was this highly bureaucratic element of the Soviet organization following more top-down instructions, the *komintern* was this political bridge between local experiments and a global orientation (International). Although interestingly, this inspiring homological trait between Freud and Marx raised by Lacan in this lesson needs to be further investigated in terms of political organization level, which unfortunately is something that we will not be able to pursue here.

Well, the history of the field shows us that Freud's secret committee was composed by his most trusted psychoanalysts: Sàndor Ferenczi, Hanns Sachs, Otto Rank, Karl Abraham, Max Eitingon, and Ernest Jones, that it lasted almost a decade and it was dissolved in 1924 (Gay 1989). Although recognized as a "childish and romantic" (Gay 1989: 230) move by Freud and Jones in an exchange of letters, in a way, this could be interpreted as an attempt to consolidate a certain consistency in the psychoanalytic practice. But in another way, this attempt could easily become politically partisan and questionable—ulterior motifs and capricious determinations could easily infiltrate and reign over this institutional blindspot. Nonetheless, Lacan does not directly criticize this political move as such, what he does is to question Freud's necessity behind it—this is actually what he was aiming at here and how he hunts down this ghost. And why did Freud need this? Because of a romanticized notion of control over psychoanalysis which politically eventually created this ghostly element to the field. There is an agency, a control, over the *how* an analyst should or could operate in order to truly be considered a psychoanalyst as such, and this is what Lacan wants to address and to question: Is this what makes a psychoanalyst? Is it the blessing of the secret group on top of a psychoanalytical organization that determines if a psychoanalyst is formed or not? Lacan sympathizes with Freud's concern with the multiplication of the technique, implying a different quality of transference between Freud's inner circle to the crowd of the psychoanalysts which were started to be created on a industrialized pace by International Psychoanalysis Association (IPA). This is why he acknowledges this difference between Jones and the others who dealt with the secret group as a *kominterm*, differently than the more *nomenklatura* like institutionalized level of organization held by IPA.

The point he is making in this lesson about Jones (Ernest Jones) and the impacts of the inner circle concerns the formation of psychoanalysts. And diving into the *Écrits*, there are around 37 different passages when Lacan mentions Jones and it is safe to defend that the text he is alluding to here is *The Situation of Psychoanalysis and the Training of Psychoanalysts in 1956* (1956: 459). The ghostly element mentioned earlier concerns the non-addressed political influence of agency and control of the field which did spook posterior psychoanalysts formation; Lacan explains that it has something to do with the "voice of a dead man," metaphorically this dead man is Freud. Recall Edgar Allan Poe's tale of "The Facts in the Case of M. Valdemar," where a man on his deathbed is hypnotized (mesmerized in the original) by doctors and brought into an undead zombified state. The story portrays that the cadaveric body of the man was kept intact, while he was under the hypnotic control of the doctor. And only his tongue, his voice, kept on functioning—for a few months—providing this uncanny condition, until the doctor finally allowed him to die, waking him up and ending the experiment. Lacan finishes this text defending that "the association created by Freud metaphorically lives on in its collective being, but here it is a voice that sustains it, the voice of dead man 'and' (i)n such a case, however, the operation of waking that association up-using the Master's words in a return to life of his Speech—can be confused with the care involved in providing a decent burial" (1956: 406). The uncanny and psychoanalysis have a rather complex and formidable relationship,[1] but we will skip this discussion here, since the point of the ghostly voice of a zombified Freud seems to have already provided the point needed to present Lacan's criticism concerning the association and the formation of psychoanalysts. Needless to say, Lacan is concerned with the institutional power of dictating what a psychoanalyst is, completely devoted to the standpoint of imaginary formations and moralism.

Paradoxes of Transference

Lacan throughout this entire lesson sustains a dialogue with Ludwig Jekels and Edmund Bergler, because of the article *Transference and Love* (1931), praising the authors for standing out from the mass-produced analysts, mostly for their capacity for defending a certain intellectual freedom something which Lacan could relate to and was keen on. In this article, the authors articulate the "miraculous" character of object of cathexis and its conflict with the Freudian notion of narcissism considering a much viable line of questioning—considering the economical point of view of the Freudian psychoanalysis—why would anyone "invest" toward something outside of herself or himself, instead of neurastenically satisfying himself or herself narcissistically? Lacan follows their discussion on this lesson, also praising the authors for digging into the Freudian render on Eros and Thanatos, as major forces at stake in the organization between ego, superego, and Ideal Ego. Remarking an interesting position on love that he "takes" from the authors—"Just observe what you see, it is not simply that love is often guilty, but that one loves in order to escape guilt" (Lacan 1961: 318)—it is even more interesting to learn, that this is an interpretation from Lacan, which is not *ipsis litteris* (and actually quite far from it) from the original article by the authors. The possible passages that could have inspired Lacan toward this interpretation are the following:

> Is love then a consequence of a feeling of guilt? This opinion may seem peculiar, but we maintain it. We also believe that it is substantiated by the phenomenon of transference. Let us emphasize at this point the decisive characteristic which distinguishes the latter from love. We are sure of the assent of all experienced analysts when we emphasize the following

> symptoms of transference as especially striking and characteristic: 1, the infallibility of its occurrence despite the absence of choice as regards the object, manifesting itself with a complete disregard of age or sex, and disregarding every personal quality or its absence; 2, its impetuosity which, though often veiled, betrays itself in some instances before the patient has met the physician... Is guilt the only difference between transference and love? Psychoanalytically, the difference is that in the case of love, only the ego ideal is projected onto the object, whereas in transference the superego, the ego ideal and the daimon, are projected. Transference is also very different from love in that the object is not only the object of love but perhaps to an even greater extent an object of anxiety. (1931: 337–339)

But, as it becomes clear, Lacan's interpretation validates Lacan's own point on the overall article about love, transference, and the relationship between psychoanalysts and analysands. The French psychoanalyst's point concerning love and transference is rather crucial, as Badiou later on defends, it is actually one of the common borders between philosophy and psychoanalysis,[2] the other one, being mathematics presentified by Lacan's *mathemes*[3] here at this lesson. So, deciding to side with Lacan's interpretation of the article, the technical aspect of transference and its importance within the psychoanalytic apparatus is what is at stake. The relationship between psychoanalysts and analysands through transference is not only the main point of this lesson, but a necessary theoretical consideration to organize the praxis of the field. When Lacan follows Freud's elaboration on certain interventions that stop working after a while, without getting rid of some other features, it becomes clear to Lacan, that Freud defends structural features and that there are elements which can be transformed through the acknowledgment of its mechanisms.

The paradoxical features of transference relate to the effects of participating within an structural illusion. As Žižek quite accurately posits, transference is a mechanism which operates as the belief "...that truth can be found in laws... transference is this supposition of a Truth, of a Meaning behind the stupid, traumatic, inconsistent fact of the Law. In other words, 'transference' names the vicious circle of belief: the reasons why we should believe are persuasive only to those who already believe" (2008: 36–37). This is why there is a double inscription to transference, a paradoxical formalization. In psychoanalysis, in order to participate within its effects, one must already be under its transferential influence in the first place (this is why establishing and dissolving transference is key to the psychoanalytic process). In this lesson, Lacan aims at refining transference as a psychoanalytic mechanism, commending Jekels and Bergler for moving pass the Freudian economical developments via their attempt of polishing it.

The Place of the Psychoanalyst

This final subset of investigations on this lesson relates to Lacan's opening question, which is: "where is the analysand situated, where should the analyst be in order to respond appropriately to him?" (1961: 311). And this led his investigation toward the hypothesis of the Ego-Ideal or Ideal Ego functioning in the relationship between the psychoanalyst and the analysand. First of all, Lacan addresses the problem of confusing those two elements and the importance of distinguishing between them. If the Ego Ideal (*Idéal du Moi*) and the Ideal Ego (*Moi Idéal*) do have different effects upon the subject, it is necessary to differentiate them, as Lacan cares to explain. Basically, Lacan wants to get rid of a more imaginarized embodiment of the psychoanalyst, because this presupposes a naive comprehension that there is a procedural way of behaving, which would be or could be more interesting to the psychoanalytic process. But a phenomenological reaction or a particular way to react is much different than the place of the psychoanalyst which Lacan is developing here. The psychoanalyst defends that when Freud coined the terms in *Einführung zur Narzissmus*, he was being careful with the significant at stake, so the subsequent explorations on psychoanalysis should to the same. And what will tie the transference between the psychoanalyst and the analysand is much open to Chance, there is nothing to do, besides sustaining the place of the psychoanalyst.

The Ego-Ideal and Ideal Ego sustain narcissistic functions, as Lacan portrays on the mirror stage. This means that both have different roles for the Ego, which is best disambiguated by this Lacanian construct. But, here in this particular lesson, Lacan presents how the Ideal Ego concerns the particular meaning which someone attributes to a certain subsumed signifier, based upon his or her past, provoking the subject to try to restore it. The Ego-Ideal represents a future like possibility, a certain way of interpreting the given conditions and identifications within a given reality, moving the subject toward an accomplishment. So where does transference appears here? Well, "(t)ransference is, then, an illusion, but the point is that we cannot bypass it and reach directly for the Truth: the Truth itself is constituted *through* the illusion proper to the transference – 'the Truth arises from misrecognition'" (Žižek 2008: 59–60). Therefore, the psychoanalytic apparatus conditioned by transference allows the traversing of the phantasy through its process, and this very own process is, to a certain extent, a subjective experience of the agency of time and re-appropriation of it.

Although these notions will be further explored in the subsequent lessons, in here we find already a very interesting distinction. Considering the relationship between the psychoanalyst and the analysand, Lacan states that: "Very early on it was said: 'The analyst takes for the analysand the place of his ego-ideal'. This is true or it is false..." (1966: 313). As further explained, it is true that this dimension occurs under transference, but this is far from being the whole point of the process. So, the "actualization of the reality of the unconscious", which is another good definition for transference (Žižek 2008: 58) allows that the psychoanalytic apparatus be put to work in the relationship between the analysand and the psychoanalyst. And this is what Lacan addresses here, the psychoanalyst being placed as the Ego Ideal occurs indeed, but also because of the imaginary charge of the crowd of psychoanalysts which is socially established. And of course, the whole point must be its counterpart in the psychoanalytical procedure toward the remission of symptoms and toward an ontological transformation (Dunker 2015), since what really moves an analysis comes from the analysand's side.

In this sense, the operation of borrowing the imaginary aspect of the Ego Ideal must only be the beginning of the procedure or of the process, but not its end. And once the illusion gets established, once the analysand believes that the psychoanalyst has what it takes to address his or her symptoms, the effects of transferences start to work and positively and negatively operate within the analysis until it gets dissolved. The crucial element in here, only briefly commented by Lacan in this lesson, concerns the desire for analysis. Well, this is crucial since the traversing of the phantasy relates to becoming an analyst of himself or herself. And this desire for psychoanalysis, from the analysand, is what moves the transference in order to participate in its effects, until he or she becomes able to switch places with the psychoanalyst.

This is what Lacan talks about when he mentions the contribution of psychoanalysis concerning action. He comments on the philosophical discussion about it, but considers that a contribution concerning action from the standpoint of the psychoanalyst is possible. He relates to the logic of the unconscious at stake for the analysand and also to the clinical demand of a clearer interpretation when an acting-out occurs. This is a call for interpretation of a demand to reintroduce the analysand toward the symbolic and an invitation to Speech. Such clinical insight also relates to the end of this lesson, where Lacan briefly comments on a clinical case and addresses one of the demands for occupying this place, the place of the psychoanalyst. A psychoanalytic process can turn out to be revolutionary process for the Subject, if in its process the analysand manages to seize the zombified means of his or her symbolic production and becomes able to break down the imaginary constructions between the Ego Ideal and the Ideal Ego, thereby sustaining his or her's desire for analysis.

Conclusion

Through the investigation of the following elected subsets: (1) *The psychoanalysts and their crowd*; (2) *Paradoxes of transference;* and (3) *The place of the psychoanalyst*, it becomes clear that Lacan's investigation on transference in this lesson is formidably clinical. And also that Lacan displays concerns which transit between three different levels—particular, group and social—throughout his presentation. There is a theoretical appreciation of Freudian formulations such as the Ego-Ideal and the Ideal Ego, as well as their relationship to narcissism. Such investigation toward the psychoanalytic treatment considering the Ego-Ideal and the imaginary component as implications toward the process is crossed-examined by Lacan's criticism toward the clinical. Lacan defends the role of love within psychoanalysis throughout his research on transference and explores the paradoxical effects of this mechanism which were deepened here in this lesson.

Notes

1. For more about this discussion, see Freud's *The Uncanny* (1919), Royle's *The Uncanny* (2003), Dolar's "I Shall Be with You on Your Wedding-Night": Lacan and the Uncanny (1991), and there is previous appreciation of this on Gonsalves' *Ethics and Monstrosity on Psychoanalysis* (2016).
2. Badiou defends two crucial thesis to further explore this point in *Conditions*: "Thesis 3: The inauguration of a truth-process is exactly what Lacan referred to as an 'encounter' when he said that in an encounter 'it is love that approaches being as such'. This inauguration, incidentally, is what Plato in his *Symposium* called *exaiphnès*, the 'sudden'. It is what I call 'event'. The event is undecidable... Thesis 5: Philosophy and psychoanalysis have a common border to two procedures that are external to one another: mathematics, on the one hand, and love, on the other. The knot of these components forming the outer border of philosophy and psychoanalysis consists in the localization of the void in the link, or the relation, that might be supposed to 'hold together' the Idea and the thing, or being the knowledge of being. Love undergoes the void of relation, because there is no sexual relationship. Mathematics undergoes it, because it exhausts it in pure literalization" (2008: 209).
3. Lacan's mathemes are his formalizations attempts toward that which words lack in order to fully portray.

References

Badiou, Alain. 2008. *Conditions*. London: Continuum.

Dolar, Mladen. 1991. "I Shall Be with You on Your Wedding-Night": Lacan and the Uncanny. *October* 58, Rendering the Real (Autumn): 5–23.

———. 2008. "Freud and the Political." *Unbound*, 4 (15): 15–29.

Dunker, Christian. 2015. *Mal-estar, Sofrimento e Sintoma*. São Paulo: Boitempo Editorial.
Freud, Sigmund. 1919. "The Uncanny." In *Freud Complete Words* (1953–74), vol. 17, 219–56. London: Hogarth Press.
Gay, Peter. 1989. *Freud*, 229–230. London: W. W. Norton.
Gonsalves, Rodrigo. 2016. *Ethics and Monstrosity on Psychoanalysis*. https://egs.academia.edu/RodrigoGonsalves. Last accessed 1 November 2017.
Jekels, Ludwig, and Edmund Bergler. 1931. "Transference and Love: Read Before the Vienna Psychoanalytic Society." November 8. First published in *Imago*, XX, 19 M, 5–31.
Lacan, Jacques. 1961. "Transference". In *Le Séminaire - Livre VIII*, 543–567. Paris: Seuil.
———. 1966. "The Situation of Psychoanalysis and the Training of Psychoanalysts in 1956." In *Écrits. Le Champ Freudien*, edited by Jacques Lacan, 396–397. Paris: Editions du Seuil.
Royle, Nicholas. 2003. *The Uncanny*. Manchester: Manchester University Press.
Žižek, Slavoj. 2008. *The Sublime Object of Ideology*. London, UK: Verso Books.

20

Beyond the Mirror: Commentary on Session XXIV

Jelica Šumič Riha

Transference is one of the four fundamental concepts Lacan chose to re-examine in his *Seminar VIII* in order to be able to write, as he puts it, "a new chapter on analytic action."[1] The question Lacan is raising in this seminar is that the analyst's participation in the transference, more specifically, the analyst's place in it, and in particular the analytic relationship itself, is based on a misunderstanding. Indeed, Lacan insists, there is no overlap between the place where the analysand situates the analyst and the place where the analyst must be "in order to suitably respond to him."[2] There is then an issue here, which is the unclarity over the analyst's function in the cure. If Lacan is constantly interrogating the concept of transference, this is because the question of transference is not only a theoretical one, but also a technical one, that of its handling in the cure. According to Lacan, transference is to be considered as that which "directs the way in which patients are treated."[3] It should be noted that, for Lacan, it is not the analysand who is to be guided; rather, as Lacan goes on, "the

J. Šumič Riha (✉)
Research Center of the Slovenian Academy of Sciences
and Arts, Ljubljana, Slovenia
e-mail: jsumr@zrc-sazu.si

G. Basu Thakur and J. Dickstein (eds.), *Reading Lacan's Seminar VIII*,
The Palgrave Lacan Series, https://doi.org/10.1007/978-3-030-32742-2_20

way in which [the analysands] are treated governs the concept."[4] This is why transference could be considered as compass that signals not only the analyst's orientation, but also his blundering. Setting out from Freud's contention according to which "[t]ransference, which seems ordained to be the greatest obstacle to psychoanalysis, becomes its most powerful ally,"[5] Lacan goes on to show how the position of the analyst is decisive in the handling of the transference.

For Lacan, it is clear that this handling of the transference does not come to appealing "to some healthy part of the subject thought to be there in the real,"[6] as the ego is "precisely this part that is concerned in transference, [...] this part that closes the door."[7] As a consequence of this confusing the subject of the unconscious, the symbolic function, with the ego, the imaginary function, the main question for the post-Freudian orientation in psychoanalysis became the question of the ego-ideal, which for Freud is the mainspring of narcissism, insofar as the ego-ideal was considered to be "the pivotal point of the kind of identification whose impact is fundamental in the production of transference."[8] This has particular bearing upon the possibility of the subject to exit from the narcissistic sphere, or, in Lacan's words, "to leave behind his narcissistic self-envelopment."[9] This is why, for Lacan, any conception of analysis that defines its end as identification with the analyst inevitably makes analysts loose their compass and lead their analysands astray. It is in view of arriving to, what Lacan calls, his "perhaps daring goal," namely "to formulate what the analyst must truly be in order to respond to the transference – which also implies knowing what he must be and what he can be later on [in analysis],"[10] that he sets out to identify the impasses and the risks involved in the theory of narcissism developed by authors of the article "Transference and Love" which, for him, perfectly illustrates the post-Freudian position that broaches the issue of the analyst's role in terms of love and identification.

While Lacan himself may well designate the "initial infatuation" or Freud's *Verliebtheit*, that inevitably emerges at the beginning of the treatment, as "a pivotal role in the transference,"[11] this love transference is nevertheless situated at the level of the imaginary. Indeed, the function of this love is "[n]othing but to fill the emptiness of this standstill with a lure. But [...] this lure serves a purpose by setting the whole process in motion anew."[12] Yet what is at stake, for Lacan, especially in *Seminar VIII* in which

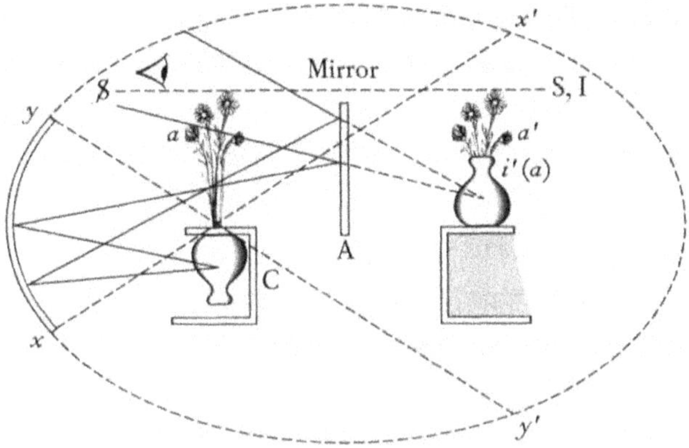

Fig. 20.1 Complete schema

he develops at length the issue of love, is to establish, what place love has in the analytic treatment—if transference is, indeed, love, although not just any love. For there is a theoretical point here that is worthwhile disengaging for discussion, insofar as transference presents itself as a paradox: On the one hand, its development is a necessary condition for interpretation and on the other, it closes the door to the unconscious, thus remaining the site of a "permanent conceptual crisis […] in analysis,"[13] a crisis that puts into question the very possibility of psychoanalysis.

In Chapter 24 of *Seminar VIII* that centers around the question of identification, Lacan sets out to restore the constitutive function of the symbolic by using the optical model, already presented and discussed an length in his article "Remarks on Daniel Lagache's Presentation"[14] as well as several seminars. This "bulldozer-schema,"[15] as Lacan himself calls it, is introduced in order to account for the difference and relation of dependence between two irreducible functions, the symbolic function of the ego-ideal, and the imaginary function of the ideal ego (Fig. 20.1).

The main interest of this schema can be seen in the fact that it introduces the function of the Other—presented in the schema in the form of the flat mirror and designated by the letter A—as it is precisely this function that renders the distinction between the ego-ideal and the ideal ego necessary. It is in the space of the Other that the subject sees himself/herself and the point from which he/she looks at himself/herself is also in that space.

It is then in the field of the Other that the subject is constituted as the ideal ego, that is to say, by regulating via the ego ideal the completion of what will become the ideal ego, he/she will constitute himself/herself in his/her imaginary reality. What the schema renders visible is that where the subject sees himself/herself, namely where that real, inverted image of his/her own body that is given in the schema of the ego is produced, it is not from there that he/she looks at himself/herself.

Crucial for Lacan's elaboration of identification in Chapter 24 is what Freud termed the second type of identification, identification via the *einziger Zug*, via the unary stroke. Thus, for Lacan, "[w]hat is defined by this *ein einziger Zug* is the punctual character of the early reference to the Other when it comes to narcissism."[16] As the term "punctual" makes it clear, this kind of identification avoids any attempt to integrate the whole reality of the person that incarnates the role of the ego-ideal, abstracting the variety and multiplicity of qualities that constitute the other, focusing instead on isolated, contingently chosen traits, each of which is unique, and it is due to this unicity that the unary trait has some affinities with the signifier. However, the unary trait, as Lacan conceives of it, is, strictly speaking, a sign rather than a signifier. Cut off from the chain of signifiers, the unary trait operates all alone. But precisely as such, in its abstraction from the diversity of other traits or qualities, the unary trait constitutes the "primordial symbolic term," preparing the subject for the entry into the symbolic register. But the *einziger Zug* is constitutive not only of the ego-ideal, it also regulates the subject's relation to others as well as to the external world: "In the world of a subject who speaks – in other words, in what we call the human world – we purely and simply encounter a metaphorical attempt to attribute a trait in common to all objects; it is purely and simply by decree that we can try to attribute a common feature to their diversity."[17] This operation of unifying is gratifying for the subject to the extent that it promises the eventual unity and completeness of the self. But since the ego comes into being only by identifying with something outside the self, it follows that the relation to the Other precedes the subject's self-being. At stake in the handling of the transference is precisely this possibility of modifying the tendency to maintain the illusion of autonomy of the ego, with its murderous misrecognition, by uncovering that absolutely contingent *einziger Zug*, "primordial signifier" on which the subject's coming into being depends. The crucial question then becomes: How can the identification with the unary trait function as a mediation between narcissism and love insofar as love relates to the Other?

Lacan's ambition was, from the outset, to situate psychoanalysis at the level of the symbolic, rather than that of the imaginary. This move is particularly relevant when it comes to dealing with the relationship between (little) others, because such relationships are structured by the paranoid logic of the mirror stage necessarily involving a dimension of aggressiveness. This is why, for Lacan, love cannot involve only the small other, my mirror image, but must also include the dimension of the Other. However, for the subject to embody the Other for someone else, this is one of the main theses in *Seminar VIII*, the beloved must retain a precious object, *agalma*, this being always the lost object, the object that the one in love always tries to refind in the Other.

In *Seminar VIII,* Lacan develops a radically different logic for love in psychoanalysis—a logic that does not aim at the imaginary unification, but interrogates instead the relationship between love and knowledge. Indeed, Lacan takes a very important step that brings not the answer, but at least helps us to formulate the question of the possible articulation of love and knowledge on the basis of the transference. The connection between love and knowledge indicates that it is not enough to articulate the state of being in love simply by the ego-ideal (I) and the ideal ego (*i(a)*). The ego-ideal is the point from which the subject sees himself/herself as lovable, while *i(a)* designates the imago of the ego, as seen from this point of view. To include the function of knowledge means that it does not suffice to posit the state of being in love from the point of narcissistic satisfaction: "I only love you in order to see myself as I love myself," but rather, "I love you for something that is in you, which is what you lack." It is this precious object that, according to Lacan of *Seminar VIII*, is the cause of the love that one has for the Other: The Other has what the subject has lost, and because the Other has it, his/her image acquires a consistency that the subject feels he/she lacks.

In *Seminar VIII*, Lacan situates this agalmatic object at the level of being: To the extent that the subject can come into being only by entering the field of the Other, i.e., by being represented by a signifier for another signifier, which is why the subject lacks being, he/she can regain some of his/her being through object a, which will give him/her, in the imaginary register, the consistency that he/she lacks in the symbolic. The subject will therefore love the one who seems to hold the truth of his/her being. This also explains why Lacan, at least from *Seminar VIII* onwards, insists on the affinity between love and unconscious knowledge. This affinity between love and unconscious knowledge is crucial to Lacan's reading of Socrates' position in Plato's *Symposium*: For Lacan, Socrates, for being the one who knows all there is to know about love, is also the one who refuses to comply with the metaphor of love. And, vice versa, to respond to the love another has for me amounts to consenting to being loved for something I don't know about myself and which causes the other's love. Hence, if Socrates does not comply with the metaphor of love, this is because he cannot admit something that is not governed by the logic of the signifier, which Lacan recognizes as the originality of the Socratic discourse. To love someone is not only to grapple with a hole in knowledge, it is also to consent that the Other is in possession of what one lacks. Thus, if love has something to do with transference, as Freud and Lacan claim by insisting that transference, while being artifice, is a genuine love, this is because love relates to something which remains obscure to the subject in love. This is precisely Lacan's claim which allows him to broach the phenomenon of transference in psychoanalysis.

While love is no doubt inevitable consequence of the analytic setting and, as such, a condition of possibility of the cure, it can also disrupt an analysis if it is not elaborated logically. The logic of love needs to be elaborated so that transference may be handled in a treatment that will lead the subject to reconcile himself/herself with the singularity of his/her subjective position. Because of the presence of the subject supposed to hold the truth of my being, the analytic situation inevitably triggers transference love in the analysand: The latter loves his/her analyst because the analyst is supposed to hold something the analysand lacks, which is why it causes his/her desire. In the analytic setting, this desire takes the form of a desire articulated to the lack-of-being. The analysand wants to know something about himself/herself, and this self-knowledge will make him/her hole. By being the agalmatic object for the analysand—for Lacan the analyst is not present as unconscious but as object a, i.e., with his being, not his lack thereof—the analyst raises the analysand's hope that he/she will regain what he/she has lost, whether the truth of his/her being or the mythical, yet unattainable jouissance that would make him/her whole again.

So, how does the analyst avoid the trap of identification and narcissism, detected by Lacan in both, theory and practice, of the post-Freudians? By avoiding the position of the ego-ideal, the analyst has to occupy that of the object a. The analyst has to draw a clear line of demarcation between offering his/her body to incarnate the agalmatic object that the analysand is desperately demanding, while returning him/her to the real of his/her libidinal body, fragmented by the drives. This, of course, is nothing but a lure, which is why Lacan concludes *Seminar VIII* by claiming that the analyst must mourn love, since no object is more valuable than another, or, rather, he/she must accept to stop being agalmatic for the analysand, he/she must accept to lose his/her agalma, becoming nothing more than a waste product of the cure, he/she must consent to a radical mutation of the object a: form *agalma* to *palea.* Only by accepting to become a residue, *palea,* the analyst will succeed in guiding his/her analysand to the point at which he/she will reconcile him/herself with the inexorable logic of the drive.

Just like Socrates, the analyst, through what Lacan describes as the metaphor of love, renounces to be in the position of the loved (*eromenos*), setting instead the analysand, the one in love, (*erastes*), to work on his/her desire. In keeping the gap open between the ego-ideal and the object a, Lacan provides us in the final part of *Seminar VIII,* with a first formulation of what he calls an "absolute point" and what will be developed in *Seminar XI* in terms of the desire of the analyst, modeled on Socrates' *atopia*: By refusing to give any indications as to his desire, he turns the subject to take up the path of the logic of the signifier in order to face that "before which the subject sees himself being abolished when he realizes himself as desire. In order for the subject to accede to this point beyond the reduction of the ideals of the person, it is as desire's object *a,* as what he was to the Other in his erection as a living being, as *wanted* or *unwanted* when he came into the world, that he is called to be reborn in order to know if he wants what he desires."[18]

Notes

1. Jacques Lacan, *The Seminar of Jacques Lacan. Book VIII: Transference*, trans. B. Fink (Cambridge: Polity Press, 2015), p. 334.
2. Ibid., p. 329.
3. Jacques Lacan, *The Seminar of Jacques Lacan. Book XI: Four Fundamental Concepts of Psychoanalysis*, trans. A. Sheridan (London: Penguin, 1977), p. 124.
4. Ibid.
5. Sigmund Freud, "A Fragment of a Case of Hysteria," SE VII, p. 117.
6. Jacques Lacan, *The Seminar of Jacques Lacan. Book XI: Four Fundamental Concepts of Psychoanalysis*, p. 131.
7. Ibid.
8. Jacques Lacan, *The Seminar of Jacques Lacan. Book VIII: Transference*, p. 346.
9. Ibid., p. 348.
10. Ibid., p. 344.
11. Jacques Lacan, *The Seminar of Jacques Lacan. Book I: Freud's Papers on Technique*, trans. J. Forrester (London and New York: W. W. Norton, 1988), p. 282.
12. Jacques Lacan, "Presentation of Transference," *Écrits: The First Complete Edition in English*, trans. B. Fink (New York and London: W. W. Norton, 2006), p. 184.
13. Jacques Lacan, *The Seminar of Jacques Lacan. Book XI: Four Fundamental Concepts of Psychoanalysis*, p. 131.
14. Jacques Lacan, "Remarks on Daniel Lagache's Presentation: 'Psychoanalysis and Personality Structure'," *Écrits*, pp. 543–574.
15. Jacques Lacan, *The Seminar of Jacques Lacan. Book XI: Four Fundamental Concepts of Psychoanalysis*, p. 145.
16. Jacques Lacan, *The Seminar of Jacques Lacan. Book VIII: Transference*, p. 355.
17. Ibid., p. 395.
18. Jacques Lacan, "Remarks on Daniel Lagache's Presentation: 'Psychoanalysis and Personality Structure'," pp. 571–572.

References

Freud, S. 1955. "A Fragment of a Case of Hysteria." SE VII, In *The Standard Edition of the Complete Psychological Works of Sigmund Freud.* trans. J. Strachey, 24 vols. London: Hogarth Press.

Lacan, J. 1977. *The Seminar of Jacques Lacan. Book XI: Four Fundamental Concepts of Psychoanalysis.* Translated by A. Sheridan. London: Penguin.

———. 1988. *The Seminar of Jacques Lacan. Book I: Freud's Papers on Technique.* Translated by J. Forrester. London and New York: W. W. Norton.

———. 2006. "Presentation of Transference." In *Écrits: The First Complete Edition in English,* translated by Bruce Fink. New York and London: W. W. Norton.

———. 2006. "Remarks on Daniel Lagache's Presentation: 'Psychoanalysis and Personality Structure.'" In *Écrits: The First Complete Edition in English,* translated by Bruce Fink. New York and London: W. W. Norton.

———. 2015. *Transference: The Seminar of Jacques Lacan, Book VIII.* Edited by Jacques-Alain Miller and Translated by Bruce Fink. Cambridge: Polity.

21

Mind the Gap: Commentary on Session XXV

Gautam Basu Thakur

Introduction

Topic of the twenty-fifth session in Seminar VIII is the relationship between anxiety and desire. But there's a stumble at the very outset: "[t]he beginning of this session is missing."[1]

This absence might be the result of an accident, such as failure to record or transcribe the first part of the live session, but for those interested in reading Lacan for content as well as form this offers a titillating opportunity, one which emerges from within a slip in the work or via the labor of preparing the text. This makes necessary, therefore, a few words regarding the metatheoretical and pedagogical potentials of this stumble. Accordingly, here are three broad observations about the missing text.

1. This lack is appropriate given the subject matter of this session, namely, what is missing or lacking in our understanding of anxiety or "the meaning of anxiety."[2] Thus, Lacan submits at the outset, if one must

G. Basu Thakur (✉)
Boise State University, Boise, ID, USA

G. Basu Thakur and J. Dickstein (eds.), *Reading Lacan's Seminar VIII*,
The Palgrave Lacan Series, https://doi.org/10.1007/978-3-030-32742-2_21

talk about anxiety—the relationship between anxiety and desire—then, one has to pay attention to what has remained absent so far in habitual readings of Freud.

2. This absence is a stumble. Or, it should be read as such, i.e., as a disruption in readerly satisfaction/enjoyment. Interestingly, disruption is at the center of Lacan's focus in this lesson for two reasons. One, he explains anxiety as resulting from a sudden unbearable irruption in the subject-object dialectic. Two, this entire session can be characterized as a disruption in or deviation from the rest of the Seminar because, as Lacan makes clear at the end of the session, this session was a detour about the "subject's relation to the ideal ego and to the ego-ideal."[3] In this, the twenty-fifth session itself is a gap between the sessions of June 7, 1961 and June 21, 1961. To a reader as myself, this session is a veritable hole that is prefaced by another hole—the sentence noting the lack of the beginning.
3. Lastly, when thinking in the context of his immediate seminars, this gap or what emerges in the space of this gap, namely, Lacan's discussion of anxiety as made available to readers via Fink's translation, connects his past seminars, for example, Seminar IV (on object relation), to his future seminars, especially Seminar X (on anxiety).

No less interestingly, Lacan's seminar on anxiety, which was delivered two years later, was his last at Sainte-Anne Hospital. In 1963, he was debarred from training analysts and this led to him moving his yearly seminars to École Normale Supérieure. Lacan's excommunication from the SFP and his founding of the ECF was not only a rupture in his career/teaching but also constituted a "major upheaval in the French analytic community."[4]

The argument I am striving after is this: Whatever the reason might be for the missing section, this absence gains interesting critical purchase in the context of the topic of this session, i.e., anxiety, and Lacan's definition of anxiety as resulting from the constriction of the gap between desire and jouissance. In other words, the replacement of the lack sustaining desire by the real as an irredeemable gap inaugurates anxiety. Anxiety is the anxiety over a real object taking the place of a fantastic object. It is around this peripeteiac, termed the "moment of moulting" in Seminar X, *l'angoisse,* that is, a moment marked by the disappearance of an imaginary "situatable," "locatable," and "exchangeable" object and the appearance in its place of a "private, incommunicable [or real] object," that anxiety surfaces as a response to the constriction of a gap between desire and jouissance.[5] As Lacan elaborates in this session as well, the sudden emergence of nothing between the subject and the object of its desire is the cause of anxiety; or, anxiety is over "being faced with the other *a*," that is, "the object of his desire."[6] Anxiety is over encountering a gap between what the subject desires and what the object of desire truly is. The caveat or lesson of this session however is that anxiety is the last defense of desire.[7] What follows is a brief selective summary of my understanding of Lacan's theorization of anxiety.

Section 1: There Is No Anxiety Without the Ego

Lacan begins by drawing attention to a sentence in Freud's *Inhibitions, Symptoms, & Anxiety*: "The ego withdraws the preconscious cathexis from the *Triberepräsentanz* [.] It transforms it in order to release unpleasure and *Angst*."[8] Lacan considers this sentence as critical for understanding Freud's explanation of the relationship between anxiety and desire.

According to Lacan's reading of Freud's text, anxiety results from the status of the *objet a*, which in transferring to the subject the condition of its objectness, or by making the subject recognize itself as object, produces anxiety. Put differently, anxiety is over the constriction of the imagined gap between the self and the other. We find a key toward this point at the top of this session when we read the formula: $a \neq i(a)$. Or, the other I imagine as the alterity apropos whom I consolidate my identity is never really what I imagined it to be, and, therefore, when the real other (*a*) appears in its true radical alterity, we experience anxiety as defense against this traumatic other. Anxiety erupts when the "cathexis of little *a* is transferred to \$."[9] Insofar as the ego/I is built on the basis of misrecognition and misidentification, and insofar as "the specular nature of the imaginary order is ultimately dependent upon a real element which cannot be specularized"—"a nonspecularizable remainder, a void ('hollow') that resides at the frontier between the Imaginary and the Real"—anxiety signals the contingency or fragility of an imaginary founded on (the) nothing.[10] Point to be noted here is that anxiety does not lead us toward the traumatic object but away from it. It is also not a simple collapse of the symbolic order. But, rather it is what defends us from the real object thus sustaining the symbolic and us as desiring subjects.

There is no anxiety without the ego. Anxiety is a defense against a threat to the ego. To elaborate, the self identifies in the other an attestation of its ego (say, bodily unity) but the eruption of the real in the locus of the self-consolidating other reflects back to the ego its essential condition as lacking. Anxiety is a defense against this threat. Consider as example the scene from Jonathan Demme's *Silence of the Lamb* (1991) where Jame Gumb/Buffalo Bill dances naked in front of a home recording camera with his penis tucked between his legs. What Gumb wants to see in the recording is his image as a woman, as castrated, therefore an attestation of his wish to become a woman by wearing a suit made out of the skin of (m)other women.[11] If the subject is located between Gumb's biological real and the image he scripts for himself via the recording, this subject remains ungraspable and/or empty, and "anxiety as a signal is [...] produced in response to the call [for something to fill it]."[12] Lacan ends "Section 1" by stating that his aim is to explicate further what Freud means by "anxiety as a signal is produced at the level of the ego?"

Section 2: *Mitleid*—Be Wary of Your Humanity

In this section, Lacan explains Freud's text further by noting that "anxiety as a signal is produced" in the place "occupied by *i(a)*" and, insofar as the ego is the image of the other or misrecognized in the image of the other, anxiety surfaces at the level of the ego. This could warrant the impression that Lacan is talking about anxiety over the dissolution of the external image constitutive of the ego. But he quickly clarifies by noting that anxiety is not related to the dissolution of the image but to the position the image occupies relative to the self. Put another way, anxiety does not indicate the end of desire. But, in order for anxiety to emerge, there has to be a relationship at the level of desire, which Lacan notes can only mean that anxiety represents a defiant effort to preserve desire.[13]

What is the relation of the ego/I to the other? And where does anxiety feature in this relation? According to Lacan, the ego is constituted via and is contingent on the other. "The subject sees his being in a reflection in relation to the other," that is, the loved object which "through its captative effect on the subject" is "strictly equivalent to the ego-ideal." The subject *is* in relation to the *Ichideal*.[14] Anxiety marks the moment when the other's specular image transforms into the real other—the intractable object of desire as substantiation of the subject as lack—unraveling thus the fragility of the ego/I. In this sense, the subject receives the signal from the other.

* * *

I find "Section 2" exciting for Lacan's discussion of pity or *Mitleid* insofar as the enumeration of pity in relation to the ego or imaginary proves important in the context of our global present, especially the (neo-)liberal (Romantic) push toward caring for the other, identity politics, charity, and tolerant pluralism.

Lacan's critique of altruism or *Mitleid* as an idea (or, ideology) that satisfies or consolidates the ego by preserving the image of the other as helpless, needing help or incapable of taking care of its own, develops Freud's theory of the narcissistic origin of love for the other.[15] However way we might conceive *Mitleid*, that is, either as "love for the other" or as "brotherly love" or "love thy neighbor" or, pressingly in the contemporary era, as "love for the refugee," it is an expression of self-love or narcissism. As Lacan puts it, when someone helps a person because she is poor, our imagination helps to construct as well as retain the other in an irredeemable image of poverty. This image functions to both sustain our ego as well as veil the radical alterity of the other.[16]

Postcolonial critics would be quick to remind that this is othering albeit a less innocuous mode. And though Lacan himself might not be thinking in terms of ideology critique, his reference of *mitleid* as responsible for bringing strangers together through identification, a moral force predicated on the possibility of knowing the other by identifying with the other's suffering, proves useful in the context of our contemporary ideology of feel-good multiculturalism. As I see it, the strength of Lacan's hypothesis lies in the structural point being made here and should not be questioned for dismissing material conditions of poverty. That is to say, Lacan is not saying that poverty is imaginary, but, rather, that the monolithic imagification of the other as victim functions to satisfy the ego/I of the savior. In rescuing the other from its depredation, the subject performs its imaginary vanguardism without directly confronting either the other in its heterogeneity or unsettling the already consolidated privilege of the Self.

* * *

None of this should make us forget that Lacan is speaking here to trainee analysts, and that the aim of this session and seminar is to impart lessons useful to the clinical practice of psychoanalysis. We should accordingly refocus on Lacan's theorization of anxiety via the "leaps" he claims to have put on Freud's original contribution to the subject. Notably, these leaps are:

Firstly, for anxiety to emerge there has to be an "absolutely necessary connection with the object of desire."[17] Anxiety erupts only when the image veiling the other is suddenly withdrawn revealing the other instead as incomprehensible to imagination. In Seminar X, Lacan would name this time as the "moment of moulting."

Secondly, Lacan stakes that while anxiety indeed warns the subject about the trauma of the object and urges it that the time has come to take flight, unlike this quintessential animal reaction to an external threat or danger, anxiety in the context of humans functions more to preserve the subject's desire. Anxiety is the "radical mode" via which the subject continues to maintain its relationship to desire at a time when it is in risk of disappearing completely by confrontation with the real object ("an uncertain, undecided, or indefinite object") as substantive of the fundamental emptiness of the self. Simply put, anxiety is over recognizing "we are in a relationship of not having it [the object]." At this stage, "anxiety is the final or radical mode in which the subject continues to sustain his relationship to desire, even if it is an unbearable mode."[18]

Section 3: The Purpose of Psychoanalysis

The purpose of psychoanalysis is (a) to distinguish between desire and need and (b) to establish desire as a threat or danger to the subject who desires.[19] In analysis, this means the analyst must keep her analysis free from anxiety situating herself in a "pure place," namely, the place of "pure desirousness."[20] And, in order to further explain how a subject can manage to occupy the place of pure desirousness, Lacan turns again to Plato's *Symposium*, especially to the exchange between Socrates and Alcibiades.

Other commentators have already discussed this *affair*. Therefore, without repeating the details, I will summarize what Lacan says about the relationship between anxiety, desire, subjectivity, and otherness on this particular return to *the Symposium* . But first let us recount what we know about anxiety so far.

We know that anxiety results from the constriction of the gap between the ego/I and the other or when the subject ($) and the object (a) appear transferable. This happens when fantasy responsible for making reality bearable fails to continue its function. This collapse leaves the ego without any defense against the other, thus pushing the subject to recognize it in the position of the object.

Lacan wants his audience to see this moment in Alcibiades's loud profession of love for Socrates, and in Socrates' refusal to accept the position of Alcibiades's object of desire. Instead of returning love with love, that is, by not accepting Alcibiades's demand and becoming his desired object, Socrates does something interesting. He pushes Alcibiades to confront the truth about his desire, namely, Alcibiades is incapable of knowing what or whom he truly desires. For Socrates's action reveals to Alcibiades that the real object of his desire is lost/veiled/displaced in his demand that Socrates love him back.[21] It is thus by abstracting himself from the position of the other that Socrates manages to uphold the enigma of pure desirousness as pure excess.

The Socratic maneuver is therefore twofold. One, by refusing the position offered to him by Alcibiades, Socrates abstracts him from being reduced to an object in someone else's fantasy. Socrates will not be a feather in someone else's cap. Two, by showing that Alcibiades's demand veils his real desire, namely, that Socrates desires him and that Agathon becomes his beloved, Socrates alienates Alcibiades in his own desire. By reducing Alcibiades from the subject-who-knows to the subject-dispersed-in-desire, Socrates initiates Alcibiades on a path toward traversing his fantasy and recognizing his own existence in terms of ontological lack. As such, the desiring subject in speaking about her desire only risks being reduced to the status of the demanding subject, therefore far afield from being the subject in possession of desire. But when the subject departs from enunciating desire or accepting being the object of desire, as Socrates does in this case, she only edifies the fantasy of the place of pure desirousness as the enigma of the question (*che voi?*) that no one can answer. Socrates exposes the impossibility of love, its predication on *ab-sens*, that is, the non-relationality of the self and the other and the positing of the beloved (the other to be loved) for foreclosing the primary negativity, the Thing in-itself, of this ab-sense.[22] Socrates surfaces as the unmanageable object that is neither in desire nor outside but exsists—a real gap—as the constitutive limit of desire. The lesson here is simple and applicable equally to trainee analysts and those engaged in theorizing knowledge[23]: "Interpretation is directed not so much at the meaning as towards […] its irreducible and senseless character *qua* chain of signifiers."[24]

Notes

1. Jacques Lacan, *Transference: The Seminar of Jacques Lacan, Book VIII*, ed. J.-A. Miller and trans. B. Fink (Polity, Cambridge, 2015), p. 360.
2. Ibid.
3. Ibid., p. 371.
4. Shepherdson, "Foreword," to Roberto Harari's *Lacan's Seminar on Anxiety: An Introduction* (New York: Other Press, 2001), p. xi.
5. Jacques Lacan, *Anxiety: The Seminar of Jacques Lacan Book X* (2004), trans. A. R. Price (Polity, 2014), p. 88.
6. Lacan, *Transference*, p. 364.
7. Ibid., p. 366.
8. Ibid., p. 360.
9. Ibid., p. 361.
10. Lorenzo Chiesa, *Subjectivity and Otherness: A Philosophical Reading of Lacan* (MIT Press, 2007), p. 106.

11. Gumb desired his "big" neighbor. This woman (or, girl) was his way out of his mOther's desire. Failing to realize this wish and escape his mOther's desire, the film suggests, he focuses on tailoring the suit that would transform him completely into the object of his wish thus curtailing the mOther's desire.
12. Lacan, *Transference*, pp. 361, 362.
13. Ibid., pp. 363, 365.
14. Jacques Lacan, *Freud's Papers on Technique 1953–1954. Seminar Book I* (1975). trans. John Forrester (Norton, 1988), p. 126.
15. Jacqueline Rose, "The Imaginary," in *Jacques Lacan: Critical Evaluations in Cultural Theory*, vol. I, ed. Slavoj Žižek (Routledge, 2003), p. 17.
16. Lacan, *Transference*, p. 364.
17. Ibid., p. 365.
18. Ibid.
19. Ibid., p. 368.
20. Ibid., p. 369.
21. This is one possible way for reading Lacan's presentation of the Alcibiades-Socrates affair. As Fink reminds us, there's more than one explanation given by Lacan about this affair, and quite a few hints regarding what might have been at play in the exchange between Alcibiades and Socrates thereby making different and paradoxical interpretations of love, desire, and anxiety possible. See, Bruce Fink, *Lacan on Love* (Polity, 2016), p. 194.
22. Lee Edelman, "Learning Nothing: Bad Education," in *Differences*, vol. 28, no. 1 (2017): 125, 133.
23. Lacan, *Transference*, p. 361.
24. Jacques Lacan, *The Four Fundamental Concepts of Psychoanalysis. The Seminar of Jacques Lacan, Book XI* (1973), trans. A. Sheridan (Routledge, 1981), p. 212.

References

Chiesa, Lorenzo. 2007. *Subjectivity and Otherness: A Philosophical Reading of Lacan.* Cambridge: MIT Press.

Edelman, Lee. 2017. "Learning Nothing: Bad Education." *Differences*, 28 (1): 124–173.

Fink, Bruce. 2016. *Transference: Lacan on Love. An Exploration of Lacan's Seminar VIII.* Cambridge, U.K./Malden, MA.: Polity.

Lacan, Jacques. 1981. *The Four Fundamental Concepts of Psychoanalysis. The Seminar of Jacques Lacan, Book XI* (1973). Translated by A. Sheridan. London: Routledge.

———. 1988. *Freud's Papers on Technique 1953–1954. Seminar Book I* (1975). Translated by John Forrester. New York: Norton.

———. 2014. *Anxiety: The Seminar of Jacques Lacan, Book X* (2004). Translated by A. R. Price. Cambridge: Polity.

———. 2015. *Transference: The Seminar of Jacques Lacan, Book VIII.* Edited by Jacques-Alain Miller and Translated by Bruce Fink. Cambridge: Polity.

Rose, Jacqueline. 2003. "The Imaginary." In *Jacques Lacan: Critical Evaluations in Cultural Theory*, vol. I, ed. Slavoj Žižek. London: Routledge.

Shepherdson, Charles. 2001. "Foreword." To Roberto Harari's *Lacan's Seminar on Anxiety: An Introduction.* New York: Other Press.

22

The Movement of the Pendulum and the Spiral Turn: An Analysis of Lacan's XXVI Lesson from Seminar VIII: Commentary on Session XXVI

Ivan Ramos Estevão

Introduction: The Class of June 21, 1961

Miller called the June 21 class: "*Dream of a Shadow, the man.*" This present exercise though is much more of a commentary than necessarily a reading guide to the class. Every lesson from any of Lacan's seminars lends itself to many possible threads that can be pulled and read through many different emphases. Therefore, there are no possibilities of analytically exhausting any of Lacan's classes, especially because Lacan was given to the enigmatic and catchy phrases which convene a certain decipherment and/or an interpretation from the part of the reader.

It is always good to remember that Lacan has two modes of transmission, oral and written, and that even if they have points of interlocution—they are not the same thing.[1] Lacan's purposeful hermeticism is accentuated in the written form of his production, especially in post-1950s texts.[2] Such

I. R. Estevão (✉)
School of Arts, Sciences and Humanities and Institute of Psychology, University of São Paulo, São Paulo, Brazil
e-mail: irestevao@usp.br

G. Basu Thakur and J. Dickstein (eds.), *Reading Lacan's Seminar VIII*,
The Palgrave Lacan Series, https://doi.org/10.1007/978-3-030-32742-2_22

hermeticism has many reasons, one regards the production of a text which cannot be easily read and that requires a certain positioning when removing a more simplistic interpretation of the scene. Just like *Bebop* which cannot be easily played because of its accelerated rhythm, to read Lacan's writings require an imaginary decentration from a didactic reading.[3]

The same effect happens occasionally in the seminars where is more common to find a certain didacticism, since we can follow the construction step-by-step of his work. Moreover, there is also the problem of establishment behind the seminars, that goes through a certain filtering from the one who is in charge of officially establishing Lacan's seminaries. Because of this, the reading of the seminars should hold the following question: If whether the rigor of transmission is on the one who transmits the seminars or if it is on the one who establishes them in a chosen form.

All oral transmission carry immediate eventual effects: It is under construction and at a crossing between the subject from the enunciation to the subject of the statement. Lacan said that in his seminars he spoke from the position of the analysand. In other words, in his writings he chose both the words and textual organization. While the advantage of accompanying his seminars, in spite of the problems mentioned previously, concerns the possibility of reading/listening to his very own thinking movement in its development. The class discussed in this chapter accompanies a double movement: On the one hand, it presents moments of didacticism that makes crystal clear the logic which governs the construction of the Lacanian psychoanalytic theory, on the other hand (and at the same time), alternates between puzzling and decontextualized sentences, that trace back to a certain free association common to an analysand. But, what we choose to extract from the proposed lesson, in general terms, concerns that which contains the structural form of advancement for psychoanalysis (both Freudian and Lacanian). Even if this class does not allow us to clearly exemplify and see such movement, it is important to point out it occurs continuously in all of Lacan's seminars and writings. We will clarify what this movement is all about in the next section.

The Movement of a Thought

In Luiz Roberto Monzani's book *Freud, o movimento de um pensamento*, the author states that Freudian thought can be metaphorized by two figures—a pendulum and a spiral—serving to account for the difficulty of conceiving the movement within the construction of Freud's work, which contains both continuity and theoretical rupture. Monzani tells us that: "(...) the Freudian discourse appears clearly to be *pendular*, i.e., a few times emphasizes one pole of the question, sometimes its opposite. (...) Following (...) this pendular movement, we will perceive that it ends up, when we penetrate this complicated theoretical network which is the Freudian one, a *spiral* movement, with the condition of thinking this image both in space and cylindrically, where the same issues are addressed, 'forgotten', resumed, but not at the same level as how they were being treated earlier...."[4]

What it means is that there is an intimate relationship between theory and the clinic, but the concepts that arise from the development of these two fields could be incubated or seemingly left aside, only to return elsewhere when the theoretical body has changed. (Thinking here about the concepts of repetition, seduction, drive, Oedipus complex and castration, among others.)

We are defending here that psychoanalysis generally moves in the same way, occasioning the sensation to anyone who constantly studies the field, that there is an eternal return to concepts that once seemed discarded or "outdated." They return to the extent that the theory finds itself on impasses, problematizations or yet, at a stagnation concerning metapsychology and the clinic itself.

It is precisely from the Lacanian diagnosis that psychoanalysis stagnated—or worse—that Lacan himself proposes the famous return to Freud.[5] Recovering the central texts, the logic of thought and the foundations of the field in order to be able to advance in this substrate. Our argument is that Lacan uses the same pendular and spiral model to produce and advance in psychoanalysis.

In XXVIth session, another shift happens when Lacan takes up Freudian concepts in light of another theoretical moment. Having advanced in his return to Freud, emphasizing texts and central concepts (such as desire,

Oedipus, object relations, the Ego, the unconscious, the psychoses, among others), Lacan focused now at the return to the concept of *transference*. This return regards largely on the conceptualization from the referential standpoint of four elements extracted from Freud, but that were not established by Freud himself, namely, the three registers: Real, Symbolic, and Imaginary, and also, the concept of subject. One can say that it is in light of these four concepts that Lacan returns to the Freudian theory.

Lesson XXVI

So, the main idea is to trace a theoretical point and also to notice certain shifts and turns which Lacan provides to a few concepts. Lacan emphasizes a delimited group of concepts which, with the exception of one, are all present in Freud's *Introduction to Narcissism.* The concepts are identification, narcissism, object, Ego-Ideal, Ideal Ego, and desire. The concept Lacan uses in the lesson but which is not in the text on narcissism is the *phallus*, only thought later by Freud.

Let's follow the overall sequence of this turn: Starting with Freud and his concept of narcissism, we go to the resumption of narcissism in the Mirror Stage, followed by the proposal of the optical scheme and the schema L and finally, we approach the idea of the *objet petit a*, which will be presented at the next year's seminar on identification. All of this against the background of the registers and the subject.

In Freud's *Introduction to Narcissism,* we find a curious statement: "(…) is a necessary assumption, that a unity comparable to the ego does not exist from the beginning in the individual; the ego has to be developed [*entwickelt*]. But the autoerotic drives [*Triebe*] are primordial; then there must be something that adds to autoerotism, a new psychic action, to form narcissism."[6]

So, acknowledging one of the early starting points of Lacan's reading of Freud—already implies the effort to think the problem which Freud himself proposes here, that is, what provides conditions to usher the passage from autoerotism to narcissism. And this is far from being resumed to this, since the initial process of constructing an image of itself or rather, of constituting the Ego itself, implies what Lacan will later on formulate as the two processes of the subject's causation: alienation and separation.[7]

But, the Lacanian answer to Freud's enigma proposed here comes in the form of the *Mirror Stage*, first psychic movement of what will set fundamental basis for the process of *identification*, which from a Freudian standpoint concerns the first form of loving.

The starting point of the spiral lies here: In the *Introduction to Narcissism*, Freud articulates the whole range of concepts we have listed previously. And Lacan resumes some of these concepts with the Mirror Stage, as a process of identification where the subject assumes an image which precipitates the *infans* at the symbolic matrix in a primordial way preceding the identification with the other.[8] Here in this text, Lacan advances the idea of narcissism, Ego, the Ideal Ego, and the identification, while articulating with his theoretical shift. The constitution of the "I" is a matrix for thinking the construction of the Imaginary and also the capture of being in the mirror image proposed by the Other (which is here metaphorized as a mirror). This Other provides signifiers and supports the bodily image. In this process, two elements immediately emerge: the subject, which disappears at the moment it arises, in order to become an evanescent point among the signifiers and also, the "I" (*Je*), operating at first as a bodily image, but which is also the image that will become basis for secondary identifications, assuming traits that will serve in order for the Ego to be able to state itself. The Ego displaces the subject, being referenced to the Other.

But going back a little, we can already notice on Freud an effort to think of narcissism in two stages: primary and secondary, much like Lacan also proposes identification[9] on two levels, referring to the concepts of Ideal Ego (primary identification) and Ego-Ideal (secondary identification). And, still according with Lacan throughout this lesson, it is not appropriate to confuse those two levels, first because there is a passage which leads from one to the other and second, because this is the same passage which renders possible for the assumption of the desiring subject as well as a certain objetal relation. The idea of not confusing both levels comes from Freud himself. Although Gaufey emphasizes how in Freud both concepts—along with the idea of Superego—are clearly mixed back in 1914, an example of this confusion.[10]

But, after all, what is the I (ou I (A)) and the i ('a) that Lacan refers to in this class? Well, they are the *mathemes* that serve to locate the Ego-Ideal (or the Other's Ideal, in case the "I") and the Ideal Ego (i '(a)). The Ideal Ego is an imaginary effect from the structuring operation which occasions the overcoming of primary narcissism. While passing through the logical operation of the Oedipus complex and castration, a fictional temporality is constituted: The subject operates from a mythical past, a past where the subject was the object of the Other in a relation of supposed complementarity and completeness. The Ideal Ego implies a certain image of the past of what the subject supposedly once was, and it nods to a certain happiness which was lost, and that the Ego aims to recover. It becomes a matrix which steers both desire and demand, a vector of meaning which operates the recovery from a loss. So, the "I" (from the matheme) is the second element of this fictional temporality and it is projected as a future possibility of recovery from the once lost complementarity.

The step that allows us to retrieve such concepts and circumscribe them a bit better is provided by Lacan in 1953, when he uses Henri Bousse's mirror diagram in order to think the relation between the Symbolic and the Imaginary. He modifies the diagram but maintains its essential features: There is a construction of a virtual image of an object that can be seen but which is simultaneously intangible, or in other words, an image without material consistency. It is a model that says about the virtual reality of the Ego, which is constituted from a set of mirages and that finds in a mirror (which Lacan considers a metaphor for the Other (A)) a support in the construction of the self-image. The optical scheme, which appears repeatedly as a way of locating the subject in its modalities of identification from the Other, will also find its resonances in the L schema and later on, in the R schema (Figs. 22.1 and 22.2).

From the terms presented by the Mirror Stage, both the optical scheme and the L schema are ways of articulating what happens at the encounter between two registers: the Imaginary and Symbolic. In class XXVI, Lacan tells us that: "In order to follow with all rigor Freud's teachings, if the field of narcissistic investment is central and essential [the field of the Imaginary formed in the Mirror Stage], if it is around him that decides the whole fate of human desire, there is not only that field."[11] Here, there are some comments to be made, since this seems to be the center of this

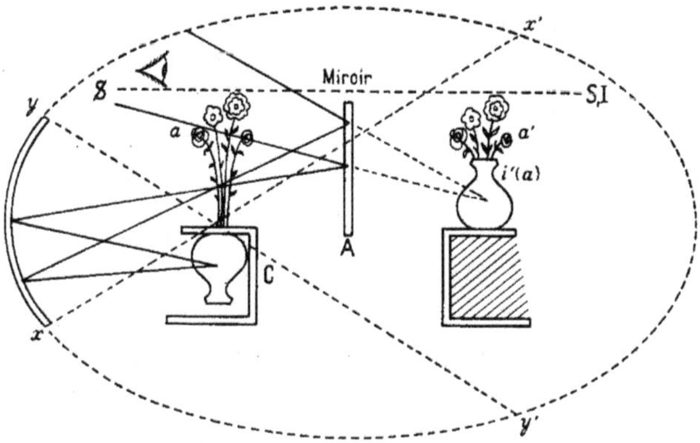

Fig. 22.1 The Optical scheme

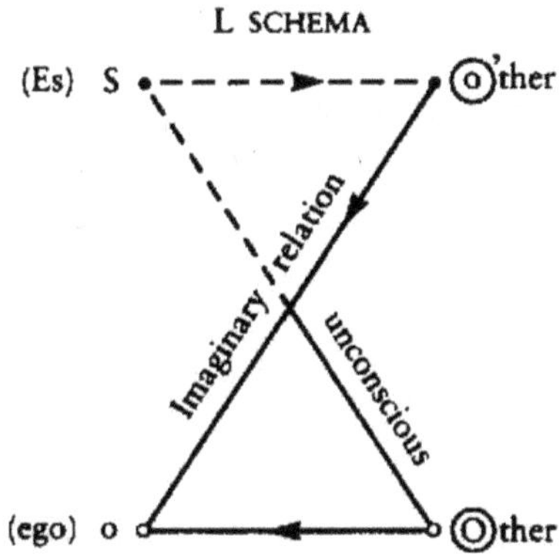

Fig. 22.2 The L schema

lesson: It is in the Imaginary field articulated by the construction of a virtual image of the Ego, created from the traits provided by the Other, that decides the destiny of desire. It is in this fictional temporality which involves a mythical past (i'(a)) and also an impossible future (I(A)), that one can formulate something about desire. But what precipitates the entrance into this desiring logic? Or, why not stay at the mirage of complementarity within the Imaginary field?

Lacan tells us that "(i)t is thanks to her [the significant function] that what comes from this field [Symbolic] opens to the subject the possibility to leave the pure and simple capture at the narcissistic field."[12] Desire is regulated by the narcissistic field, while the Imaginary can only be articulated thanks to the significant function (and here Lacan speaks, indirectly about the Name-of-the-Father).

If the Imaginary field opens space for the regulation of desire, it also offers that which Lacan, in more than one opportunity calls the object of desire—not to be confused with object *cause* of desire—but "the object [which] is found through objections."[13] So, the Real of the desire, the point when one awakens from a dream, is the satisfaction of the demand, which reveals precisely the vanishing of the object, and desire is that which remains from the operation of satisfying the demand in a dream. Thus, the object partially appears.

If in Freud the shadow of the object falls upon the Ego, in Lacan the shadow of the Ego falls on the object, which remains.

The Ego, Ego-Ideal and Ideal Ego are shadow modalities, a certain "eclipsing" of the object, which can only appear as partial object such as the breast, feces, and which is also present in the phallic object. About this, Lacan states: "The phallus is the pivot function, I would say, which allows us to situate that which distinguishes from it, that is, *a*, and in the small *a* as small *a*, the general function of the object of desire."[14]

We have an entire sequence where Lacan maintains in many ways that: Desire is the effect of the signifier; the signifier that intervenes in the narcissistic Imaginary; making possible from the Other the construction of an Ideal Ego and Ego-Ideal, that become mirages of the object small *a*. The Real appears in the text as an allusion to this object.

The fact is that Lacan is about to take another turn, he is about to formulate an other object, the small object *a*, which displaces from object of desire to the object *cause* of desire. Such object is the very own intangibility experienced when one approaches the virtual object of the optical scheme. But that does not take place here. What Lacan will do next, concerns a movement that begins in Seminar VII, which is to increase the emphasis on the third register, the Real, and also where Lacan can finally locate the object *a* not only as an objection.

Conclusion

If we return to our idea the upward spiral, we will have here three times to consider and what we also find in this class is a referral to a fourth one:

1. The introduction of narcissism in Freud is what makes it possible to situate Ego-Ideal and Ideal Ego; concepts which are obscure even in Freud.
2. Lacan's later proposal of the Mirror Stage, which renders possible to re-situate Ego-Ideal and Ideal Ego, acts now as elements of the identification process and of the constitution of the Ego, articulated by the registers of the Symbolic and the Imaginary. And, here we have the schema L and the optical scheme to support it.
3. In a third moment, now under the light of the conception of object, what the Ego-Ideal and Ideal Ego allow to move forward in order to locate the essential point of the problematic of the object: an object which is veiled.
4. The fourth movement of the spiral will come later, with the locating of the object no longer as object of desire—which implies some materiality—but, as an object *cause* of desire.

Finally, from this point on Lacan continues his work thinking more emphatically the register of the Real, which cannot be treated except from under the light of the other two registers, maintaining the pendular and spiral system of its production.

Notes

1. In this respect, it is important to visit the work of J.-C. Milner, *A Obra Clara*. trans. P. Abreu (Rio de Janeiro: Zahar, 1996), pp. 11–25.
2. There is an interesting example of this narrated by Catherine Millot, in *A vida com Lacan*. trans. André Telles (Zahar, 2017), p. 88. But, Foucault addresses his considerations on Lacanian hermeticism. Cf. M. Foucault,

"Lacan, o 'Liberatore' da Psicanálise," in *Ditos & Escritos I: Problematização do Sujeito: Psicologia, Psiquiatria e Psicanálise.* trans. V. L. A. Ribeiro (Forense Universitária, 2006), p. 330.

3. Hobsbawm defends that *Bebop* was set up as a revolutionary and consequently a revolting form of jazz expression, built to be a song "so difficult that 'they' - the whites who always ended up earning the profits of the conquests of the blacks – 'could not steal it.'" Thus, its very fast rhythm and its improvisation form could only be repeated for those who had excellent instrumental ability. E. J. Hobsbawm, *História Social do Jazz.* trans. A. Noronha (Paz e Terra, 1989), pp. 98–99.
4. Luiz Roberto Monzani, *Freud, O Movimento de um Pensamento* (Campinas: Editora da Unicamp, 1989), p. 303 (Not translated to English).
5. Jacques Lacan, "Situation de la psychanalyse et formation du psychanalyste en 1956," in *Écrits* (Seuil, 1966), pp. 459–491.
6. Sigmund Freud, *Introducción del narcisismo* (1914), in Sigmund Freud *Obras Completas.* vol. XIV. trans. J. L. Etcheverry (Amorrortu, 2006), p. 74.
7. Jacques Lacan, "Position de l'inconscient," in *Écrits* (Seuil, 1966), pp. 839–844.
8. Jacques Lacan, "Le stade du miroir comme formateur de la fonction du Je," in *Écrits* (Seuil, 1966), p. 94.
9. Jacques Lacan, *Le séminaire, livre VIII, Le transfert* (Seuil, 2001), pp. 437–438.
10. Jacques Gaufey, *El lazo especular.* trans. G. Leguizamón (Edelp, 1998), p. 92.
11. Jacques Lacan, *Le séminaire, livre VIII, Le transfert* (Seuil, 2001), p. 441.
12. Ibid.
13. Ibid., p. 442.
14. Ibid., p. 445.

References

Foucault, M. 2006. "Lacan, o 'Liberatore' da Psicanálise." In *Ditos & Escritos I: Problematização do Sujeito: Psicologia, Psiquiatria e Psicanálise*, trans. V. L. A. Ribeiro. Rio de Janeiro: Forense Universitária.

Freud, S. 2006. *Introducción del narcisismo* (1914) in Sigmund Freud *Obras Completas*, vol. XIV. Trans. J. L. Etcheverry. Buenos Aires: Amorrortu.
Gaufey, G. 1998. *El lazo especular*. Trans. G. Leguizamón. Cordoba: Edelp.
Hobsbawm, E. J. 1989. *História Social do Jazz*. Trans. A. Noronha. Rio de Janeiro: Paz e Terra.
Lacan, J. 1966. *Écrits*. Paris: Seuil.
———. 2001. *Le séminaire, livre VIII, Le transfert*. Paris: Seuil.
Millot, C. 2017. *A vida com Lacan*. Trans. André Telles. Rio de Janeiro: Zahar.
Milner, J.-C. 1996. *A Obra Clara*. Trans. P. Abreu. Rio de Janeiro: Zahar.
Monzani, L. R. 1989. *Freud, O Movimento de um Pensamento*. Campinas: Editora da Unicamp.

23

The Transmission of an End: "Mourning the Loss of the Analyst" Commentary on Session XXVII

Cindy Zeiher

What happens upon the realization of the moment that transference is no longer transference; more specifically, when transference has run its course and when there is nothing further to say? Or rather, how does one deal with an end, the end of something so profound that the banalities of everyday life are made poignantly liveable? The analytic procedure is unique in that it unapologetically asks the analysand to make a specific demand, wherein language is forced to contend with the analysand's enjoyment of investment in her symptom. However, as Lacan reminds us in his last session of Seminar VIII, this interrogation of the symptom will and must end. Moreover, an ending occurs when a realization is made and the traversal of fantasy is undertaken in order to confront a different desire, that of passing from the position of analysand to that of analyst who bears the mark of castration and of know-how about her symptom.

C. Zeiher (✉)
School of Language, Social and Political Sciences; Sociology and Anthropology, University of Canterbury, Christchurch, New Zealand
e-mail: cindy.zeiher@canterbury.ac.nz

G. Basu Thakur and J. Dickstein (eds.), *Reading Lacan's Seminar VIII*,
The Palgrave Lacan Series, https://doi.org/10.1007/978-3-030-32742-2_23

Facing an end is strange because the "libidinal waves" Lacan speaks of no longer transmit in the same way. They have surpassed their enclosure, which had allowed the symptom to be handled throughout the analytic procedure. Moreover, the enclosure had provided the space where the *objet a* was played out. Throughout this last session, Lacan ponders Freud's 1937 seminal text *Analysis Terminable and Interminable*, picking up on Freud's ambivalence toward whether one can ever ascertain a natural ending to analysis. For Freud, psychoanalysis is a talking cure, one which aims at making more bearable the traumas and anguish suffered by the patient. If following extensive analysis one has the desire to be in the position of an analyst, then Freud contends that analysis must continue. Thus, there is really no end to one's analysis. However, in revising Freud's position Lacan prompts us to face its logical conclusion: that Freud's theorization of the "end" of analysis is simply a realization of one's lack:

> Simply as readers of Freud, you should all the same already know something of that which in its first appearance at least may present itself as the paradox of what presents itself to us as end, telos, as the completion, the termination of analysis. What does Freud tell us if not when all is said and done that what the one who follows this path will find at the end is nothing other essentially than a lack? Whether you call this lack castration or whether you call it *Penisneid* this is the sign, the metaphor. (Seminar VIII 1960–1961, pp. 38–39)

It is unsurprising that Lacan chooses to end his seminar on transference with how it began—with a consideration of Plato's *Symposium* and the nature of love. At this stage of his theorization, Lacan describes love as a narcissistic shadow, which he quickly links to the libidinal attraction one inevitably encounters in life, as a way of contemplating this shadow. What follows is most striking; Lacan maintains that in the end all that one is left with is this very shadow. Perhaps in the clinic this is the point of love—that analytical love unlike amorous love is configured by the fact that it will end. After the end, the analysand has to live with the shadow, a remnant of the enclosure of the symptom which falsely attested to subjective wholeness. Of course, the symptom does not go away, it is simply handled less rigorously because there is no longer the demand.

Interestingly in Session XXVII, Lacan abruptly abandons the *Symposium*, instead referencing Genet's *Le Balcon* as having an implicit parallel with the analytic situation:

> It seems, rather, that this truly leaves the *I* in abeyance. It leaves it so well glued [*collé*], in any case, in fantasy that I defy you to find this *I* of desire anywhere else that where Jean Genet points it out in *The Balcony* [italics in original]. (Seminar VIII 1960–1961, p. 392)

It could be said that there is an obvious and somewhat comical connection between Lacan and *Le Balcon* in that *Le Balcon* is set in a bordello, a place where libidinal exchange occurs and therefore much like the psychoanalytic clinic, both places where exchanges are made between words, money, bodies, and affect.[1] Sometimes the exchanges are exciting, sometimes boring, often repetitive and always tinged by fantasy about subjects inscribing themselves into a dialectic of desires. Although the motives of these exchanges are not always shared, they nevertheless resonate with one another. Libidinal meetings are frequent and yet marked by explicit exchange and intervention which leave a trace, the start of the formation of the shadow even. On leaving the encounter, that is, the libidinal exchange, one returns to previously lived and known actualities, which are certainly more familiar, better known perhaps, but not necessarily more true if for no other reason than that life is always in a state of flux, even if imaginary. The situation outside the clinic is comparable to the situation outside the brothel—for both contexts one can logically assume that a revolution (or at least a transformation) is taking place both *inside* and *outside*. The libidinal space is always there to be returned to; it is a reminder that one remains a barred subject in relation to one's particular object of desire, a relation where meaning and belonging collide (even if momentarily) as a will to *jouissance*.[2]

> You must now go home, where everything -- you can be quite sure -- will be falser than here…. You must go now. You'll leave by the right, through the alley…. (Genet 1957)

It is here that we consider Aristophanes' "myth" of love, to which Lacan later refers in *Encore* (1972–1973, p. 205):

> Aristophanes' myth illustrates man's pursuit of his complement in a moving, yet misleading way, by suggesting that it is the other, one's sexual other half, that the living being seeks in love. For this mythical representation of the mystery of love, analytic experience substitutes the search for the subject, not for his sexual complement, but for that part of himself, lost forever, that is constituted by the fact that he is only a sexed living being, and that he is no longer immortal.

Lacan explicitly invokes Aristophanes, whose concept of splitting—that love is split between two bodies who need to find each other to make one love—Lacan regarded as profound. Love is a central focus for psychoanalysis for which Lacan makes a distinction between analytic and amorous love. What Aristophanes' love represents is the repression of the subject's fundamental loss, "one's sexual other half". Lacan seeks to rectify this repression through a focus on desire, in which the function of fantasy cannot be ignored. This is beautifully captured by Genet's play where desire is actualized through the gifting of the libidinal body, that which exists in the Real and fundamentally cannot be known:

> The Woman: Reality frightens you, doesn't it?
> The Bishop: If your sins were real, they would be crimes, and I'd be in a fine mess. (Genet 1957, p. 10)

According to Lacan, unlike in the clinic and with our lovers, we repress explicit libidinal desire. He contends that this repression belongs to the time and space of the ancient worlds and so should not be seen as particular to contemporary, Post-Freudian times. Drawing on Genet and the psychoanalytical clinic as the metaphorical bordello, Lacan says that we can here cultivate a space to ponder the function and effect of desire. While both venues focus on libidinal exchange, its transmission is procedurally different. Of course, both the bordello and the clinic take advantage of language as a form of sovereign enjoyment.[3] It is important however to recognize that Lacan's emphasis is exploring the truth of desire which eclipses the signifier (of the Phallus). Neither the brothel nor the clinic are necessarily authentic places for the play of fantasy, but rather they both place the subject as one already *in* fantasy before she or he even walks through the door. As one of the prostitutes, Irma attests to the punters, "They all want everything to be as real as possible..." (Genet 1957, p. 35). As contexts, although the bordello and the clinic obfuscate longing and meaning they nevertheless propagate the intersection of their illusion, the very intention of which is to remind the barred subject of the Other, as close attention to the crux of Genet's play reveals, "Would it perturb you to see things as they are? To gaze at the world tranquilly and accept responsibility for your gaze, whatever it might see?" (ibid., p. 72).

Lorenzo Chiesa (2015) notes that Seminar VIII and, in particular, Lacan's brief commentary on Genet's play, signifies his turning away from the Oedipus complex toward the subject as one of *jouissance*. Lacan's uptake of the subject of *jouissance* as paramount becomes indisputably clear as he ponders the relation between the "I" (ego-ideal) and the *a* (desire) as one which is not either/or but rather a function of the Other's desire (Seminar VIII 1960–1961, p. 393). He then claims that the function of the ego-ideal is to preserve the *a* as the ideal-ego (p. 394). He talks about this in metaphorical terms, as the moisture [*de l'humide*] trapped within a vessel. Such interrogation of what is trapped within the image is the very lesson of psychoanalysis. In *Le Balcon*, this is comically put to the test when the General wants to be seen as the epitome of the authority he seeks to represent:

> The General: (He looks at himself in the mirror) Austerlitz! General! Man of War and in full regalia, behold me in my pure appearance. Nothing, no contingent trails behind me. I appear, purely and simply. (Genet 1957, p. 62)

Looking in the mirror, the General sees his "I", his own "fullness" or "wholeness" as it were. This misrepresentation is his true pleasure: He is both the moisture (the metaphysical essence) and the vessel (the object which captures the essence). He is his own narcissistic liminal image, which he unashamedly declares and which is, as Lacan would describe it, a ridiculous affirmation to himself. This brings to mind Lacan's overt criticism of the position of certain IPA analysts: that the analysand submits to the analyst as ideal and that analysis is the procedure wherein the analysand cultivates identification with the analyst. For Lacan, psychoanalysis is not a masquerade which models the ideal-ego in a mistaken transference. However, a masquerade such as that purported by Genet's General is undertaken enthusiastically by nearly everyone in the play—the prostitutes enjoy masquerading as passive slaves to paradoxes of ideal femininity and the men enjoy dependence in repetitively activating their ideal-egos of authority. Lacan confirms this for us when he says in *Four Fundamental Concepts* that "the masculine ideal and the feminine ideal are represented in the psyche by… the term masquerade… [which] is precisely to play not as the imaginary, but at the symbolic level" (1964, p. 193).

It is here tempting to turn to Hegel's master/slave dialectic which is so startlingly illustrated in Genet's play. As the punter who wishes to be the Bishop states in negotiating a *ménage à trois*:

> We are bound together, you, he and I. For example, if he didn't hit, how could I stop him from hitting? Therefore, he must strike so that I can intervene and demonstrate my authority. And you must deny your guilt so that he can beat you. (Genet 1957, p. 15)

Here is an example where *jouissance* is channelled into a use for language, or language-use. There is, of course, the obvious *jouissance* of the slave being more powerful than the master—she can simply stop the show and knows that if she does, good-bye to everyone's *jouissance*. This is her hold on the paying punters. But what about the punter wishing to masquerade as the Bishop? He cannot exercise anything, let alone his authority, without an act and her obedience to his command. His interventions can be only provisionally anticipated and are conditioned by the other punter and prostitute acting out in the particular way he directs. Here, his *jouissance* is one of dependence, not merely on the slave's obedience (which is not entirely reliable) but on the entire setup of interaction with a particular slave, a particular time, and a particular place. This is the perfect illustration of Lacan's ego-ideal I(A)—ideal-ego i(*a*) dialectic, that it is desire which in preserving the *objet a* defends the specular image. It is also a reminder, thanks to the slave, that the *objet a* is not, for everyone all of the time, a universal nonexistent object of fantasy. This is wittily illustrated by Irma's sharp retort to the one who considers himself a Master (of morality), the Chief of Police:

> Chief of Police: ...Out there rebellion is tragic and joyous, whereas in this house everything's dying a slow death. So today's my day. By tonight I'll be in a grace or on a pedestal. So whether I love you or desire you is unimportant. How are things going at the moment?
> Irma: Marvellously. I've had some great performances.

Irma goes on, providing her parting punch...

> Irma: ... My dear, your function isn't noble enough to offer dreamers an image that would enshrine them. Perhaps because it lacks illustrious ancestors? No, my dear chap... You have to resign yourself to that fact that your image does not yet conform to the liturgies of the brothel. (ibid., pp. 45–46)

The propping up of the image and the objects needed for such a masquerade to continue is not lost on Lacan when he says in *Écrits* (1966, p. 97), "Freud, let it be recalled, in touching on the feelings involved in the transference, insisted on the need to distinguish in it a factor of reality." Of course, props are central to the internal workings of the bordello, its costumes, and accessories which provide for the libidinal transference to take place, as noted by the two prostitutes Carmen and Irma:

> Carmen: And what'll the authentic detail be?
> Irma: The ring...
> Carmen: What about the fake detail?
> Irma: It's almost always the same: black lace under the homespun skirt. (Genet 1957, p. 35)

Such ready-made objects are positioned as ready-to-enjoy (*pret-a-jouir*), but are at the same time merely contingent in fulfilling the fantasy of the desire itself.[4] This is because it is transference and not identification with authenticity which is paramount. Whether objects are real, fake, or a bit of both is inconsequential. Here, authenticity is not a category which measures the value of objects, but rather an indication of whether one is seen to be included in the transferential relation. Thus, the Police Chief, miffed at initially being excluded (no one wants to take on the boring fantasy of his particular authority!), claims that "brothel tricks are mainly mirror tricks" (Genet 1957, p. 48). He is of course correct (after all, are not most institutions in some way a parody of themselves?) but in saying this he is not declaring any profound insight but simply stating what everyone else already knows and goes along with. Confronting his discomfort in being marginalized, he props himself up with his own narcissistic symptom; his virtue signaling and his so-called honesty in declaring the falsity of the spectacle before him, as if he is the one who sees the truth while everyone else is playing dress-ups. This is exactly what Lacan alerts us to in Session XXVII: that in the pursuit of subjective wholeness we conflate the ego-ideal with the ideal-ego, that we enter the clinic as the Police Chief and through the process of analysis, hopefully become a bit less stupid by seeing objects for what they really are—simply props for fantasy.[5]

Lacan refers to *Le Balcon* earlier in Seminar V. The brothel in Genet's play offers authority figures during the French Revolution unmitigated jouissance of which Lacan says that

> comedy manifests by this kind of inner necessity this relationship of the subject, from the moment that he is signified…. (Seminar V 1957–1958, p. 11)

Is Lacan here drawing on Genet's play in order to examine how the concept of political power encapsulates unconscious forces, or is he negating the concept of power as unable to encapsulate unconscious forces? Perhaps a bit of both. As a psychoanalyst, he privileges the unconscious, and thus, it makes sense to conclude that any play of power is also one of unconscious libidinal investment. But if we look at Lacan's last session more closely, the clinical procedure (as a complete trajectory) is not directed by the analyst, but by what the analysand brings to the couch. This includes the unconscious will to pursue an end. The power in the clinic, it seems, is with the analysand. But of course, it is more than this. Genet's play is about staging subjects of authority, such as the Bishop, the Judge, and the General. They enact various erotic scenarios by punters with prostitutes' while outside the brothel political insurrection is continually building.

After attending the first performance of the play in Paris, Lacan makes a very curious observation, that the perverse intentions and rituals of these subjects of authority are mimicked by other patrons, but not those of the Police Chief whose role in keeping the brothel safe during this politically unstable time is nevertheless central to the play. Lacan notes that the Police Chief represents "… simple desire, pure and simple desire, this need that man has to rejoin his own existence in a fashion that can be authenticated and directly assumed, [and so to give] his own thought, a value which is not purely distinct from his flesh […]" (Seminar V 1957–1958, p. 17). So perilous yet impotent is the revolution—and this is the truly comical point—that everyone simply goes on fucking while the Chief of Police also continues his role of ensuring public safety.[6] As Lacan says:

> […] the chief of police consults his entourage on the subject of the suitability of a sort of uniform, and also the symbol which will be the symbol of his function. He does so not without shyness […]: indeed, he shocks the ears of his listeners a little: he proposes—a phallus. Would the church have any objection to it? [he asks]—and he in fact bows his head a little […] to the bishop who shows some hesitation. The bishop for his part suggests that after all if the phallus is changed into the dove of the Holy Spirit, it would be more acceptable. In the same way the general proposes that the figure in question should be painted in the national colours, and some other suggestions of this kind follow, which make us think that of course we are going to come pretty quickly to what is called on such occasions a concordat. (Seminar V 1957–1958, p. 22)

As Lacan alerts us in Seminar VIII (1961–1962), it is impossible to fuck the signifier, rather enjoyment here is simply re-routed. This realization points to the impossibility of two things. First, one literally can't fuck a signifier because the prostitutes are not really having sex with the Bishop or the General or the Judge, but rather with clients who are pretending to be these figures of authority. Second, such satisfaction is as afforded by fantasy is short-lived; when the enjoyment of the fake authority of the Bishop, the General, and the Judge gets a bit boring for patrons and on the realizing that the expected revolution probably won't happen after all, the authority offered by the Police Chief is then taken up. These figures of authority, arguably eventually even the Police Chief, are turned into sublimated poetic objects, which, rather than the actual act of intercourse, represent true satisfaction. So it is not who one fucks, but who one pretends to be while fucking.

A poignant moment occurs toward the end of the play when a prostitute announces that her client would like to be clad as the Chief of Police. Does not this concluding staging of impossible power align with the conclusion one reaches during analysis, that in failing to grasp the very Thing itself, one develops symptoms which mask this failure? Thus, it is the enjoyment of the symptom which gets played out in bordello, in the clinic, and in everyday life. When faced with the fact that the clothes fit the symptom but not necessarily the subject, when in the end authority's lack and failed legitimacy are revealed, what can one do?

> [...] when he has passed the test, on condition precisely that he is castrated, namely [in an action] which ensures that the phallus is once again promoted to the state of a signifier, to this something which can or cannot give or take away, confer or not confer authority. (Lacan, Seminar V 1957–1958, p. 18)

The end, it seems, is rather depressing. What does Lacan say about an end or an ending? In *Four Fundamental Concepts*, he stipulates, as he had earlier in *Écrits*, that the end is the direction of treatment and one which should remain at the forefront of the analyst's desire:

> What is certain is that the transference is one thing, the therapeutic end another. Nor is the transference to be confused with a mere means. The two extremes of what has been formulated in analytic literature are situated here. How often will you read formulas that associate, for example, the transference with identification, whereas identification is merely a pause, a false termination of the analysis which is very frequently confused with its normal termination. Its relation with the transference is close, but precisely in that by which the transference has not been analysed. On the other hand, you will see the function of the transference formulated as a means of rectification from the standpoint of reality, to which everything I am saying today is opposed. (1964, pp. 145–146)

Ends are often glimpsed even before they start to make a more marked appearance, usually through a disrupting of the Imaginary with the Symbolic. As early as Seminar I, Lacan suggests that perhaps the end is marked with the subject's ability to articulate desire:

> Where is the dialectic of the symbolic reintegration of desire going to lead? Is it enough simply for the subject to name his desires, for him to have permission to name them, for the analysis to be terminated? That is the question that I may perhaps raise at the end of this session. *You will also see that I will not leave it there.* (1953–1954, p. 193) [emphasis by author]

As of course, he does not. The concept and praxis of the end is returned to again and again during his seminars and in *Écrits*. In fact, we could say that in psychoanalysis, it is what can be counted on in the end that the analyst and analysand strive toward. In this way, the end is always being transmitted. However, this is also a specific end; *Le Balcon* shows us both that which dispels the fantasy and what marks the end. At last the Police Chief gets a punter, a lowly mechanic who wants to give his "clothes" of authority a go. This is significant as the *jouissance* provided by the authority of the Bishop, General, and Judge is waning libidinally and within the imaginary, if not symbolically. The authority of the Police Chief reverses this abating *jouissance* by creating the perfect illusion: that perhaps the revolution can continue and there is no end in sight.[7] Yet throughout, language is disrupting the fantasmatic relation between the prop and the subject. The authority of language is insufficient to fully capture the fantasy of authority; just as the revolution is failing so *jouissance* is diminishing. Fantasy attempts to take on a further libidinal horizon of recovering fading *jouissance* of the revolution.

What does the end reveal to us? In psychoanalysis, it is confrontation with the masquerade under which one operates, specifically the subject's acceptance of castration. This confrontation is the final part of something which nevertheless continues in a different direction; It is not a happy end; indeed, Lacan dismisses that psychoanalysis should be a quest for happiness, "It is in such a context that analysis appears to be... and the analyst sets himself up to receive, a demand for happiness... There is in Aristotle a discipline of happiness... Please note the one finds nothing similar in psychoanalysis" (Seminar VII 1959–1960, pp. 292–293). Lacan is saying that psychoanalysis is a handling of investment in this masquerade, and as this becomes no longer needed, the subject is confronted with the difference between a position in the world which is not contingent on good, well-being, or happiness, and "a responsible position relative to an analysis" (ibid., p. 303). Luis Izcovich calls this the mark of a psychoanalysis:

> The stake of analysis can be understood in terms of an operation on *jouissance.* More exactly, it is an operation through [which] the analysand accedes to know-how with his symptom, a know-how that did not exist.... In other words, analysis carries the marks of the subject.... (2017, p. 223)

Such a mark is unmistakable as it bears a specific pronouncement, first used by Freud, *Wo Es war.* Lacan takes this up later in *Écrits* as

> [w]here it was, I must come into being. This goal is one of reintegration and harmony, I might even say of reconciliation [*Versohnung*]. (1966, p. 524)

He continues

> 'I must come to be where it was'. It is very precise, it is this *Ich* which is not das *Ich* which is not the ego, which is an *Ich*, the *Ich* used as subject of the sentence. Where it has been, the place where it speaks. Where it speaks, namely where a moment before there was something which is unconscious desire, I must designate myself there, there I must be this I which is the goal, the end, the term of analysis before it is named, before it is formed, before it is articulated, if indeed it ever is, because as well in the Freudian formula this *soll Ich werden*, this 'it must be, this I must become', is the subject of a becoming, of a duty which is proposed to you. (ibid.)

As we know from Genet's play, there are moments when the end is accelerated, such as when the Madame, Irma, instructs her client that

> It's time. Come on! Quick! Make it snappy! (Genet 1957, p. 9)

It seems that such scansion encouraging the end of the act is just as explicit in the bordello as in the clinic. Of course, scansion is also a rhetorical device designed to startle rather than elicit a retort. Yet at the same time such "strategic punctuation," as Bruce Fink (2007) puts it, is the key to interruption and breach of social etiquette often used in the clinic (and, according to Genet arguably also in the bedroom). It is striking because scansion has the function of calling out any potential avoidance. Interestingly while scansion is allowing for a certain kind of interruption in discourse, it is also reminding us of the end to come. For Lacan, linking Genet's *Le Balcon* with the clinic signals that the end is marked by Eros as claimed earlier in Seminar VIII:

> Again is it indeed a question of underlining this 'making use of Eros'. And to make use of it for what purpose? Here indeed is why it was necessary for me to recall to you the reference points of our articulation from last year: to make use of it for [the] good. We know that the domain of Eros goes infinitely further than any field that this good may cover, at least we can take this as understood.... You should indeed not have in any preconceived or permanent way, as a first term of the end of your action, the supposed good or not of your patient, but precisely his Eros. (1960–1961)

Once this is revealed to the subject, grappled with, and thereby laid to rest, so to speak, mourning inevitably follows because the subject can no longer recognize her former self reflected in the image previously projected. But it is more than this, the object so crucial to this procedure, the analyst, is no longer available in the same way. That is, the specific transference between analyst and analysand has ended. To be clear it is an ending, and not a liberation from the symptom per se, which has taken place. Here, a realization has occurred, one that settles the symptom and which can be worked around. Moreover, it is a realization that one does have some minimal agency as to how the symptom is transmitted. Lacan unapologetically offers a pessimistic position on the end, but that is more useful than any vitalist alternative:

> As I believe I have shown here in the sphere I have outlined for you this year, the function of desire must remain in a fundamental relationship to death. The question I ask is this: shouldn't the true termination of an analysis – and by that I mean the kind that prepares you to become an analyst – in the end confront the one who undergoes it with the reality of the human condition?

> It is precisely this, that in connection with anguish, Freud designated as the level at which its signal is produced, namely, *Hilflosigkeit* or distress, the state in which man is in that relationship to himself which is his own death – in the sense I have taught you to isolate it this year – and can expect help from no one. (Seminar VI 1959–1960, pp. 303–304)

He then suggests that the end is a procedure which is marked by mourning, an experience of death:

> At the end of a training analysis the subject should reach and should know the domain and the level of the experience of absolute disarray. It is a level at which anguish is already a protection, not so much *Abwarten* [waiting] as *Erwartung* [expectancy]. Anguish develops by letting a danger appear, whereas there is no danger at the level of the final experience of *Hilflosigkeit*. (ibid.)

Tracy McNulty (2019) asks "what is delivered in this mourning?" She posits that transmission too leaves a mark, an inscription that the analyst is capable of acting upon another body, namely the analysand. Here, we can say that at the end of analysis, the analysand is weighed down by transmission, a transmission which has the effect of confirming the experience of destitution and which as McNulty rightly points out, is a pre-condition to think the procedure of the pass.[8] This is echoed in Genet's play in which the balcony of the bordello is a transitional estimate space in which fantasy is revealed for what it really is. Lacan ends Session XXVII with positing a way in which the ego-ideal can be recuperated: that in mourning there is the possibility that the analysand glimpses a different desire, *le désir de l'analyste.* Mourning contributes to the testimony of the analysand that something profound and transformational has occurred. Such a desire to analyze, one which should not be confused with pure desire, also rests upon the *objet a*—the unknowlable and nonexistent object. However, the desire to analyze is one which is not repressed. This kind of mourning relieves the subject from the unknowable object because analysis is the passage to the act, not a passage to the *objet a.* It is a full realization and acceptance of castration, one which is a recognition of transmission from the vantage point of subjective distance.

Notes

1. As Carmen, one of the prostitutes in Genet's play unapologetically states, "entering a brothel means rejecting the world" (1957, p. 44).
2. Such a parallel does not assume that the distance between inside and outside the brothel is flattened, but rather that it is comprehensible as an invention of transgression. The reign of the image taking place within the brothel also allows for its destruction.
3. There are however no explicit sexual acts in *Le Balcon* (rather is it a prosaic *double entendre* word-play of innuendo), notwithstanding it is situated very much at the intersection of sex and politics. The same (for the most part) can be said of the clinic. But more interestingly, what *Le Balcon* and the clinic both propagate is that sex and the masquerades we harbour about being a sexual subject are integral to one's subjectivity and place in the social world.
4. At the end of Session XXVII, Seminar VIII (1960–1961, p, 398), Lacan somewhat comically implies that religion did not wait for science to confirm *pret-a-jouir*, nor was it reluctant to take up the ready-made enjoyment available. Thus, he does not dismiss *pret-a-jouir*, but rather, suggests that it allows the work of analysis to occur.
5. Interestingly Badiou (2002, 2013) suggests that we should look to our inner Police Chief as a form of pure power—our moral compass—as a way of navigating politics. For Badiou, the Police Chief is an imageless figure in the midst of the repetition of images. He is the inscription of pure essence. Further it could be argued that it is this alienation which the Police Chief enjoys; being located as beyond not being sexy enough for the punters.
6. Badiou (2002, 2013) argues that the visibility of dominant social orders and ideological conditions is upheld by idealised emblems. The excessive staging of such emblems, whether they be architecture or authority figures, serves to keep any real struggle for change obfuscated and even socially invisible. It can be argued that a retreat into perversion, such as the bordello affords, delegitimizes authority rather than enhancing it. Thus despite its de-legitimisation, it is the bordello and not public governance which holds the greater revolutionary potential.
7. This can be linked to question of the revolution as within the realm of the real and perhaps this is the reason Lacan took up Genet's play in the first instance. It offers way of asking what is possible in upholding a Lacanian interpretation of real change or conversely, no real change.

8. It is notable that the Police Chief confesses to Irma, one of the prostitutes that his "function weighs [him] down" (Genet 1957, p. 47). He desperately wants to detach himself from this image which has enveloped him in order to transmit a different one. This desire to traverse the fantasy is a shared one among the punters, the Bishop stating much later, "It lies with us for this masquerade to change" (ibid., p. 84).

References

Badiou, A. 2002. *Le Balcon du present.* Lecture given at 'Returns to Marx' Colloquium, Tate Modern Gallery, May, London.

———. 2013. The Pornography of Democracy. *Verso.* Originally published in *Nouvel Observateur, 'L'Année vue par… la philo'.* Accessed from https://www.versobooks.com/blogs/1223-the-pornography-of-democracy.

Chiesa, L. 2015. The First Gram of Jouissance. *Comparatist,* 39, 6–21.

Fink, B. 2007. *Fundamentals of Psychoanalytic Technique: A Lacanian Approach for Practitioners.* New York: W. W. Norton.

Freud, S. 1937. Analysis Terminable and Interminable. *International Journal of Psycho-Analysis,* 18, 373–405.

Genet, J. 1957. *Le Balcon.* Translated by B. Frechtman. London: Faber & Faber.

Izcovich, L. 2017. *The Marks of a Psychoanalysis.* New York: Karnac.

Lacan, J. 1953–1954 [1991]. *Seminar I: Freud's Papers on Technique.* Edited by Jacques-Alain Miller. Cambridge University Press.

———. 1957–1958 [2017]. *Seminar V: Formations of the Unconscious.* Translated by R. Grigg. Hoboken, NJ: Wiley.

———. 1959–1960 [1992]. *Seminar VII: The Ethics of Psychoanalysis.* New York: W. W. Norton.

———. 1960–1961 [2015]. *Seminar VIII: Transference.* Translated by Bruce Fink. Cambridge: Polity.

———. 1964 [1981]. *Seminar XI: The Four Fundamental Concepts of Psychoanalysis.* Edited by Jacques-Alain Miller and Translated by A. Sheridan. New York: W. W. Norton.

———. 1966 [2002]. *Écrits.* Translated by Bruce Fink. New York: Norton & Norton.

———. 1972–1973 [1998]. *Seminar XX. Encore: On Feminine Sexuality, the Limits of Love and Knowledge.* Translated by Bruce Fink. London and New York: Norton & Norton.

McNulty, T. 2019. *Separating from Separation.* LACKiii Conference, 9–10 May. Clark University.

Index

G. Basu Thakur and J. Dickstein (eds.), *Reading Lacan's Seminar VIII*, The Palgrave Lacan Series, https://doi.org/10.1007/978-3-030-32742-2

B

C

D

GPSR Compliance
The European Union's (EU) General Product Safety Regulation (GPSR) is a set of rules that requires consumer products to be safe and our obligations to ensure this.

If you have any concerns about our products, you can contact us on

ProductSafety@springernature.com

In case Publisher is established outside the EU, the EU authorized representative is:

Springer Nature Customer Service Center GmbH
Europaplatz 3
69115 Heidelberg, Germany

www.ingramcontent.com/pod-product-compliance
Lightning Source LLC
Chambersburg PA
CBHW071745210725
29917CB00005B/319
9783030327415